Suzy Gershman
BORN TO SHOP
LONDON

The Ultimate Guide for Travelers Who Love to Shop

7th Edition

MACMILLAN • USA

For Ian Cook, with thanks for ten years of Anglo-American definitions, driving on the wrong side of the road, and pizza dinners, not to mention all the pix.

Although every effort has been made to ensure the accuracy of prices appearing in this book, please keep in mind that with inflation and fluctuating rates of exchange, prices can change. Dollar estimates have been made at the rate of exchange one pound sterling (£) = $1.50 U.S. Whenever possible, prices are quoted in sterling to more accurately reflect the local price.

MACMILLAN TRAVEL
A Simon & Schuster Macmillan Company
1633 Broadway
New York, NY 10019

Copyright © 1995 by Suzy Gershman.

All rights reserved. Printed in the United States of America. No part of this book may be reproduced or transmitted in any form or by any means, electronic or mechanical, including photocopying, recording, or by any information storage and retrieval system, without permission in writing from the Publisher.

MACMILLAN is a registered trademark of Macmillan, Inc.

ISBN 0-02-860659-0
ISSN 1065-0563

Editor: Erica Spaberg
Map Editor: Douglas Stallings
Production Editor: Matt Hannafin
Copy Editor: Douglas Elam
Design by George J. McKeon
Digital Cartography by Ortelius Design

SPECIAL SALES
Bulk purchases (10+ copies) of Frommer's travel guides are available to corporations at special discounts. The Special Sales Department can produce custom editions to be used as premiums and/or for sales promotion to suit individual needs. Existing editions can be produced with custom cover imprints such as corporate logos. For more information write to Special Sales, Macmillan Publishing, 1633 Broadway, New York, NY 10019.

Manufactured in the United States of America

CONTENTS

	To Start With	v
1	The Best of London at a Glance	1
2	London Details	8
3	Sleeping in London	30
4	Dining in London	41
5	Money Matters	52
6	Shopping Strategies	65
7	London Shopping Neighborhoods	83
8	Basic London Resources—A–Z	109
9	Home Furnishings & Design Resources	223
10	Antiques, Used Books & Collectibles	252
11	London Shopping Tours	296
	Size Conversion Chart	314
	Index	315

MAP LIST

London Underground	19
London Postal Codes	85
West End/Soho/Covent Garden	87
St. James's and Mayfair	95
South Kensington & Chelsea	101
Tour #1: Mayfair Mayhem Day Tour	299
Tour #2: Knightsbridge & Chelsea	303
Tour #4: The Home Day Tour	309

TO START WITH

Welcome to a brand new edition of *Born to Shop London*, a book that is not only totally revised, reorganized and rewritten but which comes to you from a new family. As you may have noticed from the new cover design, I have joined Frommer's.

I don't get to take Arthur Frommer shopping for $5 a day ... or even £5 a day. How could I? I spend more than that on the underground these days! But I do get to add my take on the worlds of shopping and retail to some of the Frommer's city guides.

As for the *Born to Shop* guides, they have several new features. The first benefits your pocketbook directly. A few stores and hotels listed in these pages are doing their best to welcome you to London by offering *Born to Shop* readers special discounts and other benefits; the specifics are woven into the establishment listings—so read carefully!

The second new feature is a chapter that provides a quick overview of the best shopping experiences in London. Titled "The Best of London at a Glance," it gives you all my favorite tips in an instant and is great for those who are dashing to meetings, airport connections, or other parts of Britain. Of course, those off to other parts of the British Isles might want to consider packing along *Born to Shop Great Britain*, too.

Which brings me to something else I'd like to mention. To make sure that you always have completely fresh, up-to-date material, we are now publishing the two U.K. books in alternate years. A new edition of the London guide will appear in odd-numbered years; Great Britain in even-numbered. While *Born to Shop Great Britain* has only a small section on London, some addresses and secrets are updated after this edition goes to bed, so you can always be absolutely on top of everything in London if you consult it as well.

None of the updates, ideas, or changes in this new edition would be possible without the help of the team at Frommer's—especially Mike Spring, my publisher, and Erica Spaberg, my editor—who have given me free rein to really have fun and re-do this book.

Ian Cook, who has been taking my picture for over 10 years now, continues both as cover-guy and as British correspondent. Maggie O'Sullivan and Ruth Jacobs, two of my British girlfriends who work in media in London, have also done a lot to keep me on the right side of the road in this revision.

And speaking of the cover, this one is rather simple. That's me waltzing into one of my regular hotels in London—The Dorchester—in my John Boyd bargain hat, bought last year for £23 at a secondhand shop. You'll be proud to know that I bought the hat first and was then able to find a matching dress at the discounter TJ Maxx, down the road from my home in Connecticut. I paid all of $25 for it. May all your bargains be as satisfying.

Chapter One

THE BEST OF LONDON AT A GLANCE

Hot flush! Hot *what?* Well, you're off for Britain now, luv, and there they say *hot flush,* not hot flash. So it's bullets from Broadway and tons to tell, especially if you're an American about to hop the pond.

If your time in London has pulled the short straw and you are really dashing between meetings, business appointments, or even other cities, this chapter is for you. In an easy-to-read fashion, it brings you the best of London's diverse shopping scene, including a few suggestions for gifts or personal trophies to take home with you, faster than you can say, "Trafalgar Square, please."

All the choices in this chapter appear later on in the book. And, of course, I hope even those in a mad tear will find a moment to read the rest of the book because it lists many more stores as well as tips for finding good values and other shopping strategies. Bargains in Britain are often hidden and those on a flash dash don't always get the best buy.

You won't go home empty-handed, however. Prices in London are high—sometimes frighteningly high—but there are good buys out there. If you give it a try, I promise you not only great fun, but the opportunity to shed a few pounds!

You Have One Hour between Meetings to Shop

Obviously, this depends upon where you are. If I have a heavy day, I try to get people to come to me at my hotel or to keep my meetings in the Mayfair area, so that I can at least get some fresh air, even though a walk along Regent Street or Oxford Street gives me more than a breath of fresh air ... it gives me credit card debt!

If you're the type who has to know what's hip and hot, your one hour probably has to be spent on the two parts of Bond Street (Old and New) because they're both new these days, with tons of new faces and lots of exciting retail going on.

If you find yourself in Mayfair with one hour to shop and you only want to go into one place, your best bet is **Liberty of London**, if only to visualize. But, once you're there, you'll want to shop 'til you drop, too.

I'll tell you what I generally do with my hour (and what I suggest for any die-hard shopper):

- Head for **The Body Shop** (next to **John Lewis**) and buy everything I need since it's almost half the U.S. price.
- Dash into **Boots the Chemist** for everything I need that can only be found in Britain (such as their cucumber face mask).
- Dash into **Tesco Metro**—yes, it is a supermarket—for bottled water and snacks for my room, my next flight, and any other personal needs. Then I sniff around for new products and buy gifts, ranging from a Cadbury Flake candy bar for my husband to a six-pack of Virgin Cola for any businessman in any foreign country who has never heard of such a product and will howl with amusement and delight when I present it.

- Finish up my hour at **Marks & Spencer,** as time allows.

You Have Only One Hour to Shop Knightsbridge

If you are in Knightsbridge and want to spend your hour there, I suggest a trip to **Pandora,** the designer resale shop, a quick perusal of **Cheval Place,** which is lined with even more designer resale shops, then a quick whizz through **Harrods** or at least a stop for souvenirs and a Stilton to go in the food halls.

You Have a Few Minutes to Shop but Everything's Closed

Assuming it's not Sunday night, there are a few places you can still have a little fun. (Remember, most shops in London close early by New York or Hong Kong standards; usually 7 P.M.) The **Boots** at Piccadilly is open until 10 P.M. most nights; **Tesco Metro** is open until 8 P.M. most nights and 9 P.M. on Thursdays. On Sundays, they close at 6 P.M

You Have No Real Shopping Goals but Want a Quick Spree That's Very London

- Head for **Covent Garden.**
- Explore the entire marketplace but don't forget that if you need a few gifts, there's a tiny branch of **Hamley's** (great gifts for kids) and a **Culpeper the Herbalist** (wonderful bed and bath products, including aromatherapy gifts) here as well.
- Visit the **Dr. Martens Department Store.**
- Walk away from **Covent Garden** out the front end (see map on page 87; pass Covent Garden tube; you are walking *away* from The Strand) and go to **Neal Street** for an eyeful of cutting-edge British street fashion and shoes you just can't believe.

The Best Place for Royal Souvenirs

BUCKINGHAM PALACE GIFT SHOP
Sorry, only open August and September (Tube: St. James's Park or Green Park).

The Best Museum Store

VICTORIA & ALBERT MUSEUM
(Tube: South Kensington).

The Best Children's Store

HAMLEY'S
200 Regent Street, W1 (Tube: Oxford Circus).

The Best Teenage Hangout

DR. MARTENS DEPARTMENT STORE
King Road, Covent Garden (Tube: Covent Garden).

The Best Store for Inexpensive Shoes

SHELLY'S (VARIOUS BRANCHES)
Regent Street (Tube: Oxford Circus).

The Best Show for Trendy Shoppers

HYPER HYPER
Kensington High Street (Tube: Kensington High Street).

Great Gifts for Loved Ones

- Aromatherapy fan from Culpeper the Herbalist, £8; with the scent of your choice, an additional £2–5; pre-packaged with lavender scent, £12.
- Silk knot cuff links, £5, from **Thomas Pink.**
- Filofax or Filofax inserts. Prices range with selection but are basically one-half the U.S. retail price.
- Desk gadgets and accessories from Smythson of Bond Street. I buy the tiny magnifying glass as a 50th birthday gift for loved ones, £25; with an engraved case, £35.
- Scent from Jo Malone, £20.

The Best Gifts under £5

- A **tabloid newspaper,** with at least one tacky headline and news of yet another royal scandal, 20p.
- A can or a six-pack (depending on your ability to carry it) of **Virgin Cola,** £3 per six-pack.
- **Monogrammed Victorian sachets** that either display the initials of the recipient or spell out a short name or title, $2.50 each.
- **Bath by Chocolate,** bubble bath foam from **Tesco Metro,** £3.
- Anything from **The Body Shop.**

The Best Gift for the Person Who Has Everything

The Dorchester Hotel now has gift certificates for afternoon tea! They come wrapped in an elegant box that is perfect for presentation. Full tea is about £15.50 and champagne tea is about £21.50. If you would like the vouchers sent to you or sent directly to your gift recipient, phone 171-629-8888, and ask for The Promenade. Credit card orders can be taken over the phone, however there is an additional charge for international mail.

Quick! You Need Something for the Kids!

- Corgi metal cars from Hamley's.
- British football team merchandise, sold at every souvenir stand.

Chapter Two

LONDON DETAILS

LONDON ON FIRE

Chocolate!

I'm shouting "chocolate" because I'm just old enough to remember that classic Smothers Brothers routine in which Dickie shouts "chocolate" because he thinks people will pay more attention to that word than to "fire."

It doesn't matter what you shout when you get to London because truth be told, the town is on fire; the flames of the new London retail scene will sear your heart . . . and your pocketbook.

HEATING UP?

It's way past that. Paris may sizzle; London is on fire. Again.

Remember the recession? Whether you personally came out of it for better or for worse (or for richer or for poorer), you can bet your Ascot that London town has come out on top. Maybe the average Londoner doesn't have more pence in his pocket and maybe he still dreams of shopping in America for true bargains, but the real estate developers have got to be happy. And tourists should be grinning from ear to ear. From 'ere to there.

Heating Up? 9

All of the bankruptcies and vacancies caused by the recession have now turned over, so that every time you take a step, a new store is opening up. London just about dazzles these days with the flash of all that cash.

- Designers who had *one* store in London took advantage of the availability of empty storefronts in fine locations and now have *two* stores. If they had *two* stores, now they have *three*. Or *four*. **Christian Lacroix** and **Giorgio Armani** are just a few examples. Wait 'til you see the new Mulberry digs.

- Americans have invaded the high streets. If you think I am referring to the arrival of **The Gap**, excuse me, but that's old news, old chap. Ditto **Disney**—they've been there for years now. I'm talking **Donna Karan** and **Levi's**. To name just a few. In no time at all, Mayfair may resemble your local mall. Would you believe that **Rochester Big & Tall** has opened shop across the street from Harrods?

- American-style retailing has made an even bigger impact on the scene, leaving even Sloane Rangers—those trendy fashion yuppies who wear pearls with their Wellies—to shop in places like **Jerry's Home Store**, which, as any American can tell you faster than you can say Jumpin' Jack Flash, is, uh, highly influenced by **Pottery Barn** and **Crate & Barrel**.

- There's a new James Bond on the screen and a new Bond Street on, yep, Bond Street. Don't forget London has New Bond Street and Old Bond Street and anyone with a dribble of dash and an ounce of cash will be bonding in high style. Several of the old faithfuls have reopened after closing for renovations, so **Celine** and **Hermès** are back in style. Other faces are new: **Donna Karan, Joan & David,** and **Emporio Armani**. Blink and someone new has arrived on the scene. Bond: shaken and now quite stirred.

10 LONDON DETAILS

- Grocery stores have taken up some of this expensive real estate in key trading areas, so that suddenly one of the best places to go shopping on Oxford Street or in Covent Garden is—can you stand it?—Tesco, the largest grocery chain in the U.K. Some of the best and most affordable gifts you can get for friends are going to come from Tesco. Honest. See page 156.

London was hurt, no question about it. Meanwhile, the comeback tastes better than any other victory because it comes with a change in local lifestyle.

After all, if the Queen could open Buckingham Palace to the public to make a little scratch, then it's got to be okay. No more stiff upper lip. London is out to woo you and win you and offer you a whole lot of bang for your buck so that you'll come back again and again.

- Airfares (both transatlantic and, in some cases, from London to other European points) are actually lower than they were a few years ago. Even peak summer airfares average $500 per economy seat, round-trip; off season seats go for less than $400 RT!
- Hotels have rebates, promotional rates, deals in dollars, and all sorts of enticements to get you to come visit and spend a few of your hard-earned dollars. I just read of an American Express promotion that offers free limo transfer to and from the airport to guests who arrange to stay only three consecutive nights or more in a certain hotel in London.
- Package deals are becoming more flexible, so you can have the benefits of a fixed-price trip without being herded onto a bus and having to suffer through with some first timer who wants to know who Big Ben was named after.
- The dollar may be dancing a little bit, but there are enough deals to go around. You'll want to

make your choices carefully and shop as any educated consumer would, but you can have your steak and kidney pie and eat it, too.

BOOKING LONDON

The number of guidebooks to London is staggering. I'll point you only to the ones I find essential.

- *London A to Z* (say "A to Zed"): This is a map guide that everyone, absolutely everyone, uses—locals and tourists. It's an in-depth detailed street finder which will even tell you which tube stop to use.

    Look up the addresses you desire in the index in the back, turn to the map indicated, and find your spot. No one can survive a serious stay without this gem, which is available in any bookstore or newsstand in London. There is a tube map on the back cover.

- *Antiques Diary:* This is a little booklet that lists flea markets and jumble sales throughout Britain, divided into regions. Buy the "London & Southern" edition at the Monday flea market at Covent Garden, or write Peter Allwright, P.O. Box 30, Twyford, Reading, England RG10 8DQ. This booklet has blossomed from sort of a homemade job with invaluable information to a full color booklet with editorial and listings and everything Martha Stewart would kill to know. Actually, I think the ads for the fairs are the best.

    This guidebook now has a competitor, which you may prefer: *The Antique Trade Calendar.* The publisher is GP London, 32 Fredericks Place, North Finchley, London, England N12 8QE. I buy mine in Greenwich over the weekend.

- *Time Out*: This is a weekly magazine with cultural listings. Each edition also has a shopping column which is always worth checking out when you visit. I wouldn't suggest you buy the magazine just for the shopping column, but if you need theater listings and a complete run-down of goings-on about town, this is your bible. *Time Out* has now gone into publishing in a big way; they have guidebooks as well as a magazine called *London Visitor's Guide*, which, for £3, is not a bad buy if you get a current issue. They are dated by the year.

Also note that the British Tourist Authority (BTA) has a few offices scattered around the U.S. and they give away tons of free brochures. They have an excellent bookstore but they also have tons of maps and goodies that are totally free in the U.S. You pay for these same items once you walk into tourist centers in Britain.

GETTING THERE

From the U.S.

There are a number of ways to get to England from the U.S., but since there isn't yet a tunnel which connects Boston with Britain, you'll probably be best off in an airplane.

The QE2 does make the crossing every April until winter, but it takes five days to get from shore to shore. And there's not *that* much shopping onboard.

If your time is more precious, flying is your best bet. You'll find that prices from New York to London are particularly competitive because so many carriers want a piece of the action. You may actually get price breaks from new gateway cities that are launching service, so New York is not your only way to London. Ask, depending on where you are coming from.

If you find that all prices are the same, what do you base your choice on?

I think about convenience, frequent flyer mileage, overweight costs (I do a lot of shopping, remember), and perks. Now that Delta has a code-sharing deal with Virgin, it's harder than ever to sort out exactly what you're going to get and where the real value is.

BRITISH AIRWAYS I make it simple by pretty much sticking with one carrier for the New York to London run: **British Airways.** They've got use of Terminal Four and a million amenities geared to their passengers in the terminal. BA claims to be the world's favorite airline—they're certainly mine.

Every trip finds new improvements; recently I discovered they now have express passport service, so you don't even have to stand in line at immigration in Heathrow.

In-flight amenities are extended to economy, which is not true on every other airline. They give you a free toothbrush and overnight kit, even in the "back" of the plane in the World Traveller section.

Prices vary with the seasons and the competition; it's frequently less expensive to fly from New York to London than from New York to Los Angeles. Winter prices are always the best deal. They also have complete package tours with hotel rooms—in and out of London—and many specials.

My best secret: BA doesn't always advertise their rates. Watch for an American Airlines airfare war, then call BA. They will match the current lowest fares.

My second best secret: BA charges their excess baggage at a flat fee of $89. This is one of the least expensive methods of taking home your extra shopping packages in the world.

BA has almost a dozen U.S. gateway cities as well as the entire USAir network to help you make domestic connections. In the U.S., call 800-272-6433.

AMERICAN AIRWAYS I do sometimes fly American into London but actually use them for their other U.K. service more, partly because their gates are a tad inconvenient. If you are traveling on a mileage award, I'm sure you won't care.

American Airways is really trying to give BA a run for its money and therefore, they continue to increase both their number of flights and level of service—in all classes. Furthermore, they let you check three, not two, pieces of luggage. Excess baggage, beginning with that fourth piece, is billed at a flat fee of $99, New York to London or wherever. Coming back from London or Europe, the fee is the same, but it is billed in local currency. Call 800-433-7300.

DELTA If you're saying you didn't know Delta flies from New York to London, here's the big news—they do and they don't. Delta has regular London Gatwick service from Atlanta, etc., but they could only get the New York–London run by working out a code sharing deal with Virgin.

Here's the trick. Say I have a full-fare business class ticket on Delta because I am flying into, say, Lisbon. Since I am leaving from London and want my Delta miles, I can fly on Virgin (from Heathrow or Gatwick) in an Upper Class seat—the equivalent of first class—and still get my Delta miles. But, I don't get the free limo and I can't use the Virgin lounge. Call 800-241-4141.

GETTING AROUND LONDON

Buy an *A to Z*—it's a detailed street map. Walk whenever possible.

By Tube

The tube —London's famous underground system— does get you just about everywhere you need to go; some type of travel pass will be your best buy if you plan an active visit with many trips per day.

There are various tour cards and discount deals available in the U.S. that are not available in the U.K., so you must buy before you leave home. BritRail has recently been privatized, so there are deals offered to Americans that are not even known about in the U.K.

These are my rules of thumb:

- If you will ride the tube only once or twice a day and possibly not every day, pay for individual tickets as needed in London. If you can't figure out how to use the automatic machine, pay for the least expensive ticket and be prepared to pay up as you exit.
- If you are on and off the tube three or more times in a day, or going to Greenwich, buy a one-day travelcard for approximately £2.50.
- If you are spending a week in London and plan to explore it from dawn 'til dusk and don't really know what you're doing—except that you want to do it all—purchase the London Visitor Travelcard. It costs approximately $50 (you can obtain it ahead of time in the U.S.) and gives you seven days of unlimited travel on tube and bus.

By Bus

I thank Ian for putting me on the city's buses; I was always too afraid to learn the routes for fear of getting lost or get stuck in traffic. While all of these things can happen to you, the pleasure of being above ground and seeing the sights as you head to a destination is sublime.

Several of the tourist travel passes cover both the tube and the bus; so you may already be covered with one single pass.

I just hop on the bus, sit down and let the ticket taker tell me how much to pay. Sometimes I can even get Ian to pay. It's about 60p per journey.

By Taxi

Taxis are plentiful in recession, even in the rain! If you ask the doorman of a hotel—not the hotel you are staying in—to get you a taxi, please tip him 50p. If you frequently get taxis from your own hotel, tip the doorman when you leave. (See page 56 for tipping guidelines.) The flag drops at £1 and escalates quickly; taxis are not cheap in London.

You can make a daily deal with a driver, especially if he owns his own taxi. If you fall in love with a driver (this happens to me all the time), talk to him about it.

By Car

You do not want to rent a car in London. You may want to rent a car at the airport in order to drive around the countryside, but trust me, you do not want to drive in London.

If you want someone to drive you, that is an entirely different ball of wax. I keep on hand the brochure from **Capital Skylink**, which does airport pickups and transport, racecourse fares and sightseeing around town at a flat rate. They do take credit cards but there's a 10% surcharge for this, so have cash on hand. Phone 171-924-6556 or fax 171-924-5513.

GETTING AROUND BRITAIN

Since many people use London as their home base for day trips to nearby cities, I suggest you do a lot of research before you hop a train. You can buy *Born to Shop Great Britain*, for starters—there's plenty of train consumer information there.

Only the wealthy are so naive as to walk into a train station in Britain and buy a ticket to where they want to go—there are deals and saver days and special times and train passes and even something wonderful that allows you to upgrade to a first class ticket for £1 more!

Also note that with the privatization of BritRail, there's a transition period in effect which makes it very confusing as to which tickets you can buy where and how many InterCity (fast) trains are actually running. Call BritRail in the U.S. for information and consider a rail pass if you are doing a lot of train travel (phone: 212/575-2667).

GETTING IN TOUCH

. . . .

I call home frequently and find that AT&T USA Direct service is great, but not necessarily the bargain I want. Please be aware of the actual charges incurred each time you use one of these newfangled access codes that have been marketed as bargain phone fares. Yes, you get U.S. phone rates which may be less expensive than British Telecom (BT), but you pay a per-call surcharge so that if you talk for only a minute, or get the answering machine of the party you are calling, you're paying a very hefty price for those airwaves. (AT&T surcharge is $2.50 per call; MCI surcharge is $2.00 per call.)

I now buy a £4 phonecard upon arrival in London (any news agent will sell you one). This card is good for calls placed anywhere in the world. To call a telephone number in the U.S., slide the card into the proper slot in any booth marked Phonecard and dial 010 plus the area code and the number. You pay 10p per unit for the card; the card sounds an electronic beep when you have used up most of your units.

I spoke to my husband back home for several minutes for only 20 units and was quite pleased with myself and my savings. I call France; I call all over the world.

To avoid hotel surcharges and the trek to a phonecard phone from your hotel room, do use the access lines. To call the U.S. from anywhere in the U.K., dial 0800-89-0011 to get USA Direct service. To use a similar service via MCI, call 0800-89-0222.

You can also call home and ask them to call you back. If you have a good international phone plan, this offers the best savings. On my MCI plan, I pay 55 cents per minute from the U.S. to U.K. You'll have trouble beating that.

SHOPPING HOURS

Shopping hours are downright unorganized in London, so try to pay attention to what day of the week it is when you are shopping. Tuesdays seem to have later openings in the morning while Wednesday, Thursday, and Friday have slightly later closings in the evening. Note that it can be all three of these days at some stores or only one or two of them.

If the store normally opens at 10 A.M., then on Tuesdays it probably opens at 10:30 A.M.

Very few stores in London open at 9 A.M. Almost all of the big department stores and multiples open at 10 A.M.

Note: If you have a beauty parlor appointment at a department store salon, do not panic. One of the store doors is open at 9 A.M. with direct access to the hair salon.

Covent Garden stores may not open until 11 A.M.

Very few stores close for lunch.

All stores close early in London. They do not know the meaning of late. To a British store, a *late night* means they are open until 7 P.M. or possibly 8 P.M.

The biggest news in British retail is the fact that stores may now be open for six hours on Sundays! Those hours are usually noon until 5 P.M. Some stores, usually grocery stores or tourist traps, open at 11 A.M. on Sundays.

God bless you, Ma'am.

HOLIDAY HOURS

The change in Sunday retail has created a huge wave of uncertainty about the rigid laws on holidays as

London Underground

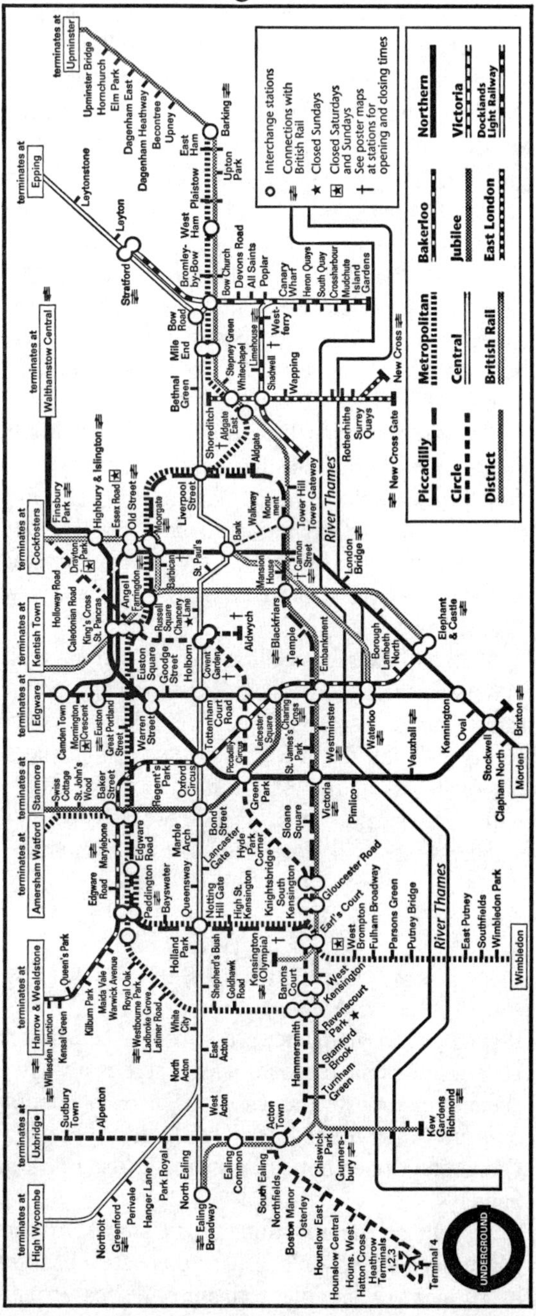

well. Used to be, stores were closed on holidays. These days, no one really knows who will do what.

I was just in London on Easter weekend and was shocked to find stores were posting hours for Sunday and Easter Monday shopping, and this includes Harrods! Yep, **Harrods** was open on Easter Monday.

France may stay closed tight on holidays, but London is getting more and more flexible. If you have your heart set on a specific errand, call the store. Also note that some branches of a store may be open while others will be closed—this was the case last Easter with **Boots.**

Who knows what Christmas will bring. Many an unhappy shopper has written to ask me to warn you: Stores are closed for as many as three days in a row right at the Christmas season—they celebrate Christmas Eve, Christmas Day, and Boxing Day (the day after Christmas). Stores also close again for New Year's Day.

Bank holidays are celebrated at regular intervals in the British calendar; they seem to fall around the same time as the feasts of the Virgin, but ever since Henry VIII split from Rome, no one in England is big on feasts of the Assumption. Bank holidays will affect retail, but in an odd way: banks and smaller stores will close; big stores and multiples are usually open.

CHEMISTS' HOURS

If you need an emergency prescription filled, or just have a late-night personal need, there is always a chemist or drugstore open somewhere in London on a later-than-usual basis. The **Boots** at Piccadilly Circus stays open until 10 P.M. and is also open on Sundays.

If your accommodations aren't anywhere near Piccadilly Circus, don't despair: there are a handful of all-night or late-night chemists dotted around town—just ask your concierge for the one closest to your hotel.

Condoms are sold in vending machines in most restaurants and in hotel gift shops.

ROYAL WARRANTS

You may wonder where the Queen shops. She doesn't. Things are "sent round" to Buckingham Palace for her to consider. Money and price tags never touch her hands. However, she asks only certain stores and factories to send round goods—these stores have the royal seal of approval, which is called a royal warrant.

Holding a royal warrant demands total discretion. The warrant holder may not talk about the royals in any way—especially to the press or public—or he will lose his warrant. So if you walk into **Turnbull & Asser** and ask them what size pj's Prince Charles wears, you will be met by an icy stare and stony silence. Royal warrants are allowed to display the royal coat of arms and to use the words "by appointment." Since there is more than one royal family in Europe, and there are several members of the Windsor family, you may also see several coats of arms on the window of any given store—appointments from various royals.

A warrant is good for 10 years and then must be renewed. If a merchant is dropped, he gets a sort of royal pink slip and has no means of redress. Every year about 20 to 30 new warrants are issued and the same number of pink slips are passed out. To qualify for a warrant, you must provide a minimum of three years' service to the crown.

There are warrants on everything from royal laundry detergent (Procter & Gamble) to royal china, and there can be several warrants in the same category. For china, HRH has as much trouble getting it down to one pattern as I do—she's got warrants at **Royal Worcester, Spode,** and **Royal Doulton;**

22 LONDON DETAILS

the Queen Mother gets her bone china from **Royal Crown Derby**. (Say "darby," please.)

And yes, the royals are also in retail. Prince Charles has been trying to get a royal warrant for his Duchy of Cornwall products and Buckingham Palace has a small gift shop selling coffee mugs to tourists for $15 a pop. There goes the neighborhood.

MUSEUM SHOPPING

THE VICTORIA & ALBERT MUSEUM SHOP I always adored the V&A gift shop and have no idea why they saw fit to close it down and completely redo it with razzmatazz. The actual shop size is the same but it has been reorganized so there is 30% more selling space. There's also an additional shop for kids in the Henry Cole Wing.

Although the usual postcards and papergoods are still for sale, the shop also sells jewelry, has some new lines created specifically to beef up the product range, and even now has a few items of clothing. They also do mail order.

A donation is suggested for museum admission; however, you can get into the gift shop without entering the museum. (Tube: South Kensington)

BRITISH MUSEUM SHOP Don't miss the reproduction gifts and the gorgeous books. This is a huge museum, it's free, it's across the street from a great sweater store (**Westaway & Westaway**), and you can walk to Covent Garden from here if you're strong enough. This store is the perfect place for unique gifts and souvenirs if you aren't into kitsch and royal souvenirs. (Tube: Tottenham Court Road or Holborn)

THE NATIONAL GALLERY SHOP Cards and calendars are the real finds, but the posters aren't shabby. The shop has been moved around the corner as a freestanding shop. (Tube: Charing Cross)

LONDON TRANSPORT MUSEUM While Covent Garden is great on Sunday, this small

How to Speak English: Shopper's Edition

Access: European firm which issues the equivalent of MasterCard
body: bodysuit
boot: the trunk of a car
braces: suspenders
brolly: umbrella
car boot sale: a tag sale held in a field or parking lot where locals sell their precious valuables right from their cars
chemist: a drugstore
chips: French fries
crisps: potato chips
deli: gourmet food market
fringe: bangs (hair)
jumble: used clothing
jumble sale: a tag sale
jumper: a sweater
knickers: underpants
loo or *W.C.*: the bathroom
mall (pronounced "mell"): shopping mall
nobs: nobilities (fancy pants)
pants: underpants
pram: baby carriage; stroller
spend a penny: to go to the bathroom. As in "I have to spend a penny; excuse me."
suspenders: garter belt
Switch: British firm which issues the equivalent of a Visa card
tat: used bric-a-brac; cheap goods
trousers: pants
torch: a flashlight
vest: an undershirt
waistcoat: a vest
Wellies: waterproof boots or shoes

museum is a treasure any day. Children will love shopping the gift area, which is also great for adults. There's a lot more here than you would expect; don't miss the thousands of postcards and posters of

24   LONDON DETAILS

Transport Art (drawings which have decorated tube and train stations since the early part of the century). Actually, the museum happens to be fun too, but the gift shop is sensational. (Tube: Covent Garden)

MUSEUM OF THE MOVING IMAGE   Part of the South Bank Arts Center at Waterloo, this is one of London's best. It's also great for kids weaned on TV and movies. Exhibits transport visitors from the earliest shadow plays to a 24-minute film that covers all of Hollywood's famous faces from Mickey Mouse to Mickey Rourke. The gift shop has a huge selection of books on movies, posters, videocassettes, notepads, postcards, Chaplin masks, movie-theme glassware, coasters, jigsaw puzzles, lamps, aprons, and other cinema tchotchkes. (Tube: Waterloo)

DESIGN MUSEUM   Sure the museum is neat, and the part of town where it's located (Butler's Wharf) is worth taking a look at to get a view of Thames redevelopment, but don't forget the gift shop or the restaurant. Products are featured heavily in the collections and are sold, along with the postcards and visual arts, in the shop. This entire complex, including the restaurant, is an example of Sir Terence Conran's genius; this is part of the New London. (Tube: Tower Hill)

BRAMAH TEA AND COFFEE MUSEUM   You know I could never resist a teapot; this museum traces the history of both tea and coffee and features many novelty teapots, as does the small gift shop. Very close to the Design Museum. (Tube: Tower Hill)

IMPERIAL WAR MUSEUM   If you've got kids—especially boys—they will love this museum and the shop, which sells model airplanes, among other things. Don't knock the name of the museum or the concept: according to Aaron Gershman, it's a great place. Also note that you must pay an admission fee if you arrive in the morning, but the museum is free between 4:30 and 6 P.M. (Tube: Elephant & Castle or Lambeth North)

Tube and Train Shopping 25

ATTRACTION SHOPPING

MADAME TUSSAUD'S Madame Tussaud's is outrageously expensive to visit and the lines out front can be thick. You can quit the scene and walk around to the side of the building, past the Planetarium, and gain access to the shop, but you'll have to knock on the door to be let in. The tour ends in the gift shop; they just aren't prepared for people who only want to shop.

The shop itself is rather large with several rooms. Much of the merchandise for sale is standard London destination souvenir stuff; however, there are some items which are unique to Madame Tussaud's. My favorite line is the group of items with the slogan "some of the people I met in London" with pictures, shirts, and coffee cups of the famous, and infamous, as created in wax. (Tube: Baker Street)

TOWER OF LONDON Get there early because the lines are fierce. And you bet there are gift shops—we counted three on our last family visit; many of the gifts were historical or educationally oriented, such as color-yourself stained glass windows, etc. Don't ask me why they don't sell paste copies of the crown jewels—makes sense to me. Maybe an Anne Boleyn Commemorative Arrow Box? (Tube: Tower Hill)

TUBE AND TRAIN SHOPPING

Retail in train stations is already pretty sophisticated. People like to be able to grab what they need as they dash to and from the train; hence there are always florists, candy stores, bookstores, and even shoe repair or coffee bean stores. I've even seen branches of **Knickerbox**, the lingerie chain, in several train stations.

Now then, what you really want to know about is Chunnel duty free. I wish I could make this answer make sense. The truth is, there is no duty free shop in Waterloo Station as you take the passenger train, Eurostar, and there are no trolleys onboard the train selling duty free merchandise. Technically speaking, the Chunnel backs the abolishment of duty free and has made many politically correct public statements along this line.

However, there is a duty free store before you drive your car onto Le Shuttle. Go figure.

SOUVENIR SHOPPING

The best place to buy London destination-specific souvenirs is from the street vendors who stretch across the "downtown" area—there are quite a few of them on Oxford Street from Marble Arch to Oxford Circle. There's another gaggle at Piccadilly Circus. The street vendors do seem to have the best prices in town. I priced those plastic bobby helmets at £1.50 in street stands and £1.99 in official souvenir shops. Just to hit the point home, the same hats were £3 at the news agent in Heathrow's Terminal Four!

Please note that if you are traveling out-of-season, you can bargain a little bit with the street vendors, except at Buckingham Palace, where souvenirs are about the most expensive in town.

Royal commemoratives also make good souvenirs, but be warned that some of these things become collectors' items and are frequently very, very expensive. At the time of a royal event (such as a wedding or a coronation), the commemoratives seem to be a dime-a-dozen, but once they dry up, they are gone forever and become collectors' items.

If you are buying for an investment, buy the best quality you can afford (branded ceramic versus cheap) and try to get something that was created in a limited edition.

On Saturdays, Portobello Road has several vendors selling souvenirs. Although some of the antiques vendors may have royal souvenirs, beware: most of what they're selling is the cheap and tacky kind that is not valuable.

Because the Harrods name has become synonymous with London, Harrods souvenirs are perfectly appropriate gifts. There are scads of them, in every price range. Souvenirs are sold both on the street floor and in the lower level.

SHOPPING SERVICES

If you think you might need some help on the ground, if you have some corporate shopping to do, or if you want more specific help than I can offer, you may want to try a shopping service.

I found Shirley Eaton through **The Bulldog Club**—she is a hostess member and has a house that is to die for. With taste as fine as hers, you know you're in good hands if you sign up for her service. You can pay £25 for a half day (9:30 A.M.–1 P.M.) or £50 for a full day (9:30 A.M.–5:30 P.M.). She will shop with you and offer her suggestions for solving your immediate needs. Shirley's specialty is antiques and interior design, but she's also keen on fashion.

Contact her directly in London at 171-581-8429 (phone) or 171-584-9874 (fax).

ROYAL MAIL: SHOPPING AND SENDING

News agents sell books of royal stamps in cute little red packages. When you purchase a book, you must specify if you want international stamps or not. There is a flat rate for all international postcards (35p), no matter where they are going. Stamps do not have denominations printed on them.

If you do decide to mail items home, you can buy Jiffy bags in the stationery department of any department store or at an office supply store. Then head for any post office, or ask your concierge to do the deed. Mark your package "unsolicited gift" and place its value at $25. (Unless it's less, of course.) You may legally send one package per day home if its value is less than $50.

International mail through stores is not tricky but can be expensive. **Thomas Goode** agreed to send some cups and saucers to the U.S.; their charge was £25! I'm sorry, but for that amount of money, I can carry them onboard. But wait, let's examine that cost without the first flush of passion.

My purchase totaled £100. I would therefore qualify for a VAT refund of more or less 18%. The cost of the shipping was 25% of my total. If I didn't want the hassle of hand carrying breakables or having to do the VAT refund myself at the airport, the price of the shipping isn't a bargain but offers a fair trade off.

A final note: If you plan to ship anything larger (such as a highboy) or are considering reserving a container, see Chapter 9 for detailed information on shipping.

DUTY FREE SHOPPING

I usually do some shopping at the duty free shop at LHR although I confess that I've gotten much more careful about it after over-paying on a bottle of Sun Moon Stars! The Saks Fifth Avenue price, with tax, was a few dollars *less* than what I paid at the duty free shop at Heathrow.

Know your prices on your favorite scents before you buy in London or in any duty free shop.

Keep the airline duty free prices with you for comparison as often airplanes are less expensive than airport duty free shops.

Look for coupons and promotional deals. The duty free shop at LHR frequently offers pound-off vouchers or does two for one promotions or price reductions if you spend a certain amount.

Although I was burned on the fragrance, I more than made up for it with the Hermès ties I bought at LHR during a recent special promotion. Here are the facts: At the time of this triumph, the dollar was trading at $1.50 to the pound. An Hermès silk tie regularly costs $135, plus tax, in New York's Hermès store, or $145. The same Hermès tie regularly costs £62 in the Hermès Bond Street store (and if you receive a VAT refund of roughly 13%, it actually costs you £55). However, when I visited the Hermès counter at LHR, the same tie was marked £55. Under the terms of a special promotion at the time (buy two, get £5 off), I bought two Hermès ties for $75 each—almost half price!

Please note that in the final analysis the London Bond Street price was more or less the same as the airport price. While I did get especially lucky on the £5 off coupon, a tie priced at £55 or approximately $85 (if the pound is trading at $1.50) is still a far better deal than what you would pay in New York.

I ran the same price comparisons with an Hermès scarf in their Bond Street store and on the airplane. When you factor in a VAT refund, a scarf bought from the store costs only £4 more than the one bought on the airplane. Considering that the store's selection is always broader than what is offered on an aircraft, most shoppers are willing to swallow the difference.

The amazing bottom line is that Hermès ties and scarves are less expensive in London—and can be cheaper yet if you shop in a duty free—than almost anywhere else, including Paris. But that's another story.

And you thought there were no bargains in London.

Chapter Three

· · · · · · · · ·

SLEEPING IN LONDON

It's not hard to find a fabulous hotel in Mayfair—or anywhere else in London—but you may want to give some serious thought to what combination of location, price, and ease of making reservations suits your budget and sensibilities.

I've found that a hotel is the single greatest factor in ensuring whether or not my trip has been a dream or a nightmare. I believe in luxury hotels, but I also believe in getting the most for my money.

- Prices in London for hotel rooms are pretty uniform and are based on the rank of the hotel—all five-star hotels cost almost the same amount per night. Therefore, one hotel with a fancier reputation is not necessarily more expensive than another.
- Many hotels have special promotions and rates. Almost every hotel discounts rooms in January when business is down, but they'll also discount during other time periods as well. When hotel rooms are empty, management gets creative. Use this fact to your benefit and don't be shy about places with hoity-toity reputations. It behooves you to spring for an international call to the hotel of your choice and to negotiate directly with them; it's unlikely that a computerized reservation service will have as much flexibility as a real live person smelling a deal.

- Look to the chains for promotions for which you might qualify. Hilton, InterContinental, and Forte (which now owns Le Meridien) all run price specials, even in the summer season. Often you can prepay for a room in U.S. dollars.
- Look for oddball locations, luxury hotels which have just been opened, bought, sold, or are rumored to be in financial trouble—frequently they have deals just to bring in cash.

LUXURY LOWDOWN

While no one can beat the prices offered by mass tourist hotels on a package, if you crave the comforts of luxury hotels, you may be surprised by the promotions some of them offer; certain luxury hotels, including the ones with the most famous names, can be more affordable than you might think. Resist the little voice inside that says you shouldn't even try to stay "at a place like that." The last time I checked, The Ritz and the Holiday Inn a half block away were priced at exactly the same amount per room. Wouldn't you rather stay at The Ritz?

The Dorchester has an add-on promotional price at Christmas and New Year's that allows guests who have booked events at the hotel to spend the night and not have to worry about the designated driver's ability to pass a Breathalyzer test or how they'll negotiate possibly slick and dangerous roads . . . last year that rate was a mere £100!

Don't be afraid to call around, to use toll-free numbers, to fax the General Manager of a fancy hotel, or to ask for a deal from all of your resources. You just may be pleasantly surprised. Don't be intimidated!

- Big chains may have gem hotels that you've never heard of—check them out on a reconnaissance trip, then book for your next stay. Think about

the InterContinental's **Mayfair**, which doesn't have the InterContinental name on the marquis, and the many Hilton hotels that are members of the Hilton family but might not be well known, such as **Hilton Mews**, a true gem.
- Weekend package deals are popular. Usually called "weekend breaks" in Britain, they are meant to generate business when businesspeople and their expense accounts have not filled the ranks.
- Combination city-country deals are sometimes offered. If you are traveling around Great Britain, consider arranging your schedule so that you spend the first weekend in London at one hotel, travel during the week (rates are lower in the countryside and in Edinburgh), and then return to London for the second weekend—maybe even to a different hotel, depending on the deal. Forte has a good program for combining destinations.

LUXURY HOTELS FOR SHOPPERS

All hotels in London are expensive. Luxury hotels can cost $400 a night for a double room. I once asked a London hotelier friend of mine why people would pay $400 a night. He explained that the room you get for $200 is frequently in such a bad hotel that you are delighted to pay twice as much to get what you want.

Most luxury hotels have promotional rates and weekend price breaks. Don't look now, but smart shoppers can have all the luxury they need and sometimes get it for as little as $200 a night. Not always, mind you, but sometimes.

THE DORCHESTER
Park Lane, W1 (Tube: Marble Arch).

The bed. The bath. The spa. Oh my. I may never be the same. I am ruined. And the spa alone is worth

Luxury Hotels for Shoppers 33

the price of admission. Actually, the spa is free when you book a room.

I met The Dorchester while writing an article for *Newsweek* on European value! One waltz through the lobby and I was hooked. That stationery with the embossed aubergine motto, "The Dorchester," makes you want to just swipe it. Indeed, even telling your taxi driver "The Dorchester" has a certain ring to it that's worth money.

I'm wild about the little shopping neighborhood directly behind the hotel (see page 93) and I don't mean in the Marble Arch direction. I am also keen on their restaurant (see page 43 for a description).

The hotel is most seriously reserved by Hollywood celebs who are very cultish about where they book; ever since Liz Taylor holed up here with her 47 pieces of luggage, the hotel has been *the* place if you are a big enough star. Or are wondering exactly how big a star you are and need a book of matches to tell you.

If you can't stay here, come for breakfast or tea. Order pancakes and coffee for £6.50 and have the time of your life. Don't forget to look at the ceiling in the Grill Room where they serve breakfast.

Oh yes, also check out their little news agent/gift shop. They sell some Dorchester logo gifts and the house brand of private label champagne. I brought this as a gift to a French hotelier once, who is still tickled. It's perfect thing for the person who has everything.

A Leading Hotel of the World. For U.S. reservations, call 800-727-9820. Local telephone: 171-629-8888.

THE ATHENAEUM HOTEL & APARTMENTS
116 Piccadilly, London W1 (Tube: Hyde Park).

A big block from The Dorchester and totally opposite in all other aspects, The Athenaeum is a very hands-on kind of small luxury hotel. It's small; it's hidden in a row of luxury hotels facing Green Park; it's not as well known as some of the big names. But therein lies its glory. This is the find that no one wants to tell you about for fear you'll ruin it. Least of all the very Hollywood crowd that stays here mainly because they know you won't stare.

Committed to shopping, The Athenaeum has several packages coordinated to the January and July sales events at Harrods. They also have a variety of other deals including full apartments, a nanny for your kids, or simply low out of season rates. Their in season rates are not as high as some of the more famous hotels and while rooms are small, you won't suffer. They have a very strong summer season promotion, usually frozen in U.S. dollars, in which you get a room for $225 per night, double occupancy. For $300 a night you can get an apartment for four. Not bad at all.

There's a small spa downstairs in the basement; the bar specializes in malt whiskeys. And the date pie with sticky toffee sauce will slay you.

Book through Small Luxury Hotels of the World: 800-525-4800 or book directly 800-335-3300. Local phone: 171-499-3464; fax 171-493-1860.

The Ritz
Piccadilly, W1 (Tube: Green Park).

The Ritz is a landmark, a nest of luxury, and a fabulous shopping hotel all wrapped into one. The location is one of its primary strengths—you're right at Piccadilly with a tube stop out the door (Green Park) and another (Piccadilly) down the block.

Part of the charm of the hotel is that it's drop-dead fancy but also intimately sized. With only 130 rooms, The Ritz is considered a small hotel. If you aren't staying here, you owe it to part of your London experience to come for a meal or for tea. Or to look at their logo merchandise gift shop.

Prices vary tremendously; The Ritz is now managed by Mandarin Oriental and often qualifies for some of their promotional offers.

For reservations in the U.S., call 800-222-0939. Local telephone: 171-493-8181.

THE LANGHAM HILTON
1 Portland Place, Regent Street, W1
(Tube: Oxford Circus).

"However did you find this place?" my girlfriend Pat asked when she inspected the lobby—and my room—at The Langham Hilton. Pat assumed that all Hiltons were created alike and that they were ugly; she would have never dreamed to look at one, let alone stay at one.

The Langham Hilton is one of those rare birds—Hilton does have a few of them—that are grande dame old-fashioned hotels which have been totally redone per modern standards but still have that old and elegant feel.

Count on more than that when you book Langham Hilton because it's got a fabulous shopping location, literally one block from just about everything. They have strong weekend promotional deals; they have a shopping weekend promotional package. For execs, there's a package with a Mansfield room which gives you a bedroom with sitting area, full English breakfast, late check out, and a corporate rate of just under £200. You need to book that one by name, Mansfield.

For U.S. reservations, call 800-HILTONS; local phone 171-636-1000.

HILTON PARK LANE
22 Park Lane, W1 (Tube: Hyde Park Corner or Marble Arch). Local telephone: 171-493-8000.

This is Hilton's big, flagship skyscraper on Park Lane, which just received a $25 million renovation.

Closer to Green Park than The Langham Hilton, it's a property to take another look at.

HOTEL SECRETS

THE MAYFAIR
Stratton Street, W1 (Tube: Green Park).

This is one of my better secrets, so get out your highlighter. The Mayfair is a luxury hotel, not in the same class as the palace hotels, but a find nonetheless.

This is a hidden hotel on a Mayfair back street, half a block from **The Ritz** and the Green Park tube station and unknown to most tourists. Furthermore, it is a member of the InterContinental chain, but it does not use the InterContinental name in its title. What this means is when you use airline miles or see a specially advertised rate offered by InterContinental, you can book this hotel and get a charmer.

I've stayed here twice; one room was uninspired, but large enough to hold a rollaway bed for my son, Aaron. The second room was not only spacious and lavishly decorated in Edwardian style, but it had a full hot tub in the bathroom. You can sometimes book this hotel for $149 a night, guaranteed in U.S. dollars, under a special seasonal offer from Intercontinental. For U.S. reservations, call 800-327-0200. Local telephone: 171-629-7777.

DUKES HOTEL
35 St. James's Place, SW1 (Tube: Green Park).

This is a hidden delight with its own special secret—when the hotel changed hands recently it was refurbished and restored to its glory as an Edwardian townhouse mansion hotel and then its rates were lowered. The Queen says she loves it; Lady Thatcher does her press from here because it reminds her of 10 Downing Street.

This small, very English hotel is a treat at any price—the fact that it's a block from Piccadilly and a half-block from Jermyn Street just makes it more delicious for intrepid shoppers. Rates are bound to go up, so watch for promotions and book immediately.

Aficionados will be pleased to note that, despite all the changes, one thing (or person) hasn't changed: Gilberto, its barman, who may make the most famous martini in the world. (His collection of cognacs and brandies will knock your socks off.) If you can't stay here, come by for tea or an after-dinner drink. Especially cozy in fall and winter but marvelously British and sublime all year 'round.

There are only 55 bedrooms and this is the kind of place that attracts regulars, so plan ahead in order to get a room. Remember to ask if they have any promotional specials. When the hotel reopened, they had the best rate in town. Rack rate for a double is £160 plus VAT.

For U.S. reservations, call 800-381-4702. Local phone: 171-491-4840. Fax 171-493-1264.

B & B BREAKTHROUGHS

If hotels aren't your thing, try **Bulldog Club**, an agency that represents private homes of elegance and taste and puts you right into a fantasy B & B with a London address that is guaranteed to be within a five-minute walk of a tube or bus stop.

Bulldog was the brainchild of a London woman with a gorgeous house and a need to keep it gorgeous. Taking in boarders has never been so glamorous.

I haven't tried this yet, but when you hear the details you'll be as intrigued as I am. There are some 20 houses in the group, all of which would be categorized as four- or five-star properties if they were hotels. Each private home is owned by a professional who is accustomed to entertaining (one of the hostesses even has a corporate shopping business; see page 27).

You receive your own key to the house and your room will be either on a separate floor from the family's bedrooms or in a separate part of the house, such as over the garage or in the coach house. There are tea- and coffee-making facilities in the rooms, robes, toiletries, and amenities galore. The real charm of this find is that you will feel as though you are staying with a friend, yet you will still have privacy.

Full British breakfast is served in the private dining room, not with the family. Perhaps the best description of this unique service is the analogy Bev Boyle, Bulldog's North American representative, offered me: "It's the reverse of 'Upstairs, Downstairs.'"

To get acquainted with Bulldog, call Bev and chat with her yourself. Tell her what you're looking for and what your needs are. (You can even specify what kind of chintz you like best.) Within 24 hours she'll make your booking and fax the details to you. You have 48 hours to decide if it suits you. Provided it does, you'll need to join Bulldog, which costs £25 annually. All major credit cards are accepted. After you're signed up, you receive a package from Bulldog's London offices with information on your hosts, their home, and its location, as well as bus and tube information and other London basics.

All rooms cost £95 a night (for two people!); £75 single, including breakfast. Expect your hostess to have a name like Lavinia. In the U.S. or Canada, call 905-737-2798 or fax 905-737-3179. In the U.K., call 171-622-6935 or fax 171-720-2748.

FLAT NEWS

If you don't want to be anyone's guest at all, you may want to consider renting a flat, which not only works out cheaper on a nightly basis, but also gives you the option of cooking some of your meals. While prices vary tremendously, you can get a nice flat with two bedrooms and two baths in a slightly suburban London neighborhood in the £300-per-week range. Expect to pay £500 minimum for a small luxe flat with a fine location.

The Barclay International Group is a U.S. firm that will book you into any of their apartments in London. A two-person studio starts at £220 for an entire week (including VAT). There are properties in Kensington and Mayfair; you can even arrange for their limo to pick you up at the airport. Their Grosvenor House apartments come with use of health club facilities. In the U.S., call 800-845-6636.

The Apartment Company is a British firm that seems to work much like Barclay with similar properties. Their hottest locale is Dolphin Square because the Princess Royal (Anne) is a tenant. Draycott House is a prestigious address where flats are frequently rented by celebrities; you're looking at £700–£2,000 a week (depending on size), plus VAT. In London, call 171-835-1144.

AIRPORT HOTELS

If you are connecting through LHR and need an airport hotel, you won't have trouble finding one. Many airlines have links with a specific hotel that offer you a price break or other amenities and privileges. I stayed at a Holiday Inn at the airport once and was lent a Virgin Atlantic bathing suit! Indeed, I pick my hotel by the spa and pool services and often go for a swim and have a massage.

What you may not realize is that the airport is very close to the town of Windsor and isn't that far from a few other English country house mansion style hotels so if you want luxury and convenience, or charm and convenience, you don't have to stay at the airport to be close to it. Many of these nearby hotels will include airport transfer in the price; ask.

Hilton's airport hotels are reliable worldwide; they have properties at LHR and Gatwick. Call 800-HILTONS from the U.S. to book.

Also note that many airport properties provide shuttle service into London for free or a small cost. Airport hotels usually cost less than London hotels per night so they may be a worthwhile alternative if you only have half a day to explore London as you connect elsewhere.

Chapter Four

DINING IN LONDON

More, please. Since Oliver Twist had the nerve to ask for second helpings, British food has improved to the point where it is hard to get reservations at certain restaurants and the French are actually coming over from Paris just to try the cooking at a few fine kitchens that have recently earned extra Michelin stars.

If you don't want to spend all your money on food and want to save a little for shopping, do not despair. London has more meal deals than almost any other city.

Those with small appetites or small budgets can rejoice: this is the city where the "jacket potato" (baked potato) constitutes an entire meal and can be eaten in any of the numerous potato fast food joints where the potato comes with a variety of toppings that turn it into quite a hefty meal.

I also like to have at least one picnic when I visit London: I usually buy prepared food for an alfresco lunch at M&S but there are now so many grocery stores that sell prepared meals in the key shopping areas of London that you'll have no trouble finding something to please your palate and your purse. The hardest part may be selecting just the right bench or stretch of lawn on which to plop yourself.

Pizza is another of my mainstays in London; Ian and I consider it a special treat to eat at almost any branch of **Pizza Express** . . . including their upmarket **Pizza on the Park.** There are almost 100 branches of this chain in the U.K. with at least 40 in the London area, so I can't list them all. Their menu lists all their London locations on the back; they'll be happy to give you one if you ask.

FOOD GUIDES

If you want to get really detailed information on London's food scene, you should be clipping from the American food and travel magazines which regularly cover it. I also clip from *Tatler,* the British magazine, and buy the annual *Good Food Guide,* although my own eating patterns are now fairly ritualized and therefore don't vary that much. All British bookstores carry this trusty tome.

BIG-TIME MEAL DEALS

The secret to dining in style in London on a budget lies in knowing about the two basic tricks that have been added to almost every upscale eatery's repertoire: the pre-theater meal and the fixed-price meal.

Pre-theater meals are usually served around 6 P.M.; note that curtain times in London vary by the production and are usually earlier than in New York. A 7:30 P.M. curtain is generally the rule. Therefore, pre-theater dinners are only available at an early hour. If this doesn't bother you (you are American, aren't you?) you can dine like a king at some of the best tables in London for the price of a song. A Little Night Music, anyone?

Fixed-price meals are offered in all the major hotel dining rooms (dancing and/or entertainment is usually included) and at the *haute*-est of tables, including London's most famous French restaurant, **Le Gavroche.**

Many of the fancier tables take some getting into, so the browse-and-book method will not work for you. You may want to fax ahead for a reservation, or several reservations, and hold them until you can check out the situation and then cancel once you get to town. Do give 24 hours notice when you cancel; this is a very polite town. Manners matter.

LUXURY MEALS FOR LESS

LE GAVROCHE
43 Upper Brook Street, W1 (171-408-0881).

Long before there was good food, let alone gourmet food, in London, there was Michel and Albert Roux. Over the years, their restaurant, Le Gavroche, has held onto its reputation as both the finest French restaurant in town and one of the best restaurants in the world. Although it's generally expensive, their fixed-price meals can be make dining here almost a bargain—if you go light on drinks and wine. Considering what it would cost you to dine at a similar table in France, Le Gavroche's three-course, fixed-price meal for £55 per person is truly memorable. This price includes VAT and service; beverages are not included. A fixed-price lunch is also available. To fax your reservation, dial 171-491-4387.

THE DORCHESTER
Park Lane, W1 (Phone: 171-629-8888).

The Dorchester, one of London's finest hotels, has several restaurants, all of which are fine and some of which are famous (and starred by Michelin). Here's the best part: Almost all of them have special fixed-price meals for approximately £25 per person, including VAT and service!

The meal I tasted at the Terrace (a dinner/dancing combination) was divine. While purists might have found the crowd and dress a little too mixed, the food was memorable. And the price, downright unbelievable!

44   DINING IN LONDON

The Grill, another dining room in the hotel, serves roast beef from the trolley in traditional style, also at a fixed price of £25 per person.

The best thing to do is to go to the hotel, check out the menus and the rooms and see which appeals to you and then book your favorite. Believe me, you will dine out on the story for years!

Also note that you can eat breakfast at the Grill at the Dorchester for under £10 and pretend you're royal.

THE RITZ
Piccadilly, W1 (Phone: 171-493-8181).

Recently, I was dining in Louis XV in Monte Carlo, which is purported to be the fanciest restaurant in the world. It was heaven, no doubt about it. But when my dining companion asked me what I thought of the room, I could only say, "It looks like The Ritz in London to me."

Indeed, the dining room in The Ritz is sheer elegance. Their fixed-price dinner and dinner/dancing packages are excellent values. Let the other tourists come here for tea; you'll be booking dinner, thank you.

THE BEST SPOTS FOR LADIES WHO LUNCH

All of the restaurants below serve dinner (except Nicole's) and are considered both hot spots and places to be seen in London. They also frequently claim to be Princess Diana's faves. I've chosen the best ones which are also located in good shopping neighborhoods so you can segue smoothly from store to table and then back again. Note that lunch often costs less than dinner. Reservations at these places are recommended; so is proper dress.

DAPHNE'S
112 Draycott Avenue, SW3 (Tube: South Kensington).

Right in the heart of the Walcot Street shopping at the edge of Brompton Cross, this has been *the* place since it opened a few years ago. The food is slightly Italian; the crowd is sleek and chic. Phone: 171-589-4257.

SAN LORENZO
22 Beauchamp Place, SW3 (Tube: Knightsbridge).

The *in* place before Daphne's opened and still not shabby. Right on Beauchamp Place in the middle of one of London's best shopping streets. Walking distance from Harrods. Phone: 171-584-1074.

CHEZ NICO AT PARK LANE
90 Park Lane, SW1 (Tube: Hyde Park Corner or Green Park).

It's the chef, Nico Ladenis, whom people are talking about—and following around London as he moves or opens another restaurant. Not to be confused with Nico Central.

This restaurant is conveniently located for Mayfair shopping and has a £25 set price lunch that goes on forever and will render you useless but contented. Phone:171-409-1290.

NICOLE'S
158 New Bond Street, W1 (Tube: Bond Street).

The place of the moment is actually inside a store (see below) and offers expensive but stylish lunch—or tea. It is *the* place to say you've been. Wear beige. No hat. Phone: 171-499-8408.

IN-STORE MEALS

Eating inside a store has become very trendy in London. Emporio Armani serves Italian food while Nicole Farhi offers her signature fare downstairs in her Bond Street flagship shop. DKNY has a snack bar that serves bagels and cream cheese and brownies and other American-style foods.

The big department stores have always had restaurants, and some have several. These used to be the places where blue-haired ladies were entertained by their daughters in a Mum and Me kind of ritual. Now, many of these store restaurants have spiffed up and are quite hip.

The best thing for shoppers about eating in a store is the convenience factor—you're already there, so put down your bags and take a seat. Get there early if you don't have a reservation.

HARRODS
87-135 Brompton Road, Knightsbridge, SW1 (Tube: Knightsbridge).

London's most famous department store has several restaurants, including a coffee shop right in the famed food halls. Phone: 171-730-1234.

HARVEY NICHOLS
Knightsbridge (corner of Sloane Street), SW1 (Tube: Knightsbridge).

The Fifth Floor of this Sloane Square institution is a gourmet restaurant where reservations are a must. There's also a small snack area in front of the restaurant and across from the food products. Phone: 171-235-5250.

FENWICK
63 New Bond Street, W1 (Tube: Bond Street or Oxford Circus).

A trendy branch of Joe's Cafe with bar and table service is here. It's okay; you can stare at the crowd. They are far more with it than anyone else you are going to see in Fenwick's. Phone: 171-629-9161.

In-Store Meals 47

BIBENDUM/CONRAN'S
Michelin House, 81 Fulham Road, SW3 (Tube: South Kensington).

Nobody combines food and shopping like Sir Terrence Conran. His state of the art masterpiece is still the rehabilitation at Michelin House that features his store and its famous companion restaurant, Bibendum. Book way in advance and hope that someone else is paying. Phone: 171-581-5817.

DICKINS & JONES
224 Regent Street, W1 (Tube: Oxford Circus).

Part of the store's remake is a new restaurant on the third floor, right near the designer clothing department. You can actually eat lunch here for £10.

FORTNUM & MASON
181 Piccadilly, W1 (Tube: Piccadilly).

They have two restaurants and while I've done the silver trolley and roast beef bit, I prefer The Fountain, where I can get in and out rather quickly. They don't take lunch reservations; if you are alone, team up with a stranger to be served more quickly. I do it all the time. Phone: 171-734-8040.

THOMAS GOODE
19 South Audley Street, W1 (Tube: Hyde Park Corner or Marble Arch).

Truth is, I tried to eat here, but the prices were so high that I thought I would faint and break all the dishes in my favorite china store. Tea is proportionately more expensive than lunch. On the other hand, they serve you on very nice dishes. Do reserve a table. Phone: 171-499-2823.

SNACK & SHOP

BERKELEY SQUARE CAFE
*7 Davies Street, Berkeley Square, London W1
(Tube: Bond Street or Green Park).*

If I'm off by myself or meeting a girlfriend for shopping in Mayfair, I love this place. They make it so easy to dash in, have a nice meal, and dash out—without spending a fortune. The food and atmosphere are sort of upmarket deli. Americans, please remember to say "Bark-clay."

Don't let the fact that it isn't right near a tube stop throw you either; Berkeley Square Cafe is located right in the middle of Mayfair. You will pass it—or circulate within a block of it—as you do your errands in the area. It's half a block from the Connaught Hotel.

PIZZALAND
Numerous locations throughout London.

I often eat at Pizzaland, a cheap Italian chain that serves pizza and basic fast Italian food. I discovered it when Aaron was two and would only eat spaghetti. I actually like their spaghetti. And I can eat lunch in a hurry for only £6. There's a Pizzaland just about everywhere. One of my regulars is on Oxford Street.

CRITERION
224 Piccadilly, W1 (Tube: Piccadilly).

This is a must-do in my book; and this *is* my book. Located in a rehabilitated theater with all the glory of a multimillion-dollar Broadway show, this restaurant serves moderately priced meals in a convenient location right at Piccadilly. Two people can eat lunch for £25! The place is huge; don't forget to look at the ceiling. You might want to book lunch (that's British for make a reservation). Phone: 171-925-0909.

TEATIME

I am a longtime believer in the English custom of taking tea for two very simple reasons:

- After you've been shopping all day, you need to plop down, drop the packages and get off those feet.
- If you want to save money, you can eat a big tea and go light on (or skip) dinner. Conversely, if dinner isn't until 8 P.M. or later, you'll never last without a sufficient tea break.

All the big fancy hotels have tea service; you can make it your job to try a different one every day. I have discovered, however, that there are several ins and outs to getting full value from teatime, so get out your highlighter. If you're British, don't blush, but I'm going to talk about money.

Generally speaking, tea comes at a set price, per person, and includes the tea (or coffee) of your choice and a three-round selection of sandwiches, scones, and sweets. There is also tea with sherry or tea with champagne.

Tea is usually served from 3–5:30 or 6 P.M. If sherry is served, it is called high tea. "Teatime," as a time of meeting someone or fixing your schedule, is usually meant to be 4 P.M.; by 5 P.M. it is socially acceptable to start drinking. I've never heard of anyone going to tea at 6 P.M.

Now for the tricky part: the finances of taking tea. At grand hotels you pay a flat fee for the total tea service, and that price is not cheap. Expect to pay an average of £12 per person, although some are £10 and prices do go higher than £12 and are often £15 at a very elegant place.

It is very unusual, especially at an elegant hotel, for tea to be served *a la carte*. However, at a few addresses, you may buy the full tea service for one and a second (or even third) pot of tea *a la carte*, thus saving about $20. Furthermore, one or two hotels allow for total *a la carte* tea service. Since very few people can eat all of what is provided at teatime, this is a money-saving device. At the Dorchester, there is a fixed price for simple tea and scones aside from the total tea price or the total tea with champagne price.

THE RITZ
Piccadilly, W1 (Tube: Green Park).

Tea at The Ritz is a *Ritz*ual that few people want to pass up. While I recommend it as a once-in-a-lifetime thing to do, I have several Ritz secrets for you. Tea at The Ritz is so popular that management doesn't even like to publicize it—the place is packed. You may not even get to sit in the main court, but in one of the fancy halls, and you *must* have a reservation.

Tea is a lavish affair; if gentlemen do not have their ties on hand, they may borrow one from the cloakroom.

The trick at The Ritz is to come for either lunch in the Palm Court or breakfast. Breakfast is served in the most beautiful dining room in London (this is general knowledge, not just my opinion) and is not as crowded as tea, so you can really relish your surroundings. Phone: 171-493-8181.

THE STAFFORD
St. James's Place, SW1 (Tube: Green Park).

Guests may sit in the parlor, in front of the fire if so desired, and take formal tea (£10), or have one large scone, without ordering the entire tea service. This Georgian house is exactly my cup of tea. Phone: 171-493-0111.

Teatime 51

BROWN'S HOTEL
Albemarle Street, W1 (Tube: Green Park).

For years I've have been sending people to Brown's Hotel for tea: There's no question that it's one of the best teas in London and that their scones are among the best. You may request one setup (tea for one) and additional cups of tea, or you may request a platter of scones to replace the tea setup (but at the same cost) and individual pots of tea. Jackets and ties for the gentlemen; be prepared for a long wait if you aren't early. Next door to **Michaeljohn.** Phone: 171-493-6020.

Chapter Five

MONEY MATTERS

For the most part, I recommend using a credit card. Plastic is the safest to use and it provides you with a record of your purchases (for Customs as well as for your books). It also makes returns much easier. Credit-card companies, because they are often associated with banks, also give the best exchange rates.

It's even possible to "make money" by charging on a credit card. That's because the price you pay as posted in dollars is translated on the day your credit slip clears the credit-card company (or bank) office, not on the day of your purchase. Of course, you can conversely lose money.

If you're getting $1.55 for your pound in cash at the hotel desk, you may get $1.50 through your credit card. Or, the pound can fluctuate in the two- to three-day period that it takes for your purchase to be officially posted to your account.

I don't like to remember this incident, but since it happened to me, it could well happen to you—I did business on a specific day in Britain when the pound was trading at around $2. I went to bed. The next morning, the pound was at $1.70. Now, this was a once-in-a-lifetime monetary accident (I hope) and I liken it to World War III—the Bundesbank forced the pound out of the EMU and England basically had to devalue. In this case, I lost hundreds of dollars.

Money Matters 53

However, if I'd bought something on a credit card on day one and they devalued on day two, I would have made thirty cents on the pound by the time the purchase was posted to my credit card.

Easy come, easy go.

Urrrrrrrrrgh.

The bad news about credit cards is that you can overspend easily, and you may come home to a stack of bills. The one extra benefit a credit card offers is the potential for delayed billing, since it may take a month or two for the London charges to appear.

Traveler's checks are a must, however, for safety's sake. Shop around a bit and compare the various companies that issue checks. I happen to use American Express traveler's checks, but they are not the only safe game in town. Just make sure the checks you use are issued by a firm that has many outlets for cashing them, so you do not have to pay an additional fee.

I like to buy American Express traveler's checks in the U.S. at the AAA Motor Club near my home. Membership has its benefits alright: there's no additional fee for buying in pounds sterling. Again, whenever you deal in two currencies, there are chances to win and to lose. I bought pounds at $1.70. Needless to say, I'll have to sit on those traveler's checks for a long time to even break even.

You can make yourself nuts over the pros and cons of the foreign money market, and I'm an expert at making myself crazy. But if you travel to England a lot, you may want to follow the rates and buy low.

I am constantly staggered at the huge amount of fluctuation there is between the dollar and the pound. I've tried to cultivate a "don't look back" policy but I still find myself shaking my head whenever faced with basic prices. Most luxury purchases bought abroad are only a bargain when the dollar is good against the pound. Never translate a price at one rate and keep the dollar price in your mind as the answer to your "how much is it?" questions.

The truth is that the price changes constantly once you have to convert back and forth.

CURRENCY EXCHANGE

As already mentioned, currency exchange rates vary tremendously. The rate announced in the paper (it's in the *Herald Tribune* every day) is the official bank exchange rate and does not particularly apply to tourists. Even by trading your money at a bank you will not necessarily get the same rate of exchange that's announced in the papers.

- You will get a better rate of exchange for a traveler's check than for cash, because there is less paperwork involved for banks, hotels, etc.
- The rate of exchange can be fixed if you buy traveler's checks in the U.S. in sterling. There will be no fee for cashing them anywhere in Britain and shopkeepers are happy to take checks in sterling, whereas they rarely know what to do with checks in U.S. dollars—or simply won't touch them.
- Expect a bank to give you a better rate than your hotel, although it may not. I've found the best rate of exchange at the American Express office. Usually they give as close to the bank rate as is possible, and they do not charge for changing traveler's checks or personal checks.

Here are some tips for your monetary transactions:

- Don't change money (or a lot of it, anyway) with airport vendors, because they will have the worst rates in town—yes, higher than your hotel.
- If you want to change money back to dollars when you leave a country, remember that you will pay a higher rate for them. You are now "buying" dollars rather than "selling" them. Therefore, never

change more money than you think you will need, unless you stockpile for another trip.
- Have some foreign currency on hand for arrivals. After a lengthy transatlantic flight, you will not want to stand in line at some London airport booth to get your cab fare.

Your home bank or local currency exchange office can sell you small amounts of foreign currency so that when you arrive in London, you have enough change to take care of immediate needs. There are usually foreign exchange booths at international airports as well. No matter how much of a premium you pay for this money, the convenience will be worth it.

Do keep this money readily available on landing—you don't want to have to undress in the taxi to reach your money belt, nor do you want the money packed in a suitcase in a very safe place.

If you are arriving at London Heathrow and plan to take a taxi into "town," have £50 minimum on hand. If you are taking the bus or the tube, £20 will be sufficient for transportation and immediate tipping at the hotel.

If you are arriving at Gatwick and plan to take a taxi into London, have a minimum of £100 on hand. If you take the bus or train, £20 will be quite sufficient.

- Keep track of what you pay for your currency. If you are going to several countries, or if you must make several money-changing trips to the cashier, write the sums down. When you get home and wonder what you did with all the money you used to have, it'll be easier to trace your cash.
- Make mental comparisons for quick price reactions. Know the conversion rate for $50 and $100 so you can make a judgment in an instant. Also know them in reverse: can you cope with an item priced at £10, £20, or £50? Have your reflexes

honed to know where your price barriers are. If you're still interested in an item, then slow down and figure out the true and accurate price.
- Expect to pay a commission—often hidden—each time you change money. Even at banks. That commission is commonly £3, but can be £5 per transaction! Compare the cost of the commission (if you have to pay one) with your hotel rate; sometimes convenience is the lesser of two evils. There is no commission for cardmembers at American Express or for Barclaycard holders at Barclays.

TIPPING

One of the most difficult things for Americans to do when they travel is to lose the concept of translating everything into dollars. Not only do you like to know what things cost, but you probably figure your tips based on your system at home.

When you travel, it works better if you plug into the local rules and denominations for tipping, because the amounts are pegged to local coins.

If you normally tip $1 per suitcase at a hotel, you are not going to stand there with your calculator and tip 73p in London.

Also, please note that Americans are known throughout the world as big tippers. Taxi drivers in particular, but people in all service businesses hope for American clients because they anticipate bigger tips from them.

On the whole, British people find the subject of money distasteful and do not even want to talk about it. Tipping is embarrassing—on both the giving and receiving end.

- In restaurants, ask if VAT and service are included in the bill. In most cases it is clearly stated on the bill. I had a dreadful experience whereby I made an expensive miscalculation and lost £20. Never be embarrassed to ask. (I was, and it cost me.)

- You tend to tip more generously and more frequently in London than in the countryside.
- You become more judgmental about tipping because you realize that the local custom is not to tip, or to tip 10%, whereas you might've been brought up to believe that 15% constitutes the minimum for a tip.

Here are my basic London tipping rules:

In Restaurants

If service is not included in the dinner price, I tip between 10% and 15% but never over 15%, and frequently at whatever number handily falls between the two, according to the sum of the bill. I do not tip maitre d's. I guess I don't hang out at the right places.

At the Hairdresser

At the hairdresser, I tip a total of 15% on the whole—that usually means £1.50 for the shampoo person and £3.50 to whoever did my hair, up to a maximum of £5 total. Please note that in Edinburgh I was told service was included. When I insisted on giving the stylist £1, which was 10% of my bill, she was thrilled but very flustered. (See page 160 for more on hairdressers.)

In Taxis

I round up the bill to the nearest number that is somewhere around 10%. If the driver has been particularly helpful, I round up a bit more.

In Hotels

- I tip 50p to a hotel doorman for getting me a taxi, if it is not my hotel. If I have been at a hotel for several days and used many taxis, I tip £5 in an envelope on which I write my name, my room

number, and my thanks. I address the envelope to "front door staff."
- If the concierge staff has been helpful, I tip another £5—more if they have been incredibly helpful.
- I tip the bellhop 50p per suitcase.
- On departure, I again tip the bellhop 50p per suitcase in person when he or she comes to pick up my bags.
- I do not tip the valet who automatically brings ice or turns down the bed. If I call down for a small but specific service—"bring me a vase, please"—I tip 50p when said vase arrives. I do not tip when a fax is brought to the room. I say "thank you."

At the Airport

They have free trolleys at London airports. Should you need a skycap, there is a fixed price of £5. I always considered that highway robbery until I needed one; he more than earned his keep!

THE EXPORT TAX SCHEME (VAT)

When you bring an item to a cash register in the U.S., sales tax is added to the sticker price of your purchase. In Europe, the tax is added before the item is stickered, so that the price on the sticker is the total amount you are charged.

This system is called value-added tax. It's known in Britain as VAT. Businesses that make over £37,000 a year must pay VAT. The cost is therefore passed on to the consumer.

If you are not a British subject and if you take the goods out of Britain, you are entitled to a refund on the VAT. You may also get a refund on VAT for hotel rooms and car rentals, but that's another subject.

The VAT is 17.5%.

The Export Tax Scheme (VAT) 59

In the scheme of things, you should be getting a 17.5% refund on purchases; however, that is a major oversimplification of the system. You will most likely get back 15% or even 13% and you may pay a fee to get this back.

The basic value-added tax system works pretty much like this:

- You are shopping in a store with prices marked on the merchandise. This is the true price of the item, which any tourist or any national must pay. (I'm assuming you are in a department store with fixed prices, not a flea market.) If you are a national, you pay the price without thinking twice. If you are a tourist who plans to leave the country within six months, you ask a salesperson, "What is the minimum expenditure in this store for the export refund?" before shopping.
- The rate varies from shop to shop—usually touristy neighborhoods and drop-dead, chichi stores have a higher quota. The law states that a refund can come your way with a minimum expenditure of £50. However, in some shops you may be asked to spend £75–100 before you qualify. Or more! I find it fascinating that the minimum at Hermès on Bond Street is exactly £62—the exact same price as a silk tie.
- More and more stores, especially the fancy ones, charge a commission for issuing the VAT refund. Expect to lose £5 of the refund.
- There are now three different companies paying out VAT refunds for shop subscribers. All three have different types of forms, but the system works the same way. One of these companies works out your refund on a chart—although I spent almost £100 at Culpeper the Herbalist, according to the chart my refund was £3.50! I was outraged. For $5, it wasn't worth my trouble to show those goods to the Customs officer in London and schlep

them on the plane with me. Check out the size of the refund before you see stars (or discounts) in your eyes.

- Once you know the minimum, decide accordingly whether you will make a smaller purchase, or come back another time for a big haul. Only you know how much time your schedule will permit for shopping. Remember that on a $100 purchase, the 17.5% minus a £5 fee may mean the savings are too little to make the VAT meaningful. The lines in summer at the VAT desk at LHR can be fierce.
- Judge for yourself if you are certain the store you are about to do business with will actually give you the refund after the paperwork is done. If you are dealing with a famous department store or a reputable boutique, there should never be a problem. I have had considerable problems with several big-name boutiques in both London and in the English countryside. More and more stores are switching to Tax-Free Europe, a firm that does the tax back for them. This is a reliable firm with a desk at the airport to give you an instant cash refund if you want.
- If you are going to another European country, consider the VAT or *détaxe* policy there. It may be smarter to wait until you get to France to purchase the same item, although the qualification for *détaxe* in France is a minimum expenditure of 1,200 FF as of January 1996.
- Sometimes the only savings you get when shopping abroad is the VAT discount. Don't knock it if you can afford it.
- If you go for the VAT, budget your time to allow for the paperwork before you leave the country. It takes about five minutes to fill out each form, and you must have them filled in when you present them upon exiting the country.
- Along with the VAT forms you will be given an envelope. Sometimes the envelope has a stamp on it; sometimes it is blank (you must provide the

The Export Tax Scheme (VAT)   61

postage stamp before you leave the country). Sometimes it has a special government frank that serves as a stamp. If you don't understand what's on your envelope, ask.

- When you are leaving the country, go to the Customs official who serves the VAT papers. Do this before you clear regular Customs or send off your luggage. The Customs officer has the right to ask you to show him or her the merchandise you bought and are taking out of the country. He or she may not even look, but by law you are supposed to have the goods with you.

If you have too much stuff to carry on board, you must allow plenty of extra time, as you'll have to exit immigration with your baggage while a security guard stands by, then get rid of your checked luggage. I dare say 17.5% just isn't worth this kind of aggravation.

Right after you've done passport control in Heathrow, go to the VAT desk (to your right if passport control is to your back) to show your goods—as you can see, you can carry them on board after all—and get your paperwork taken care of. All of the paperwork takes some preparation (filling in your name, address, passport number, etc.) which you are expected to have completed before you stand in the VAT line.

It really gums up the works for everyone else if the officer has to explain to you that you should have already done the fill-in-the-blanks part and would you please step over to one side.

Whether the officer sees your purchases or not, he or she will stamp the papers, keep a set (which will be processed), and give you another set in the envelope. You then mail the envelope (which usually is preprinted with the shop's name and address or has been addressed for you by the shop). There is a mailbox next to the officer's desk. Or, use the TAX FREE EUROPE desk for an instant refund.

U.S. Customs and Duties Tips

To make your reentry into the U.S. as smooth as possible, follow these tips:
- Know the rules and stick to them!
- Don't try to smuggle anything.
- Be polite and cooperative (up until the point when they ask you to strip, anyway . . .).

Remember:
- You are currently allowed to bring in $400 worth of merchandise per person, duty free. Before you leave the U.S., verify this amount with one of the U.S. Customs offices. Each member of the family is entitled to the deduction; this includes infants. You may pool within a family.
- You pay a flat 10% duty on the next $1,000 worth of merchandise.
- Duties thereafter are based on a product-type basis. They vary tremendously per item, so think about each purchase and ask storekeepers about U.S. duties. They will know, especially in specialty stores like furriers or china shops.
- The head of the family can make a joint declaration for all family members. The "head of the family" need not be male. Whoever is the head of the family, however, should take the responsibility for answering any questions the Customs officers may ask. Answer questions honestly, firmly, and politely. Have receipts ready, and make sure they match the information on the landing card. Don't be forced into a story that won't wash under questioning. If they catch you in a little lie, you'll be labeled as a fibber and they'll tear your luggage apart.
- Have the Customs registration slips for your personally owned goods in your wallet or easily available. If you wear a Cartier watch, be able to produce the registration slip. If you cannot

The Export Tax Scheme (VAT) 63

prove that you took a foreign-made item out of the country with you, you may be forced to pay duty on it.
- The unsolicited gifts you mailed from abroad do not count in the $400-per-person rate. If the value of the gift is more than $50, you pay duty when the package comes into the country. Remember, it's only one unsolicited gift per person for each mailing. Don't mail to yourself.
- Do not attempt to bring in any illegal food items—dairy products, meats, fruits, or vegetables (coffee is okay). Generally speaking, if it's alive, it's *verboten*. I don't need to tell you that it's tacky to bring in drugs and narcotics.
- Antiques must be 100 years old to be duty free. Provenance papers will help (so will permission to export the antiquity, since it could be an item of national cultural significance). Any bona fide work of art is duty free whether it was painted 50 years ago or just yesterday; the artist need not be famous.
- Dress for success. People who look like "hippies" get stopped at Customs more than average folks. Women who look like a million dollars, who are dragging their fur coats, have first-class baggage tags on their luggage, and carry Gucci handbags, but declare they have bought nothing, are equally suspicious.
- Laws regarding ivory are new and improved — for elephants, anyway. You may not import any ivory into the U.S. Not to worry, there is little new ivory for sale in London; antique ivory should have provenance or papers to be legally imported.
- The amount of the Customs allowance is expected to change or be modified into a different type of declaration. If you are a big shopper, check before you leave to see if there's any news.

- When the papers get back to the shop and the government has notified the shop that their set of papers has been registered, the shop will then grant you the discount through a refund. This can be done by issuing a credit on your credit card or by cutting you a check, which will come to you in the mail, usually three months later. (It will be in a foreign currency. Please note that your bank may charge you to change it into dollars.) If you are smart, you will indicate that the refund should be credited to a bank card or American Express so that you will end up with a refund in dollars.
- If you used a Tax-Free voucher, after it is stamped you can go to the Tax-Free desk in the airport and get your money. You can ask for it in a variety of currencies but the conversion rate will not be very favorable. You do best to take the cash in sterling and save it for your next trip or spend it at the newsagents on wonderful British magazines.

Chapter Six

SHOPPING STRATEGIES

LE BRIT

I was reading a French fashion magazine around the time of the opening of the Chunnel—a time during which every form of media covered every form of story related to the relationship between the English and the French—when I came across an article called "Le Brit." It was a story telling Frenchmen (and women) how to imitate traditional British style and gave sources for where to shop and illustrations with examples, all but insert tab *A* into slot *A*. After I died laughing, I was reborn to shop and realized that everyone has wanted to imitate British style for years. That's what made Ralph Lauren rich.

Indeed, while most of the European businessmen in Brussels are fighting over the definition of a banana (and whether or not one can be sold in the EU), mere mortals are borrowing from each other's closets and working on a blended fashion statement that will perhaps have the same effects as blended whiskey.

It is the very nature of the English lifestyle that changes the look from fashion into a statement—tweeds, bulky sweaters, jodphurs, and waxed jackets are part of English reality. They aren't hype or affectation; they are what people wear. It's only when these items cross borders that they take on a fantasy aspect and are suddenly mistaken for fashion.

There are British stylists who have the ability to mix a plaid skirt, a cashmere sweater, a strand of pearls, and a Barbour weatherproof and still look somewhat chic. There are men and women who can wear something that is frayed, worn, or scruffed up and make you wish you had one too.

Note that shabby chic also carries over into the home (see Chapter 9, "Home Furnishings & Design Resources," page 223).

While British shabby chic has some things in common with the Paris look, the London look is not really a continental European look, nor is it anything like an American look. If you want to blend in, you'd best study the format and adjust accordingly. Remember that English women are expected to look dowdy (unless they are Anouska Hemphill) and British men should have their hair cut with the front longer than the back, so it can be slicked straight back (with a part on the side, of course).

There is a very big difference between a city look and a country look, especially for women.

The Look

Women who want to catch the country look should:

- Carry a waxed leather handbag.
- Wear an Hermès scarf, preferably one with a horse print.
- Wear a single strand of graduated pearls (not too big!)—it's essential.
- Own at least one twin set and one pair of riding breeches.

A long, boxy, pleated skirt, corduroy jeans (baggy), and a pair of muddy Wellies complete the requirements. Oh yes, an Alice band (hairband) will do nicely, thank you.

City basics have more to do with class and status (do you have a double hyphenated last name or not? do you speak with a perfectly modulated

Oxbridge accent or do you sound like an East Ender?) and whether or not you work or lunch. Note that London basics for women include a navy blazer, a long, pleated skirt, and plain pumps or flats with horsey hardware. A silk shirtwaist dress is also safe in stripes or polka dots (for summer) and a splashy Kanga dress will always do for tea or garden parties. If it's raining (*if?*), the version of the London uniform that consists of a black cashmere pullover with black wool slacks and small black boots will do; tie Hermès scarf at neck. Add black velvet Alice band and, possibly, pearls.

Men who want to catch the look should:

- Wear suits that fit.
- Wear simple ties, but not British school ties (unless you actually attended that school).
- Carry a Burberrys.
- Wear shirts with a contrasting collar and cuffs, and no monogram; stripes are okay.

London business basics for men include a dark blue or a gray pin-stripe suit that is *never* double-breasted. A well-cut navy blazer is good for casual business, but not for The City. Good cuff links (preferably antique and witty) are essential.

The Season

Much of British style is related to The Season, which is related to the fact that the weather is dismal in Britain most of the year. While The Season can officially start any time after Easter, and events are held as early as April, everyone knows that the weather doesn't get reliable until June. Therefore, Ascot is considered the real kick-off of the season, especially for women's fashion. Wimbledon is earlier but the weather is still iffy and one doesn't really dress as seriously for a tennis tournament, or even a "drinks party" after a tennis tournament.

Along with the sporting events that comprise The Season—from horse races to boat races—this is also wedding season. It is appropriate to wear a glam hat to a day wedding.

For events such as horse races or day weddings, women wear day dresses—a term you do not often hear in America anymore. A day dress can be translated into a suit or a silk dress. White is usually not worn. Men wear morning dress, which can be rented (hired, as the British say). While many locals own their own attire, it's not unusual for a proper gent to own a good top hat (not felt!) and a waistcoat and tie and to rent the rest of the pieces of the morning suit from **Moss Brothers.**

DEAL CITY

The new London is deal city and will be until everyone gets fat and rich again.

Taxis are plentiful because locals are still trying to save money. Fixed-price menus are available at all the best places in town, including dinner and dancing packages at both The Dorchester and The Ritz.

The new London still needs cash; the new London still remembers the blitz of the recession.

- Sales begin earlier and last longer, although beware: you'll be fighting locals from all over Britain who have come to London to take advantage of these price breaks.
- People are taking in guests to their otherwise very private homes . . . and lives. They need to pay the mortgage; you get an opportunity to save on hotel rates and stay in the real London.
- Shabby chic has never been more stylish. There is less emphasis than ever before on new clothes; everyone is flocking to the car boot sales and the

secondhand dress shops. Designer clothes (and hats) from the biggest names—yes, I am talking Chanel and the like—are now the rage with local nobs. I'd dare say that the single biggest growth area in retail in terms of types of shops is in designer retail shops!
- The new London has new phone numbers (171 or 181) and phone numbers change so often (all those cellulars) that very few phone numbers are listed in this text (in fact, phone numbers only appear in hotel and restaurant listings). If you are headed to a store specifically to shop that address alone, or if a store is in an inconvenient place and you will be annoyed if it is not open when you get there, please call first. Use the phone book as your guide.

OTHER SAVERS

- Cheap shoes are the rage and no one does a more trendy cheap shoe than a British maker.
- Vintage chic remains an important part of the London fashion scene.
- Ethnic fashions are big, be they from **Oxfam**, a chain of charity shops selling both worn threads and cheap imports, or from stores like **Monsoon**, which have prom dresses made in India from local silks.
- French multiples are moving onto the British high streets in order to offer middle-class fashion at moderate prices. Mid-priced shopping in London has never been so much fun. *Vive le Kookai difference.*
- British china and dishes are cheaper in the U.K. and even cheaper if bought on sale and you don't have to pay for shipping. There are also styles available in Britain that aren't exported to the U.S., even from big firms like Wedgwood.

THE LONDON HALF-PRICE RULE

If London is twice as expensive as the U.S., then items that go on sale in London that are marked "50% off" are merely equal to the U.S. price. Let the buyer beware. Don't be fooled into a quick purchase because you think you are getting a deal.

POUNDS FOR PEANUTS

It's actually unfair to yourself and your travel experience if you constantly convert British prices into U.S. prices and try to compare value. There is no comparison. You need to judge prices and value according to local standards.

That means that you have to know enough about the price structure to understand that anything that costs £10 or less is considered inexpensive. Ten pounds can be between $15 and $20 and yet, in London, it means little. To determine value, you've got to think in British terms. This may mean spending a few days on the streets absorbing and researching local prices before you buy anything.

In no time at all, you'll take up the local hue and cry: "And it only cost 10 pounds!"

PEANUTS FOR POUNDS

Now that I've just about frightened you to death and sent your wallet into convulsions, let me assure you that there are plenty of things to buy in London and that you can still have a good time shopping. And yes, there are gift items to bring home that cost less than 10 pounds. Less than 10 pounds?

Okay, everybody, let me hear that chorus:

"And it only costs 10 pounds?"

Yes, and maybe less.

Try some of these sources for gifts in the £5–10 range.

THE BODY SHOP If you're not familiar with **The Body Shop,** see page 111 for the run-down. Since there are almost 100 Body Shop stores in the U.S., I assume you know about their line of environmentally friendly and politically correct cosmetics and health and beauty aids. Prices in London are 40–50% less than in the U.S.

Therefore, you can find numerous gift items for men, women, and children in the £5 range.

AROMATHERAPY Aromatherapy is technically a form of alternative medicine based on the restorative powers of herbs and flowers. The concept has taken London by storm (see page 109), or at least by air. There are scads of products to scent up your life and bring you long life, peace and happiness; most of them cost less than £10. You can buy aromatherapy gifts at **Harrods, The Body Shop, Culpeper the Herbalist,** and various department stores (usually on the first floor in the toiletries department).

Here are a couple ideas: A tubular metal ring that sits on top of a light bulb costs less than £2 (it holds the scent and burns off with the heat of the light bulb). I'm enthusiastic about **Culpeper the Herbalist's** aromatherapy fan, which comes packaged with lavender oil for £12.50 or can be bought *a la carte*—the fan costs about £8 and assorted scents are sold with eyedroppers; scent cards come three for £1. These fans are not available in the U.S. I must tell you that when I speak and do my "show & tell" routines, every face in the place lights up when I demonstrate this fan. It really works!

Culpeper scented candles are £4; I'm now into their sachets that you can buy with a monogram or the word MOM or MUM spelled out. They cost about $2.50 each and make marvelous gifts.

TEA FOR TWO For just under £2, you have your choice of various exotic blends of tea from the food halls of London's best department stores. Yes, you can buy teabags from **Marks & Spencer** (St. Michael's brand only, my dear) and they do make an imaginative gift for the person with a sense of humor. Personally, I suggest splurging and paying £2 to come away with something like Harrods mango tea or Harvey Nichols black cherry tea. Both come in teabag or loose tea format. I might add that at the local yuppie grocery store near where I live, mango teabags cost $9.50 for the same size box of 24. Don't forget **Fortnum & Mason** for teas and foodstuffs as gifts and **Charbonnel Et Walker**, a famous English firm despite the French-sounding name. They make a tin of cocoa that costs approximately $10 and makes a sensational gift. And, oh yes, **Wedgwood** also has tea tins for $10.

HARRODS Harrods logo merchandise does make a nice souvenir/gift. It's a tad obvious, but they have tons of choices. A key chain is fun, but to my mind, a little uninspired. For £6, I happen to like the phone message pad with the hole in it (for your Harrods pencil, sold separately, of course) or the potholders, also £6. If $10 is your budget—no problem here. If you're looking for something for less, believe it or not, you can still do it at Harrods. My best find on a recent trip: Harrods logo, olive green plastic rain ponchos for £1.50. You look like you've been wrapped in a giant shopping bag, but it's small, it's packable, it doesn't break and heaven knows, you won't go broke.

ROYAL KITSCH Royal memorabilia can be very expensive, especially if it's valuable. Royal kitsch is easy to find and rather inexpensive. You should have plenty to pick from in the under-£5 category. And no, all those wedding commemoratives from Chuck and Di's wedding are not going to be worth a fortune one day—there's simply too many of them on the market. My Charles-and-Diana tea cozy was still a steal at £3.

BUTTONS I happen to collect buttons, but I think that British military brass buttons with regimental insignias are a great gift—less than £5 for a full card. I buy mine on Saturdays at the markets on Portobello Road, but other markets sell them too. My latest prize? Buttons with pictures of Prince Charles and Princess Diana. Now there's a collectible.

TABLOIDS Trashy British tabs make great gifts for co-workers or casual acquaintances, especially if there's a royal scandal afoot. I look for *The Sun, The Mail,* and *The Express* (*The Evening Standard* is one of my regular papers, so I just save those). At 20–35p a toss, I can buy four or five newspapers on a trip and not even gift-wrap them.

THE MOSCOW RULE OF SHOPPING

The Moscow Rule of Shopping is one of my most basic shopping rules and has nothing to do with shopping in Moscow, so please pay attention. Now: The average shopper, in pursuit of the ideal bargain, does not buy an item he wants when he first sees it, because he's not convinced that he won't find it elsewhere for less money. He wants to see everything available, then return for the purchase of choice. This is a rather normal thought process. If you live in an Iron Curtain country, however, you know that you must buy something the minute you see it, because if you hesitate, it will be gone. Hence the title of this international law: the Moscow Rule of Shopping.

When you are on a trip, you probably will not have the time to compare prices and then return to a certain shop; you will never be able to backtrack through cities, and even if you could, the item might be gone by the time you got back, anyway. What to do? The same thing they do in Moscow: Buy it when you see it, with the understanding that you may never see it again. But, since you are not shopping in

74 SHOPPING STRATEGIES

Moscow and you may see it again, weigh these questions carefully before you go ahead:

1. Is this a touristy type of item that I am bound to find all over town?
2. Is this an item I can't live without, even if I am overpaying?
3. Is this a reputable shop, and can I trust what they tell me about the availability of such items?
4. Is the quality of this particular item so spectacular that it's unlikely it could be matched at this price?

If you have good reason to buy it when you see it, do so.

Caveat: The Moscow Rule of Shopping breaks down if you are an antiques or bric-a-brac shopper, since you never know if you can find another of an old or used item, if it will be in the same condition, or if the price will be higher or lower. It's very hard to price collectibles, so consider doing a lot of shopping for an item before you buy anything. This is easy in London, where there are a zillion markets that sell much the same type of merchandise in the collectibles category. At a certain point, you just have to buy what you love and not worry about the price or the Moscow Rule of Shopping.

LONDON'S BEST BUYS

No matter what the dollar does, there will always be certain categories of merchandise that remain smart purchases in London. I'm not saying these things are cheap. I'm saying that merchandise falls into three categories: designer merchandise which is more expensive in the U.K. than the U.S., designer merchandise which is exactly the same price in the U.K. and the U.S., and designer merchandise which is actually less expensive in the U.K. Here's where you'll score:

English Big Names

If you are planning on a big British buy (such as a **Burberry** raincoat), and you wanted to visit London anyway, do your shopping in January or July at the sale or head for the Burberry factory outlet shop (see page 151). Otherwise, check out prices at home before you assume a savings in the U.K.

English-made ready-to-wear should be less expensive in England, but don't get caught assuming anything. Especially if the dollar has been dancing.

Also remember the duty on ready-to-wear and stay within the $1,400 U.S. Customs limit, on which you will pay only $100 duty. After that, you'll get into higher duties on clothes, and your bargains may be tarnished. Generally speaking, you can save on U.S. prices if you buy British when it's on sale or if you get the VAT refund.

European Designer Fashions

There is a strange rule of retailing that generally only applies to sale times, but you can still score on European designer fashions at the end of the season and at big clearance sales. That's because everybody in Britain if not still broke is being very, very careful about purchases or is buying *used* designer clothing.

Regularly priced designer merchandise is surely no bargain in London, but even the sale prices on highfalutin' clothes may be too outrageously high for Sloane Rangers; so if other international jetsetters haven't beaten you to the punch, you can get lucky at a sale. Note that there are no bargains on regularly priced designer items, although you need to run the numbers carefully, as there may be concessions due to VAT and state sales tax.

China and Crystal

Even with the cost of shipping to the U.S., you will save money on china and crystal if you buy it on

Home Decor

More specifically on the home decor front: fabrics. If you crave the cabbage roses or the toile, the locally made fabrics cost less in London. Know your yardage and allow for the repeat. Few dealers will ship your order since they don't want to compete with their U.S. showrooms.

If you simply want some quick ideas or a way to spruce up a room, keep your eye on the major multiples (chain stores that seem to pop up everywhere). **Marks & Spencer** has a relatively new design department. Some British (and a few Scottish) cities have a freestanding M&S home furnishings store. **British Home Stores** has some great-looking stuff at everyday low prices. **Laura Ashley** remains a solid source for Americans who like bargains and the English look. It doesn't have to be John Fowler to be fabulous.

Needlecrafts

If you aren't already a Kaffe Fassett or Elizabeth Bradley nut, you will be when I finish with you. If you knit or do needlepoint, you should seek out Mr. Fassett's work in kit form in any London needlecraft shop, such as **Liberty,** where you'll pay a fraction of the U.S. costs. Other big-name knitting designers offer similar savings. Sweaters that cost $500 when made up cost $75 or less in kit form in London. Bradley Victorian-style needlepoint kits cost £55 in **Harrods** and $250 in New York.

Filofax

Prices are much lower in England. Even insert pages are half price. The basic leather set starts at $150 at Bloomingdale's. You can buy the whole works, top-of-the-line and complete, for less than $100 in London. Filofax items are sold in their own store, in the stationery departments of major department stores, in office supply stores, and even at the airport. I just wandered into **Filofax** a few weeks ago and discovered they had bought out the competing French firm **Le Fax**. There was a huge sale on **Le Fax** leftovers going down. I got such a headache I finally had to leave. Nothing cost more than £10 and most everything I wanted cost £1!

Dr. Martens

Basically, shoes are a bad buy in Britain. That is, regular high-fashion shoes or even moderately priced high-fashion shoes, since the British don't know from moderately priced. In Britain they sell cheap shoes at high prices.

But wait; every rule has an exception. If you are the parent of a child 12 years old on the way to 20, or are a 'tween-to-20 yourself and you or your kin wouldn't be caught red or dead (you'll only get that reference if you're young and hip, so don't sweat it) without Doc Martens, here's the deal. These shoes are a good bit cheaper in London. If you get them on sale, you may even snag a pair for $50.

You'll be proud to know that Doc Martens has opened their own retail store in Covent Garden (see page 212). Unfortunately, the store is outrageously expensive . . . on everything, especially their little giftables and souvenirs. Happily, this is not the only source in town for Doc Marten brand shoes, so don't freak.

ENGLISH SELECTION

My girlfriend Polly sent me on an errand of mercy: please buy her four coffee cups from a certain Wedgwood pattern. She didn't care about the price;

she just had to have them. As it happens, they weren't very expensive anyway and I had no trouble finding them. Yet Polly had been unable to order them in the U.S. because this particular pattern has never been exported.

One of the reasons one shops abroad is to see (and buy) things you don't even get a chance to see in the U.S. London has plenty of doozies.

BAD BUYS IN LONDON

"Moderately priced" clothes are not moderately priced in England—they are downright expensive. If you expect to find both fashion and quality for less than $50 or so, forget it.

Also check origin and quality: the £17 adorable handbag I bought on a recent trip in a middle-class department store (made in China) lasted exactly one week before the shoulder strap pulled out and snapped. Before that, I was prepared to tell readers to rush into this department store and snap up all the cheap handbags. Junk wears like junk. Don't waste your money.

Although sweaters may be pushed at you from every direction, think twice. Unless you buy from a factory outlet, get seconds or discontinued styles, or get a big markdown, you may not find the savings you expected. You can count on finding a two-ply cashmere sweater in any big U.S. department store on sale for $129; maybe even $99. Take my word for it; Brits come to the U.S. to buy cashmere. British sale prices on a cashmere jumper are rarely below £99.

American brand names. Clothes from **The Gap** have their American price code on them and the price in dollars is merely translated into pounds sterling. Honest. I'm not making this up. Something on the sale rack for 19.99 means £19.99, or about $30.

My beloved Sophie, now aged 18, recently told me she was thrilled to get a day job that paid £50 so she could buy herself a new pair of used Levi's. That's what they cost in London. You did not go to London to buy Donna Karan, now did you?

THE BRITISH AIR DARE

I've made it my business to study London's two sale periods (January and July), and have come to the conclusion that the January sales are far, far better. Even though some of the stores are offering their July sales in June these days, January is actually worth flying over for, while summer sales are not that great.

The January sales are an event, especially in recessionary times when locals have held back on their Christmas shopping and have come from far and near to mop up the bargains. The sales are far more theatrical in January; the circus atmosphere is so much fun that it creates energy in the aisles. June/July sales last year merely had an air of desperation to them.

Years ago, British Airways asked me if it was possible to fly to the January sales in London and make back expenses in savings. I dubbed it "The British Air Dare." I've now been repeating the dare on an annual basis. Even when the dollar was at $2.06 per pound sterling, I was able to break even. This past year, with the dollar at $1.50, it was downright easy.

The costs:

- **Transatlantic Airfare** I bought a British Airways ticket for just $359 round-trip! I've never found one for less than $350 and never found one for over $400 at this time of year. I always buy legit tickets because I want my air miles, but you can

- **Lodging** I booked a room at **The Ritz** in London at a special winter promotional rate.
- **Airport Transfer** I carried just a tote bag and took the tube to the hotel. On the return trip to Heathrow, with more luggage, I took the bus: £5.
- **Meals** I ate economically. One day, I had high tea instead of dinner. Another night, I ate a picnic from M&S in my room. I ate at **The Dorchester** for my big night on the town for £25.
- **Entertainment** I went shopping. I watched movies on Sky Television (free). I laid out all my shopping triumphs and gloated. I read British *Vogue, Tatler,* and *Harpers & Queen.* I didn't go to the theater (at $50 a seat I'd rather have a new handbag), and I didn't visit Madame Tussaud's.

How much did I save? Beats me. Did I have a ball? You bet. In fact, if I could only go on one trip a year, I think I'd pick London in the first week in January. Why get the blues after Christmas when you can hop a plane? Why shop at the local mall's January sale when you can get a VAT refund? Why miss out on the fact that life is a cabaret and London is forever?

Look right.

THE BRITISH AIR DARE DEUX

I wanted to take my son Aaron to London during his summer vacation, something I would normally never consider because of the high cost of peak travel. But travel to Europe, and London especially, is hot and heavy and airlines are offering deals galore these days.

So are hotels. To my utter amazement, I was able to book seats in the summertime for $500 round-trip and a Hilton hotel room with a Mayfair location for $200 a night. I could have gotten a suite for $150 a night at the **Hotel Conrad**, but I didn't like the location.

It didn't take British Air to dare me to do this; I just opened my local newspaper one day, took a look at the airfares and said, "Holy Cow!"

I am a big believer in out-of-season travel because you not only get better deals but you also have fewer crowds to contend with. But, please don't give up on in-season travel without making a few toll-free phone calls first.

Furthermore, just to make an academic point here—if my goal was a pleasant English vacation with my son and not specifically a trip to London, we could have flown into any number of other airports in England, bought a train pass, booked farmhouse overnights, and really saved a bundle.

London is a good 25–30% more expensive than the rest of Britain.

SCAMS & RIPOFFS

It's normal that in any tourist destination there will be a small percentage of the working population that is set to rip you off. I think one of the reasons Americans like to travel to Britain is that they feel less threatened; also reports of scams in Britain seem to be minimal.

However, I did get involved in an absolutely fabulous piece of hustle recently. I'm walking along Oxford Street, a half block from Oxford Circus, and there is this very large crowd gathered around a street vendor who is shouting, "Quickly please, quickly, before the police come." All of the action was to make you believe he was hustling stolen goods. Indeed, everyone in the crowd wanted to buy stolen goods.

So the guy has five bottles of perfume on a cardboard box, all major brand names. The only one I know well is Chanel No. 5, which I pick up, examine, and spritz. It looks, smells, and feels like the real thing. All the time that I am musing and looking for the scam, the guy is hurrying me along with his constant "Quickly, quickly." The price for everything is £10. I decide I'm too curious to pass this up. I hand over my £10.

I am given a shrink-wrapped box marked Chanel No. 5. The color white on the box is off and immediately you know this is not the real thing. The packaging and printing look cheap; Chanel is not embossed. The barcode looks off; the box has a price sticker on it marked £49.95. I go into several department stores on Regent Street and examine boxes. They all sell the same Chanel No. 5 for £49, not £49.95. The boxes are classier in appearance.

When I open the package, along with my own real live Chanel No. 5 for comparison purposes, I can see that the black plastic container is similar to the real thing but has the Chanel logo in different colors than on the real item. The scent is similar: Close, but no cigar.

I told this story onboard the QE2 recently as an example of a scam and a woman in the audience stood up to say I was lucky—she bought from the same guys and there was nothing at all inside the container!

Chapter Seven

LONDON SHOPPING NEIGHBORHOODS

YOURS IN A ZIP

Zip codes in London are called postal codes. They are made up of two sets of letter and number combinations. The first set actually indicates the precise part of town where the address is located, and makes a good indicator for shoppers who want to organize themselves by neighborhood.

If you'll study the map on page 85, you'll see that the metropolitan area is divided into quadrants and that these have a few subcategories, such as southwest and southeast, and so on. There is a central core; those central zones have the letter C in them for—you guessed it—"central." You can look up the general area of a store or shopping neighborhood just by using this map.

As you get more sophisticated at using this method, you'll learn the few overlapping places. For instance, Mayfair is W1, but Jermyn Street, at the edge of Mayfair, is in SW1. Practice, practice, practice.

LONDON BY NEIGHBORHOOD

London is one of the best cities in the world in which to pick a neighborhood and wander without

84 LONDON SHOPPING NEIGHBORHOODS

specific goals. Each neighborhood is distinctive because of the way the city grew out of many individual cities. Some famous names overlap (Chelsea and Knightsbridge); some are actually separate cities.

Do note that it is inappropriate to refer to London or the portion of London an American might deem to be "downtown" as *The City*. In Britspeak, The City truly means The City of London, which is a teeny-tiny one-mile area; it is where the financial institutions have their offices and the banking people—and insurance people and the other suits—do their business.

You might want to learn a few basic London neighborhoods before you arrive, just to be safe.

SHOPPING BY NEIGHBORHOOD

The marketing nobs in London always say that the McDonald's people didn't have to spend any money on market research when they came into Britain—they simply looked for a high street with a **Marks & Spencer** on it and bought space as close by as possible.

You'll note that much retail in Britain is coordinated by the same type of marketing plan—it's as though a hundred years ago some Victorian marketing genius said, "Let's find a tourist attraction and then build a store right next to it." As a result, many tourist attractions are in shopping districts, or vice versa. This makes it easy to combine neighborhoods, culture, and credit cards in one fell swoop.

The only major exception to the shop-and-see theory is that the Tower of London is sort of in the middle of nowhere. Also note that The City offers very little retail, just a few shops to serve the needs of local businessmen and -women. Furthermore, entrance to The City is restricted for security purposes.

London Postal Codes

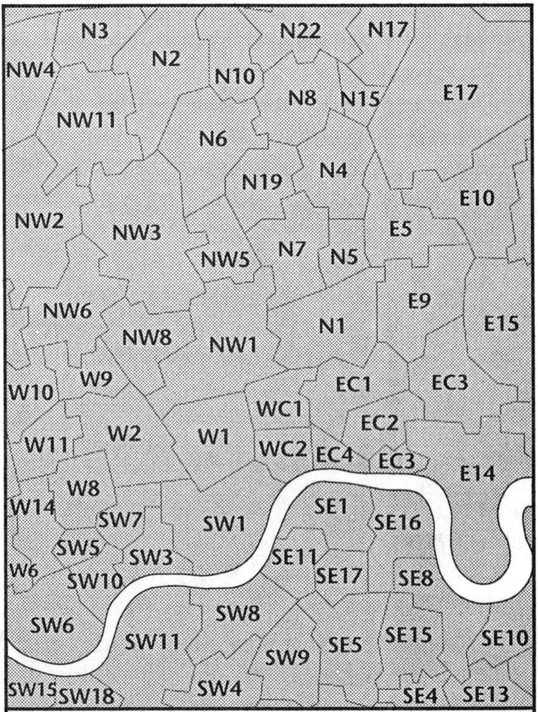

SE1:	London Bridge
SE10:	Greenwich
SW10:	South Kensington, King's Road
SW3:	Chelsea, Knightsbridge, South Kensington, King's Road
SW1:	Westminster, Belgravia, Jermyn Street, Sloane Street
SW7:	South Kensington, Knightsbridge
EC1:	Islington, Angel
E 3:	Tower of London, City of London
EC4:	Fleet Street, Old Bailey
N1:	Islington, King's Cross
NW1:	Camden, Chalk Farm, King's Cross, Euston
NW2:	West Hampstead
NW3:	Hampstead, Kentish Town
NW5:	Kentish Town, Highgate, Camden, Chalk Farm
NW6:	Hampstead, West Hampstead, St. John's Wood
W1:	Mayfair, Soho
W2:	South Kensington, Portobello Road
W8:	Kensington High Street, Earl's Court
W10:	North Kensington, Portobello Road
W11:	Portobello Road Market
WC1:	Mayfair, Soho, The West End, Savile Row, The Strand, Oxford Street
WC2:	Covent Garden, Trafalgar Square, Charing Cross Road, Piccadilly

CONNECT THE DOTS BY NEIGHBORHOOD

If you work with a daily schedule or list of shopping goals, you'll soon see that certain neighborhoods lead directly to each other, usually by foot, but often by bus. The tours in Chapter 11 are organized to move you through London in an orderly neighborhood sequence.

I have tried to organize this neighborhood section by interconnecting neighborhoods related to a larger area. To me, a person who listens to the vibes of the sidewalk, a shopping neighborhood may only hold a specific mood for two or three blocks before changing into something else. I've tried to indicate the changes and segues.

THE WEST END

The West End is the name for a large portion of real estate; a W1 address is very chic—for a store or a residence.

The major shopping areas in the West End are Oxford Street, Oxford Circus, Regent Street, Bond Street (Old and New), and Piccadilly.

Oxford Street

Most of the time I walk on Oxford Street, I hate it: it's always mobbed and it's just too real-world for my tastes. Even though they've widened the sidewalk and opened the stores on Sunday so Saturdays aren't quite so mobbed, I still feel like Oxford Street is truly the circus. And I don't mean Oxford Circus.

To enjoy Oxford Street, you have to settle into the right frame of mind (or be 22) and begin to groove on the street vendors selling Union Jacks, the fruit and flower stands, the locals in search of a bargain, and the street fashions that pass by in hurried profusion.

West End/Soho/Covent Garden

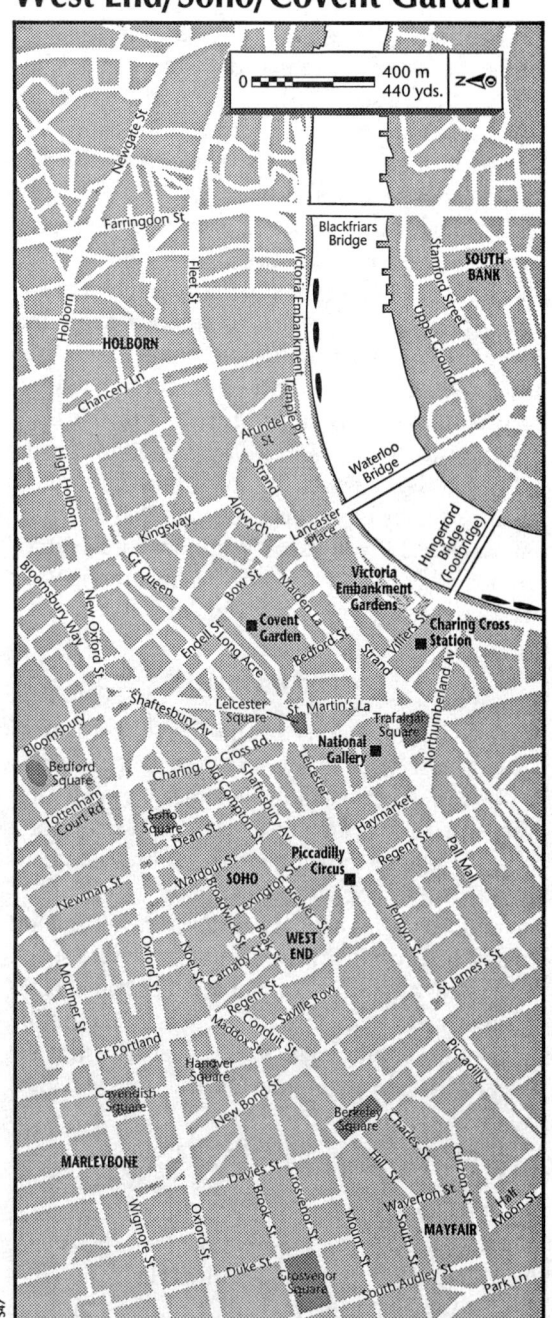

88 LONDON SHOPPING NEIGHBORHOODS

The beauty of Oxford Street is the fact that most of the moderately priced big department stores, including the flagship **Marks & Spencer**, are lined up in a row between Marble Arch and Regent Street. There's also a lot of teenybopper stores and trendy but cheap chains.

The high-rent department stores are on Regent Street, just around the corner, but a million miles away. You can also expect to find a branch store of many popular multiples such as **Body Shop** and a number of inexpensive shoe shops. There is a small **Boots** and, oh yes, there are outposts of the big record shops such as **Virgin Megastore** and **HMV**.

Many teens and 'tweens shop the multiples here, so just walking down the street may give you a chance to study London countercultural fashion like an academic. If you have a nonshopping husband, do not bring him to Oxford Street. Do bring your teenaged children or grandchildren.

Oxford Circus

To me, Oxford Street is the stretch of Oxford Street from Marble Arch to Regent Street. End of story.

Oxford Circus, and it *is* a circus, begins at Regent Street and continues along Oxford Street for a block or two toward Tottenham Court. In Roman-speak, a circus is a circle.

Oxford Circus has a decidedly more hip and hot atmosphere to it than plain old vanilla Oxford Street. The stores are still cheap, but they are selling high-fashion street looks to young people on the cutting edge of the cutting edge. These shoppers will segue over to Carnaby Street from Oxford Circus—it's just a few blocks away.

There are more multiples here, including a branch of **Marks & Spencer** that is not as big as the Marble Arch flagship and does not sell cashmere sweaters, but does have a good grocery store in the basement. You'll also find record shops such as **HMV**, the mini-mall **Oxford Place**, and my favorite multiple,

Mothercare, artfully placed between the teen fashion places and record stores to remind all of Britain's teens that safe sex is smart.

X, also known as **Department X** (although you'll only see the big X and not the rest), is a branch of the multiple **Next**. It's for teens and it's so hot that you must go out of your way to explore it. Even if you aren't a teen, or the parent of a teen, check it out: it's the kind of store that inspires ideas and creative dressing with a look that combines jeans, casualwear, and street fashion.

Regent Street

I love to walk Regent Street from Piccadilly to Oxford Circus. It's a little less than a mile in distance and each side of the street is packed with stores, but only one side of the street appeals to me—the Hamley's side (if Oxford is to your rear, you're on the left-hand side of the street toward Piccadilly). If I only have one hour in London, this is where I'll spend my hour.

You can spend a full day shopping these stores, of course, but even nonshopping husbands and kids alike will enjoy the walk to just soak up the best of the London shopping scene. If you do happen to be with kids, note that both **Hamley's**, Britain's largest toy store, and the **Disney Store** are in this stretch of Regent Street.

Frankly, I tend to ignore **Disney** and **Levi** and **The Gap** and everything else American. But they are there for those who need them. If you are with the pre-teens and teenagers, note that Carnaby Street (see page 91) is directly behind Regent Street.

Bored husbands, please note that **Laura Ashley** has a comfy armchair by the front door. Plop yourself down there if you need a rest.

Regent Street hosts the British institutions that make London retail so glorious. If there's only one store on your tour, it's got to be **Liberty**. But there's also everything from **The Gap** to **Jaeger** to **Lawley's** (china) to even the **Reject China Shop**. Also **Burberrys, Aquascutum,** and the **British Air Travel Store,** where you can confirm plane reservations, buy travel books and products, change money, and use the medical clinic.

Bond Street

While Regent Street is big department stores with big names, Bond Street is small boutiques with big names. This is where you'll find everything from **Chanel** to **Karl Lagerfeld**. The incredible **Gianni Versace** store is worth a tour; they should sell tickets to the place—it's far more interesting than Buckingham Palace. **Donna Karan** opened her DKNY store on Bond Street and is now looking for another home for her couture line. Watch this space.

You won't find any bargains in these stores, but do remember that most of them have prices that will automatically qualify you for a VAT refund.

Bond Street is divided into two parts: Old Bond and New Bond. Both are chockablock with big-name designer boutiques from all over the world. If you're a London regular but haven't been here in a year, do not convince yourself that you've been here. Bond Street feels very fresh and new with a lot of new faces; the energy is contagious and you will love coming back to see what the old neighborhood has been up to.

Piccadilly

It's hard to believe that developers can keep adding to this area but in the last little while a giant **Sogo**, the Japanese department store, and **Planet Hollywood**, the American burger joint, have opened. And someone is building a virtual reality theme park inside Trocadero where the Guinness Records Museum has been. It's really wild here.

To get to the good stuff, cut over onto Piccadilly itself and begin to walk toward **The Ritz**, where you'll find retail heaven. This is part of the Regent Street experience to me, since it is home to some special British institutions that make London the shopping mecca it is. Some of my favorites include **Fortnum & Mason, Burlington Arcade,** and **Hatchards,** the bookstore.

You can actually walk along Piccadilly until you get to Hyde Park but the storefront retail scene peters out at Green Park. On Sundays, there are vendors who set up along the park fence all the way to the Lanesborough Hotel.

SOHO

Traditionally speaking, Soho is a seedy neighborhood known for its porn shops. But here and there among the tattoo places and the massage parlors there are some hip stores. The most expensive hip stores are strung together in order to improve the real estate and make shopping easier for the customers. Newburgh Street is such a venue—it's chockablock with places such as **Gaultier Junior. Workers For Freedom** on Lower John Street looks small and uninviting, but has a reputation for high-fashion clothes that set trends.

Ian has his film processed at a professional lab in this area and I am always shocked that a few new stores have moved in. I never would have even found **Ally Capellino** except that it's a sneeze from the lab.

Last time I went there I spied a **Woodhouse** outlet shop. It was one of those temporary ones created just to clear out old merchandise, but you never know what will pop up next in this area.

Carnaby Street

The street itself has artistic banners and flags to welcome you to the rebirth of this tourist trap; there are a number of head shops selling black leather clothing (much with studs); funny, floppy hats;

T-shirts; and imports from India—with and without tie-dye. You get the picture. The teens hang out in droves.

If I haven't made it clear that I loathe these shops, let me go on to explain what I do like about the neighborhood:

- The kids and the people are fabulous to stare at.
- There's a lot of energy here and it feels like a foreign destination, which is exactly what you want from a trip to Europe.
- There are tons of postcard shops.

For my own shopping taste, there's a branch of **Boots**, there's a **Body Shop**, and there's **Muji**—a Japanese store that is known for the sublime look and feel of all their goods. There are many branches of **Shelly's Shoes**, the shoe shop for Dr. Martens and hip London looks; there's a china shop with a good selection of novelty teapots called **China Ware House**, and then there's the back street Newburgh Street, where the expensive new-wave designer shops of Soho are located.

Jermyn Street

These few short blocks of a shopping neighborhood run one block from Piccadilly and end at St. James's. Most of the stores here are small, with the exception of **Alfred Dunhill** and **Fortnum & Mason**, the back of which is on this street.

Jermyn Street represents a world that has almost ceased to exist—most of the stores are devoted to the private world of serving the upper-crust London gent. It's the home of exclusive shirt shops such as **Turnbull & Asser, Hilditch & Key,** and **Harvie & Hudson**.

Press your nose against the glass of all the shops; take in the dark wood and the aroma of old money. There are several famous stores for toiletries from **Czech & Speake** to **Trumper's** (which is in Simpson's and is actually a place for m'lord to have a shave and a haircut for more than two bits), and there's **Davidoff** for the right smoke. Cuban cigars cannot legally be brought into the U.S., but it is not a crime to smoke them in London.

ST. JAMES'S

St. James's Street stretches from St. James's Place near Pall Mall to Piccadilly, and is lined with some of London's most famous stores, many of which are a hundred years old. Or more. It all adds to the charm of the stroll.

Most of the stores have their original store fronts or have been restored to make you think they are original. Don't miss **John Lobb** (No. 9) for bespoke shoes (you can look; you needn't plunk down a thousand bucks), **James Lock & Co.** (No. 6), a hatmaker for men and women, **William Evans Gun & Riflemaker** (67A St. James's Place), and **D.R. Harris** (No. 29), an old-fashioned chemist whose brand of toiletries is considered very chic.

DORCHESTER

There's a private part of Mayfair that you will never find unless you prowl the streets or happen to be staying at **The Dorchester**, or possibly the **Connaught**. South Audley Street is the main drag of this niche to good taste and fine retail, but you will also want to wander Mount Street and end up at Berkeley Square before taking Bruton and connecting to Bond Street.

Mount Street and Bruton are known mostly for their very fancy antiques stores. South Audley has a hodgepodge of delectable goods from one of London's better spy shops (honest) to **Thomas Goode**, London's most exclusive address for china and tabletop. This shop now runs a museum service so that you can bring your coat of arms out of retirement and have it painted on your next set of dishes. Yes, it's that kind of neighborhood.

This is a part of town only frequented by rich people, which is just what makes it so much fun. Don't miss **Shepherd Market**, which is closer to Curzon Street—it's a hidden medieval alley with a few shops and pubs that looks like it hasn't changed in 300 years.

KNIGHTSBRIDGE

Fashionable and "with it," Knightsbridge crosses into a few different neighborhoods and borders Chelsea to such an extent that it can be confusing for a tourist to grasp the difference.

Once you've passed Hyde Park and are headed toward **Harrods**, you'll be on a street which is first called Knightsbridge but then changes its name to Brompton Road. This makes it especially confusing if you are watching addresses or street numbers because Knightsbridge doesn't really change its name; it just disappears into a nowhere turn. Chances are you won't realize that you've turned a corner at Sloane Street and ended up on the beginning of Brompton Road. Never mind. Pay no heed to street names and you'll be fine.

The part around **Harvey Nichols** is decidedly different than the part that comes after **Harrods**. At the Harvey Nichols end, aside from wonderful Harvey Nichols itself, there are branches of all the multiples and a number of high-end retailers as well, such as **Rodier** and **Scotch House**.

The closer you get to Harrods, the less tony the retailers become. Once you pass Harrods, on your way to Beauchamp Place, they are very standard, run of the mill places. That changes quickly again, so don't fret.

Harrods and Harvey Nichols are only a few blocks apart, so we're talking chockablock shopping here. Also note that Sloane Street (which has its own atmosphere and tempo; see below) leads off

St. James's & Mayfair

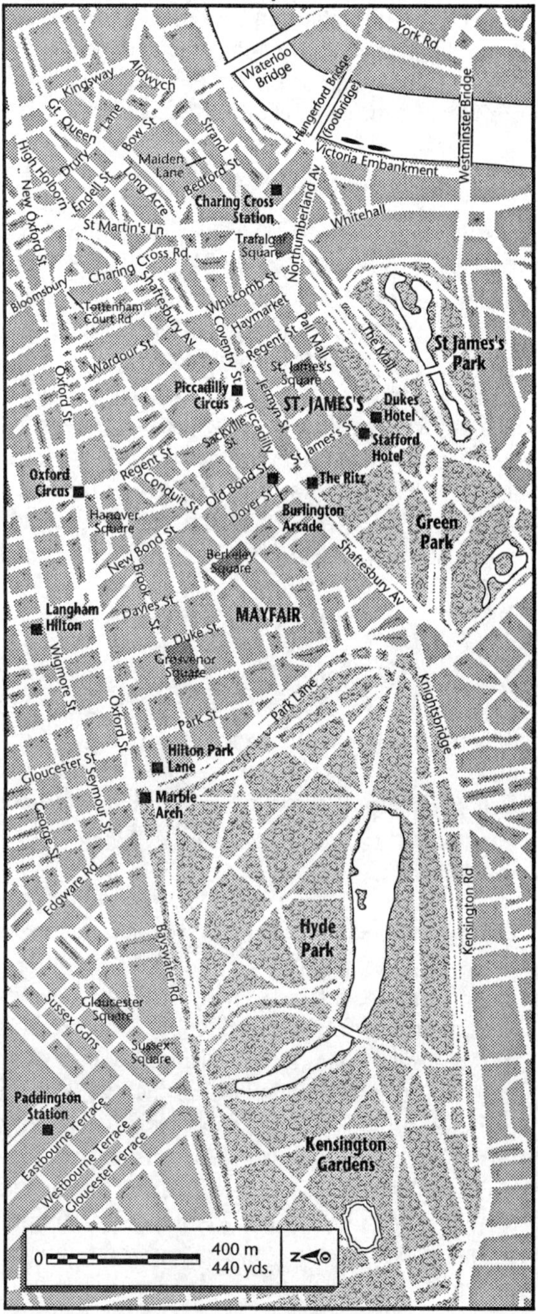

from Brompton at the corner where Harvey Nichols is standing. So you have to be organized and know where you're going because there are many directions and many, many choices to make.

Sloane Street

The juicy shopping part of Sloane Street is only about two blocks long. Yet it is two blocks of cheek-and-jowl designer chic. You could glance down the street and just rattle off an international who's who in big-name retailing from **Chanel** to **Valentino**.

Aside from the usual suspects, there's a rather well-known shoe shop, **Gina**, which I find overrated but locals seem to like. Gina has done so well that she has expanded to a second shop, across the street.

Sloane Street leads to Sloane Square and then you're on King's Road.

King's Road

If you continue along Sloane Street you will end up at Sloane Square. Here, surrounding the square, are numerous stores. On your way to the square, make sure you take a look at **Jane Churchill** and **General Trading Company**. The focal point of Sloane Square is the medium-sized department store, **Peter Jones**.

Just as Sloane Street dead-ends and disappears, you have two choices for two different retail experiences: Pimlico (see page 99) and King's Road.

For King's Road, put **General Trading Company** at your back and make a right at Sloane Square. You're now on King's Road. King's Road became famous (or is that infamous?) in the 1960s as the hot street for the bell-bottom people. It was groovy. Now King's Road is mostly a congregation of multiples, but it still has its own distinct flavor and charm, predominately design-oriented businesses. It also possesses a few of London's best antiques arcades.

The worst thing about King's Road is its lack of transportation, since there is no convenient tube station along the way. You can either go up one side and down the other and end up back at Sloane Square, or put on your hiking boots and march all the way up into the 500 block, since it is kind of interesting all the way up.

UPPER KNIGHTSBRIDGE

From **Harrods**, if you stay on Brompton Road, you'll see the London branch of **Genevieve Lethu**, a French tabletop designer who has great ideas for moderate prices, and then, in another block, a branch of **Past Times**, which sells historical reproductions commonly carried in museum shops.

In a block, assuming **Harrods** is at your back, you'll arrive at Beauchamp Place. If you stay on Brompton Road, you'll pass **Emporio Armani** and then soon you'll be at Museum Row on a street now called Cromwell Road. Brompton goes off on its own to become yet another neighborhood (Brompton Cross; see page 98).

This is all a bit tricky because there's so much going on here. Yes, you need to do Beauchamp Place; yes, you need to do the **V&A** (if only for the gift shop); yes, you need to do Brompton Cross and Walton Street and you certainly cannot miss the neighborhood that I have dubbed Pandora's Alley (see page 99).

Beauchamp Place

Whether you're going on to museums and culture on Brompton Road or yet more shopping, please take some time to explore Beauchamp (say "Beechum") Place, which is only one big block with stores on both sides of the street. There's been a great deal of turnover here because of the recession, but **John Boyd** has moved in and there's a resale shop

(Pamela) beneath him. **Kanga** (a shop carrying the line of clothes made by Lady Dale Tyron, Prince Charles's former best friend) is still here (#8), as well as **San Lorenzo**, the luncheon hotspot where Princess Di hangs out when she can do lunch, and three different branches of **Reject China Shop**.

Brompton Cross

This area was, until yesterday, one of the hottest parts of London for retail. Hard hit by the recession, this neighborhood is certainly worth the trip, but is no longer the glory spot it once was. But it's given birth to Walton Street, which is hotter than ever before.

The showpiece of the whole area is **Michelin House**, a Conran rehab which houses **The Conran Shop**, truly a good store for design ideas, home and tabletop, gift items, and even luggage. There are a few **Joseph** stores in this area and an interesting small street, which leads back to Harrods—Walton Street.

Walton Street

This district is so hip that it is actually a destination unto itself and its own little neighborhood, although obviously, as you've just read, it is part of a whole and easily connects to other great shopping areas. The street has an unusually high density of jewelry shops—the fun, funky kind as well as the terrifically artsy kind. I'm not talking cheap junk here. There's also a few famous names in decorating and in decorating accessories, such as the needlepoint shop **Tapisserie** or **Objets Extraordinaire** for embroidered pillows with witty sayings. **Jo Malone** is a must-do (see page 219 without delay) and I happen to like **Les Olivades**, a branch of the French firm famous for Provençal cotton prints. With Souleiado out of business in London now, this is your only chance for this look on the local front.

Pandora's Alley

There is no street in this part of town called Pandora's Alley; that is simply my nickname for a tiny street called Cheval Place. The street came of age when the dress agency **Pandora** moved here about five years ago. Now the block is lined with resale shops that sell used designer clothing at some of the best prices in the world. I'm talking about a Chanel suit for £450!

To get here, walk out the front of **Harrods** and look across Brompton for **Genevieve Lethu**. Cross over; you are now at the corner of Montpelier Row. Turn right on Montpelier, go only a short distance, and turn left onto Cheval Place.

Pimlico Road

This is not the neighborhood of Pimlico as laid out in your *A to Z*, but rather a street called Pimlico Road (SW1) which comes right before the real Pimlico district. To reach it by tube, use the Sloane Square stop.

For those interested in interior design, this street is filled with shops of trimmings, fabrics, and antiques. Working designers or those with a decorating need should find some useful resources here.

From the Sloane Square tube, if the station is to your back and you are facing toward **Peter Jones**, make a left on Holbein Place. This will lead you to Pimlico Road within a block; there are some shops here along the way. When you do both sides of Pimlico Road, return to Sloane Square via Lower Sloane Street, which runs parallel to Holbein Place.

KENSINGTON

This neighborhood is a must if you are in the fashion business, want to see the young hip looks, or have teens and 'tweens. It's also a must for those interested in antiques.

Kensington High Street

Like any other high street, the thoroughfare which stretches before you as you emerge from the Kensington High Street tube station is chockablock with multiples and real-people stores. There's the architecturally interesting **Barkers Of Kensington** department store, **Kensington Market** for the black-leather-and-tattoo generation, and **Hyper Hyper**, for the with-it fashion crowd.

A sneeze behind the high street is **Lancer's Square**, a mini-mall which houses **Ehrman's** for needleworks, tapestry, sweater kits, and wools.

Town Hall, around the corner from the high street, frequently hosts antiques shows and events. Eat lunch in the adorable train car cafe in **Hyper Hyper**.

Kensington Church Street

Leading up the hill from the high street (therefore meeting it in a perpendicular fashion) is Kensington Church Street, a curvy little road that is only three or four blocks long. It leads directly to Notting Hill. It hosts a few multiples, but more importantly it is home to many, many antiques shops of the high-end, but not so high-end that they are too stuffy to enjoy. Many of these dealers do the big shows, so watch out for the month of June—the stores may be closed or only open at weird hours.

Notting Hill Gate

I can't quite get into Notting Hill Gate as a neighborhood; it's more like a sigh between Kensington Church Street and Portobello Road, but there are a few multiples here as well as a good bookstore. This is your tube stop if you are going to Portobello Road. My friends Chris and Deedy lived here and they tell me it's London's answer to the cutting edge place to live, to see and be seen. Various famous names live in the neighborhood, many from art, literature, and design. There aren't any hotels here, so you can't

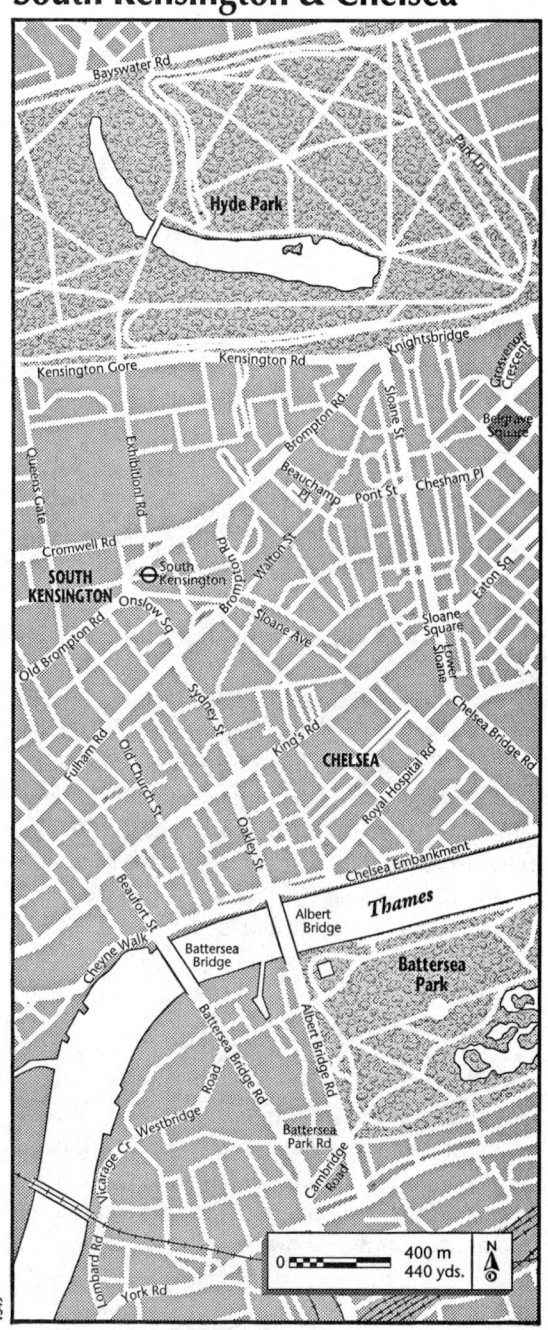

South Kensington & Chelsea

really get the feel to living here, but you can seriously browse or even hang out at **Tom Conran's Deli**—yes, *that* Conran (226 Westbourne Grove, NW8, Tube: Notting Hill).

There's a few cafes and pubs for hanging out and some specialty bookshops including one for cooks (**Books for Cooks**, 4 Blenheim Crescent) and **The Travel Bookshop**, 13 Blenheim Crescent. **Harper & Tom** is the place to buy flowers because Princess Di buys hers there, 13 Elgin Crescent.

Portobello Road

There is indeed a Portobello Road and it is the home of the Saturday market; it is also the home of many genuine antiques dealers who are open during the week. To think that Portobello Road is *just* a Saturday event is wrong. It's actually easier to enjoy the shops during the week when the Saturday throngs, the tour buses, the German tots, and the organ grinder are not in place.

Considering how famous Portobello Road is, it's not that easy to find. Please note that on Saturdays there is a chalkboard at the stairwell inside the Notting Hill Gate tube station giving specific directions for how to get to Portobello Road. The fun starts as soon as you turn right onto Pembridge Road from Notting Hill Gate and continues as you wend your way to Portobello Road. Follow the crowd.

COVENT GARDEN

The area I call Covent Garden is actually a parcel of real estate that includes Covent Garden among a handful of other neighborhoods. This part of town begins at Trafalgar, but actually backs up on one end at Mayfair and at the other, Soho.

Covent Garden

The entire area around Covent Garden is filled with fabulous little shops and pubs, which makes the whole place a super shopping area. It's also an officially designated tourist area, so stores are open on Sunday (please note that not all are open, but unlike in other parts of London, many are). Prowl everywhere, not just the festival marketplace. Include the two buildings of Covent Garden—a rehabilitation of the old marketplace—and make sure you also see the three different markets that are more or less attached to Covent Garden (between the two buildings; out the back building; and to the side of the two buildings).

Several multiples have branches in the red-brick mall stores; one of the most interesting entries is **Twilight,** a division of **Monsoon** and **Accessorize** (which is technically also a division of Monsoon) that specializes in dress-up clothes for evening, hence the name. I will admit that I flipped out when I discovered that a mere wisp of nothing but Thai silk and wire to wrap around the hair was selling for £18, but the clothes themselves are more moderately priced.

There's also a branch of **Culpeper the Herbalist,** smaller than the one in Mayfair but stocked with the same great stuff.

Across the courtyard from Culpeper is the new **Dr. Martens Department Store.** This is where every teenager in the EU is hanging out.

Neal Street

Walk out the front end of Covent Garden and pass the Covent Garden tube; you are on Neal Street, a pedestrian area that is one of the few places in London that is actually booming. A new mall (**Thomas Neals,** Earlham Court) adds to the excitement; there are pubs and people and stores galore with a funky, friendly feeling that makes the whole

Covent Garden adventure more complete. The stores here are mostly open on Sundays as well; don't miss it.

Leicester Square

Get here—to the heart of the theater district and not much of a shopping district—via New Row, so you can take in a few more charming shops. New Row is only a block long, but there's something very quaint and very Old World about it that makes its combination of bookstores, antiques stores, and crafts stores thrill you with a sense of discovery.

The Strand

This is a so-so tourist area where there are branches of the big-name shops (**Chinacraft**, **Next**, etc.), but where everything seems to have been in its prime in 1960. The Strand begins at Charing Cross and stretches along in the direction of St. Paul's Cathedral and The City. The Strand actually changes its name in a few blocks and becomes the infamous Fleet Street, but no matter.

The heart of The Strand as a shopping district is near Charing Cross and Covent Garden; here you've got the **Savoy Hotel**, **Simpson's In The Strand** for roast beef, and a handful of multiples. Stamp collectors know the area well because several famous dealers are located here; there are also a lot of **sporting goods stores** here. You can connect to Covent Garden or Charing Cross (by walking), so the location can't be ignored, and it's certainly not as intimidating here as it can be for some in Mayfair.

If you are here anyway, don't miss **The Russian Shop**, 99 The Strand, where Russian folk arts are sold at somewhat reasonable prices.

OTHER NEIGHBORHOODS

Fulham Road

Fulham Road can't make up its mind what it is, as it stretches around King's Road and closer to Sloane Square and the Sloane Ranger state of being. If you have some time on your hands, you'll be startled by the contrast between the up-and-coming and the more traditional neighborhood shops that live here. Consider **Ritva Westenius** (#153) for incredible wedding gowns; **The Sleeping Company** for the English version of French bed linens; **Divertimenti** for stylish housewares; **Oggetti** for the hard-line Italian/Memphis look in watches, knives, and teakettles; and **The Watch Gallery**, which is just plain fascinating for the variety of fun watches they have.

Camden Town

I'd just as soon ignore the fact that Camden Town exists, because, well, it's not exactly my cup of tea. That's because I am over 40. If you are 10 and under 30 (hmmmm, maybe you need to be under 20 . . .) you just may adore it here. And so, mothers of teens and pre-teens, grit your teeth. This is an entire neighborhood dedicated to buying clothes and black T-shirts and having your nose pierced. It's particularly busy on Saturday, as this is the day to shop and socialize among the many markets that line the high street.

You may have the urge to hold on to your handbag and to take a bath after you've been here, but your kids will consider this a very awesome part of town. Take the tube to Camden Town, and walk to your right.

Islington

The tube stop for Islington is Angel and you will be in heaven, especially on a Wednesday or Saturday, when you wander for a while through fair Islington. You see, Wednesday and Saturday are market days and there's an alley filled to overflowing with vendors—talk about charm galore. There's an indoor antiques market open every day, but the extra street (alley) action is what makes this fun. I also like the city market, which is for real people and is no different from any other market, except that this is where I buy my **Arsenal** team luggage. If you are looking for anti-status luggage, you too may want to stock up on the lines offered by the football vendors.

All of these marvels are within walking distance of the tube, so go and take cash. You're gonna love it.

The Docklands

The term *the Docklands* has come to refer to all development along both sides of the Thames, below Tower Bridge and stretching to Greenwich. However, the development on the south side of the river, where the Design Museum is located, is not in the thick of what is generally known as the Docklands. Canary Wharf is the heart of the true Docklands, and no one would go to there to shop.

But wait, there's hope. It's not over 'til Terence Conran sings. Across the river from the Docklands and all the things that haven't worked out, there at **Butler's Wharf**, is a lot to see and do and think about.

The best way to see it all is to go to the **Design Museum**, eat lunch at one of the several restaurants or cafes there (take your choice—they are all Conran establishments and something to behold), then pop into a few of the hot new galleries, check out the **Oil & Spice Shop**, see the museums and their shops, and then . . . take a boat and see the rest from the water.

Hampstead

To the north, and in a totally different frame of mind from the Docklands, is the wealthy suburb of Hampstead, charmingly located right off its own heath. For those who want to see what upper-middle-class London suburbs (with good shopping) are like, and for those who might be browsing for just the perfect neighborhood to move to, Hampstead is a must.

Even though McDonald's has just been allowed to build in town, Hampstead still has the feel of an English country village.

The tube station is very deep and sort of ugly; I have found it frightening. You'll only fall in love once you get to street level. Trust me on this.

After all, if it was good enough for Blake and Keats, it'll probably have something to please you, too. Beyond the immediate shopping area lies the famous Hampstead Heath, where a number of famous folk are buried.

The high street has its share of famous multiples, but it also has an American-style 1950s diner, some good food shops, and a few specialized boutiques. There is an antiques center near Louis.

Greenwich

How do I love Greenwich, let me count the ways. There's mean time and in-between time, and then there's Sundays. If you want the perfect Sunday in London, you can hightail it to Greenwich.

Greenwich is more a suburb than a neighborhood, but please don't ignore it. The town of Greenwich is not beautiful; I find it charming, but that's because I love the combination of **flea markets**, **crafts fairs**, and historical sights, and it has special family memories for me from one perfect summer when Mike, Aaron, and I lived in Greenwich.

The village is on the regular tourist beat because the *Cutty Sark* is anchored here and there are other significant sights—like the Old Royal Observatory, the National Maritime Museum, and the one-time royal residence the Queen's House, designed by Inigo Jones and restored rather recently.

If you're as interested in culture as shopping, you may want to buy a Greenwich Day Passport, which is a combined admission ticket that saves you money if you're doing the whole lot. (The Royal Naval College does not charge admission.)

A more significant sight, if you ask me, is the crafts fair held in the Victorian covered market in the center of town. There is a High Street (it leads from the train station into town), but there is no regular high-street shopping, no branch stores of any multiples . . . no, there's not even a Boots or an M&S. *Nada*. Locals have to go to Blackheath to shop, and they don't even have a lot of multiples there. Greenwich is simply a string of dealers and flea marketeers who sell crafts and vintage clothes and junk and used furniture and more junk, and I adore it. The action is on Saturdays and Sundays; forget weekdays.

Take the train from Charing Cross; the price of the ride is included in your Travelcard (see page 14).

Chapter Eight

BASIC LONDON RESOURCES—A–Z

AROMATHERAPY

Aromatherapy has been big in London for years; I'm just now accepting the fact that not only is it here to stay, but it's fun. The essence of aromatherapy is that different smells affect your mood and your body in different ways. It posits that you can manipulate your feelings and your health by surrounding yourself with certain types of fragrances.

It has become such a big business that just about every manufacturer in the world, let alone Britain, has jumped on the bandwagon. You'll have no trouble walking into Boots and finding a score of different types of aromatherapy products and treatments.

Even airlines offer samples of aromatherapy products that are designed to fight jet lag. Ian goes to Michaeljohn for aromatherapy treatments every time he returns to London from a big trip during which he's undergone a major time change; treatments are available at many other salons as well.

DANIELE RYMAN
The Park Lane Hotel, 107b Piccadilly, W1 (Tube: Green Park).

This is the brand that Ian began using after discovering it as a guest at the Langham Hilton a few years ago; **British Airways** also uses Ryman's products. I find them awfully similar to what I use from **Origins,** the Estee Lauder brand, but Ian just loves the way Asleep smells. The English product costs about £10, which is approximately what I pay ($15) for Sleep Time from Origins.

Ryman offers a variety of products for scent and skin as well as teas, candles, books, and treatments. There's a travel kit called an Inflight Comfort Kit which has things like eye compresses, rehydration gel, a nasal and sinus freshener, and a concentrated mouth rinse. I haven't tested all of these products; I usually rely on the ones provided by **British Airways,** but the just the thought of them sounds dreamy . . . and convincing. Some items are available for mail order (phone: 171-499-6321 or fax: 171-499-1965).

The shop is very tiny and is in the lobby of The Park Lane Hotel, near Hyde Park. The entrance is right next to the hotel's front door.

CULPEPER THE HERBALIST
See page 113.

BALLET & BEYOND

FREED OF LONDON LTD.
94 St. Martin's Lane, WC2 (Tube: Leicester Square).

If you are a ballet freak, you have long known of Freed of London, one of the most famous names in slippers and stuff. Freed has not stayed back in the Dark Ages of the Ballet Russe. In fact, they have *jetéd* right into the future with a dance and exercise line. When I was about eight and a ballet freak, I knew about Freed of London. The beat goes on. Bring your daughter. Celebrate tradition.

BATH & BEAUTY

The Body Shop
Covent Garden, WC2 (Tube: Covent Garden).

No trip to London is complete for me without a raid on at least one branch of The Body Shop. Usually, I decide I have not bought enough and return for more.

After a period of disinterest (I found the "green" philosophy of these stores a little too precious), I am now smitten with The Body Shop, especially since I've learned that their products are much cheaper in Britain than in the U.S.

The shops are easily recognizable by their dark green painted exterior. Inside is a world of environmentally and politically correct soaps, scents, and other beauty products; some aromatherapy products; and a full line of men's products and baby products.

Everything comes in small travel sizes for sampling purposes; I think the best fun in the world is to buy tons of these little jars and bottles either for my own travel kit or for stocking stuffers for Christmas or for making up gift baskets. I buy my niece the soaps and fruity bath bubbles and kid products.

There is a branch of The Body Shop in every trading area of London, so don't think this is the only time you can stock up. I frequent the one on Oxford Street (across from the Tesco Metro), and have even been known to use the shop at Heathrow.

Boots the Chemist
Piccadilly Circus, W1 (Tube: Piccadilly Circus).

In the Queen's English, Boots is a chemist. To Americans, Boots is a drugstore. To me, Boots is a way of life. No day in London is complete without a dose of Boots.

What a drugstore: They carry just about everything, although some stores are bigger and better than others. The best thing about Boots is that they have a huge selection of health and beauty aids, usually at reasonable prices. Their house lines offer choices in many pharmaceuticals and beauty products.

There is always a pharmacy, sometimes an optical shop, and always a selection of small appliances such as hair dryers, should you discover that your French model will not work in England. (It won't—different plugs.) You can buy pantyhose here, film, some costume jewelry, or just about any brand of makeup or perfume. They sell the **Bourjois** line of make-up from France (made in the same factories as Chanel) and have their own line of ecologically correct bath and beauty products that imitate what's sold at The Body Shop. I buy their cucumber face scrub.

There is a Boots in almost every city in England and Scotland, most often located on the high street. In London, there's a store in every major trading area. Some are open on Sundays and some are not.

CRABTREE & EVELYN
6 Kensington Church Street, W8 (Tube: High Street Kensington).

It's American; it's American; it's American. Think old-fashioned English and you've got the wonders of Crabtree & Evelyn, a firm that has been successfully selling old-timey packaged soaps, shampoos, shortbreads, potpourri, and teas seemingly for centuries. All of the shops are wood-paneled, with the feel of yesteryear; the firm is so large that there is now a multiple not only in every British city but in every American city as well. The shops are a pleasure to browse; the prices are about the same in the U.K. as at home.

Bath & Beauty   113

🛍 CULPEPER THE HERBALIST
Covent Garden Market, WC2 (Tube: Covent Garden).

Despite the popularity of **The Body Shop** and **Crabtree & Evelyn,** Culpeper the Herbalist has found its niche selling the same kinds of things in a very different manner. The Body Shop and Crabtree & Evelyn are "loud"—they practically shout their look and style. Culpeper shops are not as elaborately decorated as the competition, so the stores feel more low-key and down-home.

They offer soaps, essences, and oils, as well as other beauty products. They are very much into aromatherapy. Culpeper sells a wide range of oils (£2–15, depending on size and rarity) as well as means to distribute the scent—little pots, rings that sit on top of light bulbs (also sold in the U.S., but less than £2 at Culpeper), and what I consider to be the best-of-show: a small, white, plastic, flat, battery-operated fan which holds a paper pad (extra pads, three for £1) on which you drip a few drops of essential oil. Turn on the fan and *voilà*, the scent lasts for six hours.

You choose the scent based on what aromatherapy techniques you need to accomplish; I bought orange because I love the notion, but when I gave Olive the lavender and she told me how nice it was to sleep with the lavender scent, I got hooked. It's fabulous for jet lag.

Back to the fan itself: you can buy the fan for about £8; provide your own AAA batteries. You can buy a gift package of fan, lavender oil, and paper scent pad for £12.50. I've never seen anything like this in America; I think it's the single best gift you can give the person who has everything. I've sent these packages to people in the hospital; they are a marvelous get-well gift.

You can also buy fresh herbs in little pots in season; they have a line of spices and cooking products. Also a range of scented candles; try "Relaxing" for £4.50 in a clay pot.

🛍 Tesco Metro
Oxford Street; Covent Garden.

I haunt the health and beauty aids departments of this, the largest grocery store chain in Britain, for their aromatherapy products, bath gels (fruit cocktail is a favorite "flavor"), and bubble baths. I am particularly fond of their "Bath By Chocolate"—a foaming bubble bath product in a chocolate-colored plastic container—it's a great gift for about $4.

(See also "Foodstuffs.")

BIG NAMES
. . . .

Buying British is the very essence of shopping in London; buying British on sale and getting a VAT refund borders on genius—if you can manage to do it without going too far over your U.S. duty allowance.

This is not to say that you can't save money on non-British big names—I've already made a big point about Hermès—but British names offer the best value if the dollar is in reasonable shape and you qualify for a VAT refund. If the dollar is weak, prices in the U.S. on the same merchandise can actually be equal or less.

So what's a British big name? It's either a major designer or a clothing manufacturer whose name connotes a look that others imitate. The most famous follow in alphabetical order:

Aquascutum
100 Regent Street, W1 (Tube: Piccadilly Circus).

The "other" Burberrys, Aquascutum offers an alternative to cream, beige, red, and black plaid. Established in 1851, Aquascutum has grown from a tiny cottage industry to a major international name.

Most people who go to London for the first time want to come home with an Aquascutum or Burberrys raincoat. The Aquascutum line includes skirts, sweaters, and any accessory you could imagine. Instead of a plaid like Burberrys, Aquascutum is known for their checkered pattern.

LAURA ASHLEY
7-9 Harriet Street, SW1 (home furnishings only) (Tube: Knightsbridge).

35-36 Bow Street, Covent Garden, WC2 (Tube: Covent Garden).

256-258 Regent Street, W1 (Tube: Oxford Circus).

MacMillan House, Kensington High Street, W8 (Tube: High Street Kensington).

449-451 Oxford Street, W1 (Tube: Marble Arch or Bond Street).

120 King's Road, SW3 (Tube: Sloane Square).

Americans who love the Laura Ashley look, unite and spend your money here. Those who loathe it, please reconsider with a visit to the Regent Street store. Much of the line is made up of pure country classics and has nothing to do with little flowers.

Regular prices at regular retail in London are substantially less than in the U.S. Some of this stock is not sold in the U.S.

The line encompasses everything that has to do with the home and also a complete line of dresses, kids' wear, and sleepwear. Oh yes, they even have hats.

The home furnishings department is the best. Chintz fabrics cost less per meter here, but bed linens from U.S. makers can be cheaper at home. Each store has its own close-out policy—you may see baskets filled with discontinued wallpapers (these are sold in double rolls, for added bargains) that sell for £5. Usually there is enough of one or two patterns to paper a small room. This is one of the world's best deals.

Two extra thoughts:

- In the Regent Street store, which is the single best store Ashley has in London, there is a big armchair by the front door. Feel free to park your husband or kids here or just take a break if you're pooped. They used to have a sofa there; maybe it was too crowded.
- The Regent Street store has clothing on the street level and home furnishings upstairs; the store on Harriet Street (right off Sloane Street, around the corner from **Harvey Nichols**) is devoted entirely to home furnishings. Other branch stores do not have as good of a selection of home furnishings.

Betty Barclay
99 New Bond Street, W1 (Tube: Bond Street).

Barclay was considered one of the Brit Brat Pack of young, hip designers who made it: her clothes are spicy without being too outré to wear. Unfortunately, I was bored on my last visit there. Maybe pressure from other big talents on Bond Street will bring a more lively collection next year.

Browns
23 South Molton Street, W1 (Tube: Bond Street).

Any time you get the urge to pooh-pooh British fashion as dowdy, walk yourself right into Browns—the store, not the hotel—for a look-see at what has been London's temple of high fashion for decades. Okay, so it's not so shabby after all. And then stare really long and hard at the Romeo Gigli boutique that Browns has installed. London is not all shabby chic, now is it?

Browns is filled with a ready-to-wear selection from the top designers in Europe. **Sonia Rykiel, Jil**

Big Names 117

Sander, Jean Muir, and Missoni are all represented. Calvin Klein and Donna Karan were launched here; Karan has become a local legend of sorts with her own DKNY store and a collection store on its way. (When they get too big for Browns, they aren't too big for Bond Street.)

Yet, none of this movement diminishes Browns. In fact, the constant changes enhance their image. The store is a string of connecting townhouses; see the upstairs and downstairs levels in each of them. This can be confusing, but it's worth the trouble. This very chic and with-it shop is patronized by a very prestigious clientele that includes celebrities and movie stars.

Prices are high because these are expensive clothes—but you'll also find the velour and cotton groups in the Sonia collection, the cheap line by Jean Muir with her expensive line, and many well-priced unisex items in the men's shop.

In January, everything goes on sale; otherwise the real markdowns are across the street in a special sale shop. Sale merchandise is put in specially made shopping bags that say "Browns Sale," which labels you to the whole world as a piker with good taste. American designers are sold at Browns; there are no bargains, even on markdowns.

BURBERRY
165 Regent Street, W1 (Tube: Piccadilly Circus).

18-22 Haymarket, SW1 (Tube: Piccadilly Circus).

BURBERRY FACTORY SHOP
29-53 Chatham Place, E9 (Bus 55).

A Burberry purchase sums up the British fashion consciousness: the style is classic, the product is well-made, and it will last a lifetime (if you don't leave it on the train).

There are actually two shops in Mayfair; the line is also sold at zillions of sources and is readily available in the U.S., and even at the London airport. The big Regent Street shop is multilevel, and if you love the signature cream, camel, red, and black tartan plaid that has become a status symbol to some, you will be in heaven.

If you love that plaid but wonder what Burberrys can do to stay with the times, you will marvel at their traditional plaid done with a pale blue or pale pink ground. It's really super.

Should you be ready to make the big raincoat purchase, please come prepared with numbers (style and price) from home and, if you are really serious, come to London specifically during the sale season. With a sale and a VAT refund, you may save money. But you will also have to pay duty when you return to the U.S.

Besides all the famous rain gear, they sell traditional English fashions here as well as bespoke suits. Some items in the store, such as the umbrella, seem to be outrageously expensive ($50), while others seem quite reasonable.

The Haymarket Street store is smaller, more intimate, sort of more British, and it possesses a large children's department. It's conveniently located a few doors away from an American Express office.

If you're willing to make the trek, we've located the factory outlet store. My friend Ruth, who lives in London, says that it's very hit or miss but quite worthwhile if you hit it right. You can get there by bus but it will take about 45 minutes each way. What we have to go through to have a good time in London, amazing. See page 151 for details on the outlet.

ALLY CAPELLINO
95 Wardour Street, Soho, W1 (Tube: Piccadilly).

I had the hardest time deciding if Capellino should be called a big name or a hip and hot designer: She is actually both. Many of the big names in Britain have made their fortunes by remaining staid.

Capellino is cutting edge and has finally opened her own shop in the fringe area of Soho.

I find the clothes very inventive, exciting, and wearable but the prices beyond me. I asked Ian to buy me the ochre crushed velvet dinner dress but he said £500 was past his budget. Oh, well.

Caroline Charles
170 New Bond Street, W1 (Tube: Bond Street).

Think taffeta and silk, dress-up and Princess Diana as well as veddy-veddy-but-still-gorgeous, and you've got the edge on Caroline Charles. Think Ascot and The Season and just the right hat-and-suit combination. You're back at Caroline Charles. There is an unwritten rule with British women that you can't go wrong with Caroline Charles, so if you're trying to impress the natives, one-stop shopping will do it. Recently moved to Bond Street to be part of the new action. Has also opened her first international branch store in Amsterdam. Watch this space.

Lindka Cierach
1C Clareville Grove, SW7 (Tube: South Kensington).

If you are not familiar with this designer or her address, let's go over the quirky details first. One: her name is Lindka not Linda. It's not a typo. Yes, her studio address is 1C; that's not 10. Of course, you know all these details because you're a royal follower and you know major talent when it appears on the telly.

Lindka became famous when she made the Duchess of York's wedding gown—with the beaded thistle, thank you very much—and while she has lasted longer than Fergie in her chosen profession, Lindka remains an insider's choice for something unique, usually dressy, and possibly custom-made. If you're serious, call for an appointment: 171-224-3882.

120 BASIC LONDON RESOURCES—A–Z

JASPER CONRAN
303 Brompton Road, SW3 (Tube: South Kensington).

One of the more inventive of the young set of designers, with lines that vary tremendously from season to season, but always show a creative touch and a distinctive style. For the woman who doesn't want to look ordinary. He always does a range of simple, drop-dead chic black dresses with various necklines to flatter any figure.

PAUL COSTELLOE
156 Brompton Road, SW1 (Tube: South Kensington).

The flagship shop has opened and expansion throughout the U.K. in freestanding stores is under way. Can global acceptance be far away? This Irish designer does wearable clothes that are suitable for work, but have a nice sense of humor that's soft and pleasant. Good color palette.

NICOLE FARHI
158 New Bond Street, W1 (Tube: Bond Street).

25-26 St. Christopher's Place, W1 (Tube: Bond Street).

193 Sloane Street, SW1 (Tube: Knightsbridge).

27 Hampstead High Street, NW3 (Tube: Hampstead).

12 Floral Street, WC2 (Tube: Covent Garden).

Don't let this foreign-sounding name throw you off the track: Farhi has arrived on the scene as a very acceptable designer to provide your clothes for a British fashion statement (almost an oxymoron) that still works for the horse-and-hedge set.

This British designer does the elegant-working-woman look with New York panache and would fit well into the American scene. The tailored clothes are rich and simple, always elegant but with sporty comfort. Branch stores are popping up so frequently that she may soon be considered a multiple. For those who like Armani but can't afford it, this line is expensive but less so than Armani, and can serve the same purpose.

Farhi's Bond Street showcase is the talk of the town; her restaurant is *the* place to eat while on a shopping spree. They even serve breakfast!

Best yet, my friend Ruth has introduced me to the outlet shop (see page 152).

KATHARINE HAMNETT
20 Sloane Street, SW1 (Tube: Knightsbridge).

Once considered young and flashy, Hamnett is now an established member of the fashion establishment. Her work ranges from cute and kicky to well-cut (and pricey) suits.

MARGARET HOWELL
29 Beauchamp Place, SW3 (Tube: Knightsbridge).

Margaret Howell offers—to me, at least—the epitome of British casual classy dressing. The clothes are expensive but so chic and elegant, so much the real subtext of what Ralph Lauren has always been able to capture and recreate. There are London dress-up clothes, but this resource is best for more casual everyday clothes and for weekend chic—casual sweaters (hand-knit), twin sets, jackets, coats. One of the best in Britain for the right stuff.

BETTY JACKSON
311 Brompton Road, SW3 (Tube: South Kensington).

Known for wearable clothes, especially separates, Betty Jackson was in the forefront of the wave of hip, young London designers who could sell to U.S.

department stores. Now she's made a name for herself with clothes that real people want to buy. She likes longer skirts and snappy designs that speak loudly but don't shout.

JAEGER
204 Regent Street, W1 (Tube: Piccadilly Circus or Oxford Circus).

A basic, classic British resource—sold in their own shops and in many department stores. They have a way with wools in particular and stride the fine line between boring English clothes and high fashion. For quality, you can always trust Jaeger. I like to buy the women's wear when I can afford it; the men's clothes usually leave me cold . . . they're for thin men with European bodies.

The shop on Regent Street is almost a department store. Not only is this shop easy to find, it also has everything, including hats and accessories. One of the good things about the Jaeger line is that it is totally color-coordinated each season, so you can buy a complete wardrobe of interchangeable pieces (great for travel); the bad news is that if you don't like the color palette for a season, you're out of luck. I've seen some summer combinations that I would categorize as too British for my taste or for continental European taste.

But you'll never go wrong when they do navy and white, or with their blacks, reds, and neutrals. Many items are good travel basics.

The most Jaeger fun you'll ever have is during the January sales when you can hit department stores (**Harrods** has a good selection) and Jaeger boutiques. One warning: Jaeger may cost less in the U.S.! Shop carefully. There's a Jaeger boutique in the mall near where I live; sometimes I get better prices there, although not as big a selection.

Joseph

21 Sloane Street, SW1 (Tube: Knightsbridge).

88 Peterborough Road, SW6 (Brompton Cross flagship store) (Tube: South Kensington).

130 Draycott Avenue, SW3 (near Brompton Cross) (Tube: South Kensington).

Joseph Ettedgui is now holding his own after big changes with some of his Joseph lines. I must confess that I feel old and battered, hit hard by the financial tides, when I realize that the Joseph Tricot line and stores have bitten the London dust. But Joseph has recovered, continues to be one of the leading forces in the fashion scene in Britain, and is opening new stores with his own private label.

Joseph Pour La Maison and various other Josephs around town have survived. The man is incredibly inventive and creative; his nest of stores in Brompton Cross can still give you a visual stimulation that defines the best in hot British fashion. Joseph's look is rich, casual, inventive, and usually layered.

Mulberry

40-41 Old Bond Street, W1 (Tube: Bond Street).

11/12 Gee's Court (off St. Christopher's Place), W1 (Tube: Bond Street).

Mulberry offers a rich country look of finished elegance in first leathergoods but also clothing for men and women and accessories and now home decor. The new flagship store on Old Bond Street announces to the world what major players they are. Mulberry is keeping their small shop (right off Oxford Street; don't let the address throw you); they also have boutiques in many department stores and wide distribution of their clothes throughout Britain. Indeed, this is a look in much the same vein as Ralph Lauren's country chic, and it is rich and fabulous. It's also expensive. See *Born to Shop Great Britain* for details on the factory outlet store.

BRUCE OLDFIELD
27 Beauchamp Place, SW3 (Tube: Knightsbridge).

The Princess of Wales brought Bruce Oldfield into the spotlight, but he has been a British social secret for many years. He is most admired for his fabulous ball gowns and luxurious evening wear, which are anything but plain or simple. Most of his designs flow and rustle, and if they are black, there is always something glistening attached. Located in the heart of Sloane Ranger chic, Oldfield offers both a retail and a bespoke operation.

MARY QUANT
3 Ives St., SW3 (Tube: South Kensington).

It was a mod, mod world when Mary Quant came to fame in the swingin' sixties. When her clothes lost their cutting edge, her makeup line lived on, although it eventually went off the shelves in the U.K. Now, Quant is back and you can stop by to visit and stock up, or call for mail order (171-581-1811). Don't be thrown by the address—this is a tiny street right near Brompton Cross.

EDINA RONAY
141 King's Road, SW3 (Tube: Sloane Square).

First known for her small sweater shop on King's Road and her famous last name, Ronay began designing a full line of clothing a few years ago and hasn't looked back. The clothes are rich, lush, somewhat dramatic, and on the crease between what you would call hot London fashion and hot Milano fashion.

EMMA SOMERSET
69 Knightsbridge, SW1 (Tube: Knightsbridge).

Emma Somerset does not really belong in a list called British Big Names, but I have no list for British Medium Names. She is well-known to a small segment of the population that has money and likes to overdress. The look is what is socially acceptable for The Season and more. If you are American and are buying to impress a British audience and want advice on dressy affairs, you may want to begin here and see if you can make a match with your own style and Emma's.

TOMASZ STARZEWSKI
15-17 Pont Street, SW1 (Tube: Sloane Square or Knightsbridge).

Okay, so he's got a Polish name, but he's British and he's very hot. For those in England who still have money, this is where to spend it. Princess Di helped make the man's reputation by buying into his beaded couture; there is also a ready-to-wear line. British *Vogue* calls him "the darling of the ballroom." The reason he's such a hit, aside from his talent, is the fact that his couture costs 60% less than everyone else's. A dress that would cost $15,000 elsewhere is a mere $5,000 here. You can get a dinner suit to swoon for in the £500 price range. And you'll wear it for 20 years.

🛍 GEORGINA VON ETZDORF
Burlington Arcade, W1 (Tube: Piccadilly Circus or Green Park).

She began as more or less her own one-woman band of English Eccentric, doing hand-painted silks and scarves and items so yummy that they caught on with the upper classes and now Von Etzdorf is the darling of all with her own shop in Burlington Arcade.

VIVIENNE WESTWOOD
41 Conduit Street, W1 (Tube: Bond Street or Green Park).

6 Davies Street, W1 (Tube: Bond Street).

World's End, 430 King's Road, SW10 (take the bus).

When American fashion lion John Fairchild made up his list of the most influential and important designers of our time, Vivienne Westwood headed it up. Fairchild calls her the "designer's designer" because more mainstream designers are influenced by her bright and fresh ideas. She invents shapes, moods, and concepts of dressing and produces slightly way-out clothes that age well, though they are more for the young and monied.

The Conduit Street shop is right in the heart of your Mayfair shopping time, so pop in. They do sell off the samples at the end of the season and prices can be reasonable. This is Viv's version of a mark-down shop or factory outlet. The clothes may be outrageous but the prices may not be

International & American Big Names

No shopping mecca is more international than London; no international resource can consider itself in the big time if it doesn't list a London address on its shopping bags. But there are very few bargains in international merchandise here, unless you hit a big sale. If you do find a savings, most likely it will be less than 10% (excluding a VAT refund, which can make large expenditures more worthwhile).

While American retailers and chain stores are opening right and left in London, don't think for a minute that you might save on American goods abroad. With very few exceptions, these stores offer merchandise that is much more expensive in Britain than in the U.S. I go to Gap stores all the time just to laugh. The prices in pounds are exactly the same as the prices in U.S. dollars at home. (If you want to bring a gift to someone in Britain, buy it at the Gap in the U.S.)

The only exceptions I'm aware of are those my British friend Martine, who goes to New York a few times a year on business, has told me about. She has successfully managed to find Ralph Lauren wallpaper and DKNY blazers at exactly the same price in New York and London. Otherwise, she does better on American goods in the U.S.

I must also report that in the Adrienne Vittadini nook in **Harvey Nichols,** I did see merchandise I'd never seen in a U.S. store. Granted, I don't live in the shipping department of a major mall—but it seemed incredible to go to London to fall in love with an Adrienne Vittadini outfit. (At full British retail, no less.) Academics may want to note that one of the ways Harvey Nichols likes to differentiate itself from other London department stores is that they are heavily committed to American designers and American brands.

Oh yes, one last tacky insider tip to share: If you've ever shopped at Victoria's Secret, or used their catalog (who hasn't?), you may have noticed that they use a Margaret Street, London, address as their "headquarters." The company did this only for image-making purposes; there is no store on Margaret Street or anywhere else in London.

International Big Names

GIORGIO ARMANI
178 Sloane Street, SW1 (Tube: Knightsbridge).

AGNÈS B.
111 Fulham Road, SW3 (Tube: South Kensington).

BLEYLE
40 Sloane Street, SW1 (Tube: Knightsbridge).

PIERRE CARDIN
20 Old Bond Street, W1 (Tube: Bond Street).

Céline
28 New Bond Street, W1 (Tube: Bond Street).

27 Brompton Road, SW3 (Tube: Knightsbridge).

Cerutti 1881
76 New Bond Street, W1 (Tube: Bond Street).

Chanel
26 Old Bond Street, W1 (Tube: Bond Street).

31 Sloane Street, SW1 (Tube: Knightsbridge).

Descamps
197 Sloane Street, SW1 (Tube: Knightsbridge).

Adolfo Dominguez
57 South Molton Street, W1 (Tube: Bond Street).

Emporio Armani
187-191 Brompton Road, SW3 (Tube: Knightsbridge).

112A New Bond Street, W1 (Tube: Bond Street).

Episode
172 Regent Street, W1 (Tube: Piccadilly).

Escada
67 New Bond Street, W1 (Tube: Bond Street).

Fendi
37 Sloane Street, SW1 (Tube: Knightsbridge).

Louis Féraud
73 New Bond Street, W1 (Tube: Bond Street).

Ferragamo
24 Old Bond Street, W1 (Tube: Bond Street).

Gianfranco Ferré
20 Brook Street, W1 (Tube: Green Park or Bond Street).

Fogal
36 New Bond Street, W1 (Tube: Bond Street).

GENNY
19 South Molton Street, W1 (Tube: Bond Street).

GUCCI
33 Old Bond Street, W1 (Tube: Bond Street).

17-18 Sloane Street, SW1 (Tube: Knightsbridge).

HERMÈS
155 New Bond Street, W1 (Tube: Bond Street).

179 Sloane Street, SW1 (Tube: Knightsbridge).

ISTANTE
183 Sloane Street, SW1 (Tube: Knightsbridge).

JACADI
473 Oxford Street, W1 (Tube: Marble Arch).

KENZO
15 Sloane Street, SW1 (Tube: Knightsbridge).

KRIZIA
18 New Bond Street, W1 (Tube: Bond Street).

CHRISTIAN LACROIX
8A Sloane Street, SW1 (Tube: Knightsbridge).

29 Old Bond Street, W1 (Tube: Bond Street).

KARL LAGERFELD
173 New Bond Street, W1 (Tube: Bond Street).

201 Sloane Street, SW1 (Tube: Knightsbridge).

MAX MARA
153 New Bond Street, W1 (Tube: Bond Street).

32 Sloane Street, SW1 (Tube: Knightsbridge).

ISSEY MIYAKE
21 Sloane Street, SW1 (Tube: Knightsbridge).

270 Brompton Road, SW3 (Tube: Knightsbridge).

OILILY
10 Sloane Street, SW1 (Tube: Knightsbridge).

RODIER
106 Brompton Road, SW3 (Tube: Knightsbridge).

YVES SAINT-LAURENT/RIVE GAUCHE
137 New Bond Street, W1 (Tube: Bond Street).

33 Sloane Street, SW1 (Tube: Knightsbridge).

VALENTINO
160 New Bond Street, W1 (Tube: Bond Street).

174 Sloane Street, SW1 (Tube: Knightsbridge).

GIANNI VERSACE
34-35 Old Bond Street, W1 (Tube: Bond Street).

80 and 92 Brompton Road, SW3 (Tube: Knightsbridge).

ERMENEGILDO ZEGNA
37 New Bond Street, W1 (Tube: Bond Street).

American Big Names

DKNY
27 Old Bond Street, W1 (Tube: Bond Street).

THE DISNEY STORE
140-144 Regent Street, W1 (Tube: Oxford Circus).

ESPRIT
6 Sloane Street, SW1 (Tube: Knightsbridge).

THE GAP
208 Regent Street, W1, among several (Tube: Oxford Circus).

GAP KIDS
146 Regent Street, W1, among several (Tube: Oxford Circus).

TOMMY HILFIGER
18 South Molton Street, W1 (Tube: Bond Street).

LEVI'S
269 Regent Street, W1 (Tube: Piccadilly).

ORVIS
27 Sackville Street, W1 (Tube: Piccadilly Circus).

POLO/RALPH LAUREN
143 New Bond Street, W1 (Tube: Bond Street).

TIMBERLAND
72 New Bond Street, W1 (Tube: Bond Street).

WARNER BROTHERS STUDIO STORE
271 Regent Street, W1 (Tube: Piccadilly).

BOOKS

Below are listings of booksellers who sell recently published books, bestsellers, and other titles currently in print. If it's first editions, rare or antiquarian books, or out of print titles you seek, please see page 274 for listings of antiquarian and used booksellers. For business books, try the major multiples or **Foyles** (page 133).

DILLON'S
82 Gower Street, WC1 (Tube: Goodge Street).

In London, Dillon's is to new books what **Harrods** is to everything else. Consider that each year approximately 40,000 new titles are published in the English language. Dillon's has approximately 250,000 titles on hand at any one time. In September, the number actually increases to nearly 300,000, since Dillon's is near the University of London and must stock a vast variety of textbooks as well. While the vast majority of the stock is nonfiction, a quarter of Dillon's books are novels published in the last three years. Dillon's lays no claim to being a discounter, but its policy has led to rapid expansion. There are now about fifty shops in the U.K.

THE BUILDING BOOK SHOP
The Building Centre, 26 Store Street, WC1 (Tube: Goodge Street).

For design freaks, this is the last word. Just camp out and order in. This is a bookstore for the design trade, with specialty books for architects, designers, do-it-yourselfers, and the like. It's more industrial than crafts, but you'll find something for everyone. On Saturdays, they close at 1 P.M.

HATCHARDS
187 Piccadilly, W1 (Tube: Piccadilly Circus).

Looking for me in London? Stop by Hatchards at Piccadilly. I spend part of almost every visit to London here. Far and away the most complete of the modern booksellers, the main Hatchards is in a townhouse near **Fortnum & Mason,** and is filled with just about everything. The store is owned by **Dillon's** as a sort of boutique bookstore. There are bigger stores in London but I like the size of this one and I love their travel section.

The children's book section is a good one—this is where I discovered *James the Red Engine* before stumbling across *Thomas the Tank Engine*, which is part of the same series. If you are starting on this series, despite what you may hear, start with James, not Thomas.

Hatchards is open from 9 A.M. to 5:30 P.M. Monday to Friday and from 9 A.M. to 5 P.M. Saturday. They are also open Sunday afternoons. Holiday hours are usually posted out front.

WATERSTONE'S BOOKSELLERS
88 Regent Street, W1 (Tube: Piccadilly Circus).

99-101 Old Brompton Road, SW7 (Tube: Knightsbridge).

193 Kensington High Street, W8 (Tube: High Street Kensington).

121-125 Charing Cross Road, WC2 (Tube: Tottenham Court Road).

A chain, not so different from B. Dalton, but with a large selection of everything and many locations near the shopping areas to which you automatically gravitate. In fact, Waterstone's has invaded America and now has a few stores here and there, including Boston.

This is simply a good basic source for extra guidebooks (no one can survive in London without an A to Z), books for airplane reading, and art books.

G. HEYWOOD HILL LTD.
10 Curzon Street, W1 (Tube: Green Park).

Heywood mostly sells antiquarian books but in order to appeal to all their customers' tastes, they do have a very carefully selected section of contemporary titles. (See full description on page 275.)

FOYLE
119 Charing Cross Road, WC2 (Tube: Leicester Square).

Foyle is the largest bookstore in London, with over four million volumes in stock. It's as crowded as ever, but the somewhat lackadaisical staff has been replaced by earnest and mostly helpful college students. There are large children's and fiction sections on the main floor; upper floors are devoted to technical books, a small antiquarian library, and huge sections on hobbies, art, and commerce. The business section is particularly noteworthy. Hours: Monday to Wednesday, and Friday and Saturday, 9 A.M. to 6 P.M.; Thursday, 9 A.M. to 7 P.M. Closed Sunday.

ZWEMMER
Oxford University Press Bookshop, 72 Charing Cross Road, WC2 (Tube: Leicester Square).

ZWEMMER ART
24 Litchfield Street, WC2 (fine arts) (Tube: Leicester Square).

ZWEMMER BOOKSHOP
80 Charing Cross Road, WC2 (graphic arts) (Tube: Leicester Square).

Zwemmer has three stores in Charing Cross: (1) the Oxford University Press Bookshop, company store for one of the most respected publishers in the world; (2) a shop across the street devoted to the graphic arts—illustration, photography, etc. (there were three different books on Issey Miyake the last time we looked); and (3) a shop devoted to the fine arts (at 24 Litchfield Street). All three are open from 9:30 A.M. to 6 P.M. Monday to Friday and from 9:30 A.M. to 5:30 P.M. on Saturday.

BUTTONS

BUTTON QUEEN
19 Marylebone Lane, W1 (Tube: Bond Street).

You have to go back a little farther than the tourist mainstream to find this shop, but it's convenient enough for you to go for it—especially if you sew, knit, or collect. The small shop has everything from old to new, to hand-painted to Wedgwood buttons. The Wedgwood set is rather pricey, but other prices do begin at about a quarter per button. If you are considering making a sweater or having one made from a designer kit, come by here to get the buttons.

The store is only two blocks from Oxford Street, so don't let the address throw you. Get there through Cecil Court and you won't mind the walk.

CHILDREN'S CLOTHING SOURCES

LA CIGOGNA
6A Sloane Street, SW1 (Tube: Knightsbridge).

I am utterly amazed that La Cigogna has survived the recession: the store stands for everything the 1980s stood for—overdressed kids in expensive togs.

Children's Clothing Sources 135

This shop is loaded with all those wonderful Italian designer clothes and shoes that very few of us can possibly afford. But if you have a special occasion or are able to splurge, this is the place. If you have a daughter, the gorgeous array of party dresses next to the entrance seems endless. Also available for your princess are lovely skirts, pants, and sweaters (some hand-knits). There is a small area for infants and toddlers, and the back of the shop is devoted just to boys. Don't miss the basement for dazzling Italian shoes and dazzling prices.

MOTHERCARE
461 Oxford Street, W1 (Tube: Marble Arch).

A gigantic chain of stores selling maternity and brand-new-baby needs as well as kids' clothes and things like strollers and plastic dishes. Well-designed; good quality; moderate prices. There are some stores in the U.S., but they pale compared to even a branch store in the U.K.

TROTTERS
34 King's Road, SW3 (Tube: Sloane Square).

See page 222 for the listing on this adorable shop which sells kids' toys and clothing.

Multiples That Carry Children's Clothes

LAURA ASHLEY
7-9 Harriet Street, SW1 (home furnishings only) (Tube: Knightsbridge).

35-36 Bow Street, Covent Garden, WC2 (Tube: Covent Garden).

256-258 Regent Street, W1 (Tube: Oxford Circus).

MacMillan House, Kensington High Street, W8 (Tube: High Street Kensington).

See description on page 115.

GAP KIDS
146 Regent Street, W1 (among several) (Tube: Oxford Circus).

NEXT
160 Regent Street, W1 (Tube: Piccadilly Circus).

See description on page 189.

CIGARS

A woman is a woman but a cigar is a smoke—everyone knows that. And everyone who knows it has known it for a very long time, far longer than the current trend toward events called "Smokers," which are actually PR events created by hotels and/or cigar selling stores to boost interest and sales. Not to worry, London has long been a leading cigar capital of the world.

That is partly because Cuban cigars are not illegal in Britain.

Since it is illegal currently to sell Cuban cigars in the U.S. or to bring Cuban cigars into the U.S., my reporting on this subject is going to be limited.

However, there are a few major cigar retailers in London and you can discuss your needs specifically with them. I happen to like to hang out at Davidoff because the men who shop there are so handsome. But don't mind me. **Harrods** and **Selfridges** do also sell cigars.

DUNHILL
30 Duke Street, SW1 (Tube: Piccadilly Circus)

Alfred Dunhill is more than a cigar shop (see page 158). But they do have cigars, humidors, and smoking paraphernalia galore on the mezzanine where the atmosphere is masculine and clubby. If you're looking for the perfect gift for the man who has everything, surely one of Lord Linley's bespoke humidors will do the trick. (Non-royal watchers will note that David Linley is the son of Princess Margaret and a major force in new British design.)

Davidoff
35 St. James's Street, SW1 (Tube: Green Park).

From Geneva, Davidoff has shops in all the major capitals. Their London shop is on the corner of St. James Street right near Jeremy Street, firmly entrenched in Man Territory. The atmosphere is not as forbiddingly formal as Dunhill.

JJ Fox
19 St. James's Street, SW1 (Tube: Piccadilly).

Old cigar hands may know this shop as **Robert Lewis**. JJ Fox is the newer and proper name. Indeed, we are talking about a merger here, the joining of two of London's top cigar dealers, James J. Fox and Robert Lewis. Now then, if you think Dunhill is intimidating, you have not visited this clubby little nook where men speak Cohiba in quiet tones.

The setup is simple: there's a smoking club on two floors and the ground floor is devoted to sales. And yes, there's a cigar museum. This is the shop noted for its Churchill memorabilia—Winston Churchill opened his account here in 1900 and used it right up until a month before he died 64 years later.

COMPACT DISCS & TAPES

The London retail music scene is an accurate reflection of the music recording business itself: What was once a vital, creative maelstrom has become ho-hum and predictable, with a few giant megabuck companies dominating. Independent companies survive, if at all, by specializing. The three heavyweights—**HMV**, **Tower**, and **Virgin**—have all the amenities and services you'd expect to find in a warehouse, but they do have mammoth selection, literally something for every taste. Virgin and HMV stores open at 9:30 A.M. and stay open until at least 7 P.M. Tower is even more accessible—9 A.M. to midnight. Finally, HMV and Virgin have a total of five stores on Oxford Street, making things ever-so-convenient.

HMV
150 Oxford Street, W1 (Tube: Oxford Circus).

363 Oxford Street, W1 (Tube: Bond Street or Marble Arch).

18 Coventry Street (Trocadero), W1 (Tube: Piccadilly Circus).

Tower Records
1 Piccadilly Circus, W1 (Tube: Piccadilly Circus).

62-64 Kensington High Street, W8 (Tube: High Street Kensington).

Virgin Megastore
14-30 Oxford Street, W1 (Tube: Oxford Circus).

100 Oxford Street, W1 (Tube: Tottenham Court Road).

527 Oxford Street, W1 (Tube: Marble Arch).

Since specialty shops are often haunts for collectors, listings for record dealers and other independently owned new and used CD, tape, LP, and 78 shops appear in Chapter 10.

DEPARTMENT STORES

American department stores are mostly patterned on British ones, so you will feel right at home in just about any department store in London. All are in big, old-fashioned buildings and offer the kind of social security that enables you to know you could live in them. Most of them have several restaurants or tearooms (and they all have clean bathrooms).

During the Christmas shopping days, department stores are open later than usual, which may mean until 7 P.M. They are rarely open until 9 P.M. Other than at Christmastime, department stores have one night a week—either Wednesday or Thursday—during which they stay open until 7 P.M. or possibly 8 P.M., and just maybe 9 P.M., but a store that stays open that late is more than likely to be some kind of alternative retailing source, not a traditional department store.

All department stores have export desks that will help you with VAT forms; all department stores allow you to collect your receipts over a period of time to qualify for the VAT. Some may charge £4–6 for the administrative work they must do on their end. The minimum amount of money you must spend to qualify for a VAT refund varies dramatically from department store to department store.

When you go to the VAT desk in any given store, allow some time not only for getting your paperwork processed, but for standing in line while others ahead of you are dealing with theirs. If you can move right through, the process will take about 10 minutes. Do have your passport on hand or know your number by heart.

HARRODS
Knightsbridge, SW1 (Tube: Knightsbridge).

Quite simply, I have a love/hate thing with Harrods. I hate to send you here if you have limited time or if you think this is the best store in London, yet I love to shop here for a few brief shining moments every time I'm in London.

There is no question that this store is a landmark and that it offers one hell of a lot of merchandise. The china department and the food halls are what becomes a legend most; the children's toy department is almost as good as **Hamley's**. Pat and Steve Gross got me hooked on the wheel of Stilton sold in the food halls (£15); now, I try to stop into Harrods just to stock up on cheese. (Stilton can legally be brought into the U.S.)

What I hate about Harrods is that I think they've just stopped trying to be innovative; they just keep on keeping on. **Harvey Nichols,** which isn't anything like Harrods in reality, is at least young and alive and changing with the times. Harrods is plain old dependable vanilla ice cream. And not even French vanilla.

Before I even give you the scoop on what's inside the store, let's hope that you can indeed enter the store to see it for yourself. The store has recently enlarged its list of no-nos for visitors and enforces a very strict dress code. I got a postcard from an angry reader who said she was denied entrance because of her backpack. Jeans that are torn—even fashionably so—are also on the banned list.

Upon entering Harrods, you may find it hard to imagine that Henry Charles Harrod began his store as a little grocery business in 1849. From a small family business with a staff of two, Harrods has grown to be the most complete department store in London. But you've probably read the Jeffrey Archer book all about it.

The food halls, located on the ground floor, are internationally known, with 17 departments in all. The department store itself covers four-and-a-half acres of land and has fifteen acres of selling space. This is good to remember when your feet are telling you to stop, but you don't even feel that you've made a dent in the store.

Ground floor: food halls, men's fashions, fabrics, perfume and cosmetics, fashion accessories, jewelry, stationery, and clocks; *one:* designer clothing, a definite must-stop; *two:* china, glass, books, records, housewares; *three:* furniture; *four:* toys; *five:* sporting goods, hair, and beauty.

Don't forget that Harrods prides itself on being a full-service department store. Because of that, on the lower level, you will find a complete travel agency, export department, London Tourist Board office, bank, and theater ticket agency. There is a hair salon upstairs on five, which opens at 9 A.M., even though the store opens at 10 A.M.

When you need some refreshment, Harrods has five restaurants, three of them on the fourth floor. If you need a food hamper to complete your Season, order ahead from Harrods. Prices begin around £20 per person; kids' menu available at £12.50. There is a deposit on the traditional wicker basket, the dishes, and the cutlery. Call 171-730-1234, extension 2058.

And now for my major beef against Harrods. Their minimum for a VAT refund is £100! While this is an improvement over what it used to be (£150), this is still rather steep. And frankly, while I am the most uptight person in the world and hardly ever wear torn jeans, I think their new dress code is a little too strict. Lighten up, guys. Let's live and shop; that's what it's all about, isn't it?

SELFRIDGES
400 Oxford Street, W1 (Tube: Marble Arch or Bond Street).

They're working on the image and trying to upgrade it. I still find the store sort of boring, but for locals who live here the improvements are valued.

The real reason for an American to shop at Selfridges is that they carry many of the same basics of life that aren't flashy but may be on your shopping list, and the requirement for a VAT refund is £75, not £150, as at Harrods.

Harry Gordon Selfridge was an American who believed that the European market could benefit from a full-service department store. He was unable to convince his employers at Marshall Field's in Chicago of that fact, so in 1909 he opened his own version of the American department store. Now Selfridges covers an entire city block. Like Harrods, the store is filled with concessions of big names; there are branches of the multiples within the store itself—such as **Thornton's,** the candy chain, which has its own counter; **Holland & Barrett,** the health-food chain, which has its own department here, and so on.

Basement: housewares; *ground floor*: food halls (not as interesting as Harrods, but fine for picnic supplies), cosmetics, some accessories, some men's accessories, **Miss Selfridge;** *one*: export bureau, men's clothing; *two*: women's clothing (designers); *three*: kids' clothing; *four*: sportswear.

Selfridges has three restaurants, four coffee shops, and a juice bar. At 3:30 P.M., a gong is rung and teatime is on. It's sort of like that Colombian coffee commercial we watch on the telly: Attention, Selfridges shoppers—tea is now being served.

LIBERTY
210-220 Regent Street, W1 (Tube: Oxford Circus).

I have a simple motto that repeats itself in the back of my brain each time the Tudor-style Liberty building comes into my line of sight: "Give me Liberty or give me death."

You haven't been shopping in London if you haven't visited Liberty, and I mean the mother store on Regent Street, not a branch store.

Originally opened in 1875 by Arthur Lazenby, who did not play James Bond no matter what you may remember, Liberty is a topsy-turvy department store with nooks and crannies and salons and other parts of the store hidden up and down staircases and around corners and through glass-leaded doors.

Liberty is known worldwide for its Liberty prints, which are sold as fabrics or made up as gift items. Indeed, a basic souvenir or gift item from London is *something* made in a Liberty print. I've got scads of pairs of earrings; the little snapper doodads that hold on your mittens are one of my faves. Liberty boxer shorts are chic, but expensive.

What Liberty is best at is first drama and charm, then fabric.

The store is a visual feast and is surely the best department store in London. Don't miss it. Be sure you are in the "Tudor Building" part of the store—memories are made of architecture like this! Also check out the ready-to-sew skirts and dresses on the second floor; fabrics and needleworks are on three; linens and housewares are on four; antiques on five. The basement has the housewares, china, and exports from the Far East on which the original Liberty rep was based; there's also a bookstore on the street level *behind* the Tudor store, and then an accessories shop through a door behind that where hairbands and things like that are sold.

Because of the layout of the store, I suggest you pick up their free store plan and actually study the diagrams before you start exploring. Aside from a floor plan there is also a chart that shows the parts of the store, what's in them, and where the bridge links are between the two parts.

HARVEY NICHOLS
Knightsbridge (corner of Sloane Street), SW1 (Tube: Knightsbridge).

Although Knightsbridge's other department store is much smaller than **Harrods**, it makes up for size with quality. Harvey Nichols does not try to be everything to everyone. They concentrate their energy on the latest high fashions for men, women, and children. They are, frankly, a *real* store—not a tourist trap trading on an old reputation. Their styles are always the latest, and most of the major design houses are represented; there are lots of American designers.

Before we go any further, you must now repeat after me: Harvey Knicks. That's what you call the store. Anything else will label you a foreigner immediately.

I must admit that no trip to London is complete for me if I have not gone to the back part of the street level and spent a half hour in the hat department, trying on hats. If you're looking for weird and wonderful hats for Ascot, you may be disappointed. These hats go from bland to sophisticated, but do not pass into the weird or wonderful category. Prices range from £50–500; the selection is as good for The Season as it is in the fall, which is the best commentary and recommendation I can give anyone. I have worked the hat department of every department store in London and this is the single best one. It's not huge and it's not overly dramatic—it's simply solid.

I like the home decor floor with its own **Nina Campbell** boutique; the fifth floor—named The Fifth Floor—has the new food hall and a hotshot restaurant called, get this, The Fifth Floor. There is also a place for coffee, a snack, or quick lunch between the fancy eats and the food halls, also on the fifth floor.

I wish I could tell you what all the fuss about the food halls is. Harrods's food halls are a genuine emotional experience; this is like a trip to Zabar's in Manhattan. This is not much more than a trip to your local deli or grocery store; **Sainsbury's** (a big British grocery chain) is just as much fun. But then, it's a practical grocery store. There are ready-made-up foods that made for *le picnique*; there are exotic-blend house-brand teas (black cherry) for £2 a box—a perfect gift for someone at home.

Lower level: men's; *one*: hats, cosmetics, accessories; *two and three*: women's fashions; *four*: home furnishings; *five*: food hall and restaurants.

FORTNUM & MASON
181 Piccadilly, W1 (Tube: Piccadilly Circus).

Your visit to Fortnum & Mason actually begins before you enter the store—the clock outside is very,

very famous, so stand back and take a look. Then go through the revolving doors into a food emporium of fun.

Like many of the old department stores, Fortnum & Mason began (in 1707) as a grocery store; its founder, William Fortnum, was a footman in the household of Queen Anne. He collected and traded the used candle ends from the palace, and saved his funds until he could open his own shop. He persuaded Hugh Mason, who owned a small shop in St. James's Market, to become his partner, and thus began Fortnum & Mason.

The firm's great success during the empire's reign had to do with supplying goods not only in London, but also to the British families overseas. In the Victorian era, Fortnum & Mason also became famous for their fine-quality preserved fruits, jellies, and hams. Their hampers are a must for a status Christmas gift or for the picnics that you must eat (in the car park, no less) when you attend Royal Ascot or any of the events of The Season. Order ahead! Call 171/734-80400.

After World War I, Fortnum & Mason became a full department store with clothes and handbags and normal merchandise. That is not what I go there to buy, but you can wardrobe yourself as well as your pantry. I often eat at the Fountain, although singles beware: parties of two or more are seated more quickly, so it may behoove you to get friendly with another single in the line.

There are food tastings and various promotions; there is a midsummer sale and a January sale; there is sometimes what they call an "Account Customers Preview Day"—it's an evening event that allows you a first go at the sale goodies. You must buy a ticket to this event (£25); call 171-734-8040, extension 572 or 431.

Lower level: china, glass, silver; *ground floor*: foodstuffs; *one*: ladies' fashions, perfume; *two*: children's, nursery, toys; *three*: gentlemen; *four*: antiques.

Marks & Spencer
458 Oxford Street, W1 (Tube: Bond Street).

Marks & Spencer has built a retailing empire on the notion that you can get high quality in private label (St. Michael) goods at a fair price. I happen to think that not everything in M&S is a bargain, or even a good price, but there are plenty of items with impressive prices.

M&S is a full-service department store—they will even deliver your groceries to you at home. They have a home furnishings catalog, as well as an international mail-order hamper business. (For food gifts, not laundry.)

Only the Marble Arch store carries cashmeres—the price for a crew-neck two-ply is £79, the same price you'll pay in the factories in the Borders of Scotland. Not bad, huh?

I've been wearing a lot of twin sets lately; M&S makes them in lamb's wool at a very reasonable price. I think their men's clothing is prohibitively expensive (£40 for a pair of cords is outrageous); even men's socks are expensive compared to American discount sources. The women's underwear is famous for its quality.

I've bought bath gels and beauty products here, as well as dishes and home design elements. The grocery store in the lower level always commands my attention when I've set up housekeeping in London. Olive got me hooked on "Curiously Strong Mints," which I buy from the candy counter (they come in a green tin, 99p) and keep in my handbag. I've tried the house brand of toffee, but I like **Thornton's** better.

The important thing to remember about M&S is that the store has nurtured all of post–World War II Britain, provided quality at a price, and proved that a bargain subculture need not evolve. It's only the hard times of the early 1990s that made the U.K. reconsider this position.

Therefore, M&S has worked to inspire a fashion image, especially in its flagship London store (Marble Arch). Frankly, I don't go to M&S for fashion. I go for knock-offs of fashion, I go for the grocery store; I go for the mints. And sometimes, the cashmeres. I also go to their outlet stores in the Manchester area (see *Born to Shop Great Britain* for details).

LILLYWHITES
Piccadilly Circus, W1 (Tube: Piccadilly Circus).

Lillywhites is a department store for sporting goods. All brand names (of sportswear and equipment) are sold, including America's and Europe's finest. The sport shoe selection is flabbergasting. There aren't any bargains in this store, but the selection is enough to keep your head spinning at Olympic speed. There is also equipment and outfitting for sports that are not played in the U.S., so you can get quite an education. Snooker, anyone? Do stop by the "Outdoor Department," which is housed in what used to be a ballroom. Golf nuts may want to move into the newly renovated golf department.

Ground floor: track suits; *one*: shoes; *two*: gym; *three*: books, video, ski; *four*: racket sports; *five*: darts, snooker, water sports, shooting, riding.

DEBENHAMS
334-338 Oxford Street, W1 (Tube: Oxford Circus).

Of the few look-alike department stores on Oxford Street (there are three or so of them, all of which are virtually indistinguishable from each other), this one is the best and the most American. Debenhams was remodeled a few years ago. There's a **Keith Prowse** office for theater tickets on the ground floor; VAT desk is downstairs.

Lowest level: restaurants; *ground floor*: cosmetics, accessories; *one*: kids', ladies', Jaeger; *two*: home furnishings; *three*: furniture.

Not a must-do unless you are writing a dissertation on British retail and Oxford Street department stores.

D.H. EVANS
318 Oxford Street, W1 (Tube: Bond Street).

Just like the old Macy's, or the large department store of your coming-of-age, Evans has a good selection of their own private-label items and many designer names. The ceilings are low and the store is more dense, so it's not as glamorous as other stores.

You'll see things here that you just won't find in other shops; you'll also find that they billboard midrange designers who can get buried in glitzier stores. It's not the fanciest store you'll find in London, but if you like bread-and-butter clothes, you may want to give it a try. **Jaeger** boutiques on two floors. To make themselves stand out in the world, D.H. Evans has teamed up with the computer generation and opened a Computer Superstore on the fifth floor.

Ground floor: cosmetics, accessories, men's wear; *one*: women's fashions; *two*: kids' clothing, designers; *three*: fabrics, linens, bath shop; *four*: silver, kitchen; *five*: computers.

I'd give it a miss

JOHN LEWIS
278 Oxford Street, W1 (Tube: Bond Street).

By the time you get to John Lewis, your eyes are beginning to cross and you have no solid idea of why there are so many look-alike department stores on Oxford Street. I'm not much of a fan of John Lewis, except they have a good fabric department and this has always been a source for me to find high-fashion Alice bands (hairbands) at very moderate prices: £4–5.

BRITISH HOME STORES (BHS)
252 Oxford Street, W1 (Tube: Bond Street).

This is a big department store geared toward young families on a budget; it's snazzier than Kmart, but the fashion for career women is from hunger. The kids' clothes are cute; the home furnishings items are worth a look-see for real-people products.

The main store is on Oxford Street, but there are branches around London and the U.K.

DICKINS & JONES
224 Regent Street, W1 (Tube: Oxford Circus).

Dickins & Jones is the high-end House of Fraser entry; because it is on Regent Street. The store has just had a major face-lift and wants very much to be taken seriously by m'lady.

The store specializes in big-name designers and snazzy clothes from the middle range of these designers, i.e., variations from Yves Saint Laurent, not the Rive Gauche line; Mugler Pour Mugler, not Thierry Mugler couture. They have two hat departments: both are disappointing!

Ground floor: accessories, cosmetics; *one*: designers; *two*: executive woman; *three*: coats, British collections.

FENWICK
63 New Bond Street, W1 (Tube: Bond Street).

I have new respect for Fenwick (say "Fennick"). In fact, I almost count it as my favorite stop on Bond Street. I've shopped Fenwick top to bottom and am happy to say this is a great source for affordable designer bridge lines, cheap-junk fashion looks, and hair accessories. I've also been known to stop at Joe's Cafe for a bite to eat or a spot of tea.

The store isn't as large as a full-sized department store, so you can give it a quick once over and not be exhausted. The ground floor is one of my regular haunts.

Lower ground floor: men's; *ground floor*: cosmetics, handbags, accessories, Hat Shop, designer goods; *first floor*: Collections; *second floor*: Designer Collections; *third floor:* Weekend Collections.

🛍 Peter Jones
Sloane Square, SW1 (Tube: Sloane Square).

I really like Peter Jones for the trimmings, fabrics, and bed linens. That may sound like a strange combination, but these three departments are all strung together and make a great half-hour stop before you tackle King's Road or after you've shopped Sloane Street.

Although this is a full-service department store, I don't shop ready-to-wear here, but I love the sheets and the duvet covers.

The sheets (and duvet covers) come in colors we simply don't get at home—solid colors, but high-fashion solid colors with a range simply not seen in America. There must be five or six different shades of green alone.

They also have an excellent china department with entries you haven't seen elsewhere. I found a new range of repro majolica at low prices that had me weeping for extra arms to carry the lot home.

FACTORY OUTLETS

A British bargain can be far different from an American bargain, so look before you leap. Many bargains are by subscription only, or are hidden. If you travel to London frequently, consider joining **The FoFo Club**. It gains you invitations to private sale events sponsored by designers and other British big names. A subscription costs about $100. Write in care of Deheyser, 45 Mortimer Street, London W1N 7TD or call 171-580-9290.

There's also a growing number of outlet malls just outside London and a great distance from London. A few can be visited on a day trip from London if you have a car and are determined. See

Born to Shop Great Britain for details on the out-of-towners.

Read *The Evening Standard* faithfully during your visit and you should find out about any store promotions, sales, and even designer sample sales that coincide with your London stay.

Here are some in-town and near-town possibilities.

Browns Labels For Less
45 South Molton Street, W1 (Tube: Bond Street).

Browns is the best high-fashion specialty store in London. If you've shopped Browns's January sale, you may be disappointed in their separate sale shop—although the sale shop is open all year. It's small, offering two floors of clothes and things, but not much selection; prices are low, but not give-away.

A good bit of the merchandise is American, which means expensive (even on sale), and some is too wild to wear at any price. A pair of Pucci pull-on pants at £75 didn't strike me as a bargain; I prefer my DKNY from the outlet store in Woodbury Common, near Harriman, New York.

Burberry Factory Outlet Shop
29 Chatham Place, E9 (Take Bus number 30).

This is in a part of town called Hackney; it is past the Docklands and is easily reached by bus—although it can take 45 minutes or longer each way. Only determined shoppers should attempt this one. I have not been, but Ruth, my spy, says it's hit or miss but worth doing if you get lucky. Aren't they all.

Aside from the usual raincoats—yes, discounted—there is ready-to-wear for men and women. Is the discount worth the bus ride? Well, yes, if you find a coat it could cost about £150 (half the regular price and far less than the discounted price at the Burberry outlet in Woodbury Common in New York).

Important note: Store hours are untraditional, to say the least. The store is only open on afternoons during the week, 12:30 P.M.–6 P.M. Monday through Friday. It is open on Saturdays 9:30 A.M.–1 P.M.

To get there, take the number 30 bus and ask the driver to tell you when to get off, which will be in quite some time. You can catch the number 30 bus right near The Langham Hilton at the other end of Portland Place at Marylebone Road. I recommend calling first for precise directions from your London location and to confirm store hours. Saturday hours changed recently and could change again. Phone 181-985-3344.

Nicole Farhi Outlet Shop
75-83 Fairfield Road, E3.

Another of Ruth's finds. Her take: It doesn't have a lot of stock but can have good buys. Note that the shop sells both Farhi and French Connection (see page 187), which is a younger look made by the same company.

Hours: 10 A.M.–3 P.M. on Tuesday, Wednesday, and Saturday. On Thursdays, it's 11 A.M.–6:30 P.M. On Fridays, 10 A.M.–5:30 P.M. Closed Sundays and Mondays.

Rodier
2B Blades Court, 121 Deodar Road, SW15.

I love Rodier, a line of French knits, but I admit that I went to a Rodier outlet once in the Manchester area and could have wept. I think those clothes were made on Mars. They did not look like anything I knew or ever loved. So I send you to this one with caution and the note that it's Ruth's find, not mine.

Designer Sale Studio
241 King's Road, SW3 (Tube: Sloane Square).

I am listing this store because they advertise in the leading women's magazines and you may think it looks impressive. By not seeing the store here, you might feel compelled to check it out for me and let me know your great discovery. If you like it, do tell. I've been several times and not only find myself unimpressed, but often feel like I just don't get it. I have never seen a name that I recognize. Good luck and happy hunting.

The good news is that it's convenient.

Vivienne Westwood
41 Conduit Street, W1 (Tube: Bond Street or Green Park).

The Conduit Street shop is right in the heart of Mayfair. They sell off samples at the end of the season and prices can be reasonable. This is Viv's version of a mark-down shop or factory outlet. The clothes may be outrageous but the prices may not be.

FLORISTS

I use florists in London for two purposes: when I'm here and need to send flowers during my stay and when I'm back at home in the U.S. and must have absolute assurance that the right flowers will be sent at just the right time to a business contact or friend in London. The florists listed below also sell gift items and are status names known by those who keep track of that sort of thing. If you are looking for a small gift for the person who has everything and knows everything (and everyone), you might luck out at one of these shops.

Moyses Stevens
157 Sloane Street, SW1 (Tube: Sloane Square).

Stevens has been my regular florist in London ever since I first needed to send flowers to a business contact in London. The recession has forced Mr. Stevens from Berkeley Square into less flashy digs, but his reputation is still excellent. The look is an extravagant collection of English formal flowers arranged casually in a bouquet or basket.

You may also want to look at the specially made tulip-shaped vases (£15), which I think are super gifts.

You can phone your order from the U.S. and charge it to your credit card: 171-493-8171.

Kenneth Turner
125 Mount Street, W1 (Tube: Bond Street or Green Park).

For dried flowers, candles, home scents, or live bouquets and arrangements, this name is known throughout the world—he's even done some big jobs in the U.S. and published a book on his arrangements. The gold foil tags are to die for; the flowers will make you faint away. The new shop is not as special a space as the old shop, so when you walk in if you are not impressed, stick around and look at some of the outbound deliveries. This guy personifies talent, but the new shop does not personify retail display.

For delivery in London, call 171-355-3880. You may charge it to your credit card.

FOODSTUFFS

Charbonnel et Walker
28 Old Bond Street, W1 (Tube: Bond Street or Green Park).

If you can't get through the day without a fix of chocolate, stop by Charbonnel et Walker, which happens to hold a royal warrant. Sources outside of Buckingham Palace say that Charbonnel et Walker is the best chocolatier in the world. Prince Philip likes the Mocha Crisp. The chocolate milk mix makes a great gift. During The Season, they offer

Foodstuffs 155

"strawberries and cream" truffles. In winter, they host chocolate tastings.

Fortnum & Mason
181 Piccadilly, W1 (Tube: Piccadilly Circus). See page 144.

Harrods
Knightsbridge, SW1 (Tube: Knightsbridge). See page 139.

Harvey Nichols
Knightsbridge (corner of Sloane Street)., SW1 (Tube: Knightsbridge). See page 143.

H.R. Higgins
79 Duke Street, W1 (Tube: Bond Street).

One of the best gifts to take back home is a tin of tea, but coffee also can be brought back and since it's all the rage in the U.S., why not? H.R. Higgins is the "in" coffee provider, and since it's conveniently located in the midst of all the best places to shop in the West End, I always stop in for a sniff and a bag of beans. Listen to your friends rave about your brew and watch their faces when you tell them it's from London. (Higgins does mail order.)

Prestat
14 Prince's Arcade, SW1 (Tube: Piccadilly Circus).

Famous for their red candy boxes, their truffles, and their animal shapes in chocolate, this shop holds a royal warrant. Try the chocolate sardines—a great gift for only £5.

Selfridges
400 Oxford Street, W1 (Tube: Marble Arch or Bond Street).

Like Harrods and Harvey Nichols, Selfridges has its own food halls. They are not as good as Harrods, but fine for picnic supplies. Notable food multiples within the store itself are **Thornton's,** the candy chain (see below), which has its own counter, and **Holland & Barrett,** the health-food chain, which has its own department here.

Tesco Metro
Oxford Street; Covent Garden.

Tesco, currently the largest grocery store chain in Britain, has moved into prime retail real estate vacated during the recession and built "downtown" supermarkets. They are for the local working population but I have found them to be fabulous tourist attractions. Not only can you get a snack or cheap eats, but you can buy gifts and have a ball here, to boot.

My favorite buys include their aromatherapy and bath products (see "Bath & Beauty") and Virgin Cola, the latest product by Richard Branson (who else would think to take on Coca-Cola?).

Most Tesco Metro stores have two levels, so if the first floor looks small or unimpressive, go downstairs. I frequent the store on Oxford Street, directly across from the department store John Lewis. It is open on Sundays. There is also a branch near Covent Garden.

Thornton's
256 Regent Street, W1 (Tube: Oxford Circus).

Covent Garden, WC2 (Tube: Covent Garden).

If you're more the type who needs a candy fix and not a royal pedigree for your bonbons, there's a large British chain called Thornton's, which is popular all over the U.K.

At Easter, they will personalize any chocolate egg for free. This makes a great gift, but hand-carry yours on the airplane, because the egg is hollow and it will shatter if packed in your luggage . . . or choose the flat, egg plaque style which is an oval—not nearly as classy as the real egg shape, but easier to transport.

Thornton's has many branch stores and some counters in various department stores, such as **Selfridges** (see above).

I happen to be addicted to their toffee.

R. Twining & Co., Ltd.
216 The Strand, WC2 (Tube: Charing Cross).

R. Twining & Co., Ltd., holds a royal warrant and is famous the world over. You may drink their tea already at home. Attached to their shop on The Strand is a tiny museum of tea; it's quite out of the way but worth the trip.

Whittard's
23 South Molton Street, W1 (Tube: Bond Street).

This looks like an American chain, but is in reality a spruced up and ready-for-prime-time British chain that has taken advantage of the recession and moved into some very fine real estate. Now, they have a bevy of beverage boutiques selling packaged tea and coffee in adorable digs. It's a little too perfect to be really British, but you'll like it just the same (my English girlfriend Maggie does). There's one just about everyplace, even on Carnaby Street!

GIFTS

Asprey
165-169 New Bond Street, W1 (Tube: Green Park).

Asprey isn't a designer name, but is nonetheless one of the big names of London. Essentially, they sell expensive *tchotchkes*—pens, leathergoods, some luggage, little this-and-thats for wedding presents and presentation gifts. Just your average blue-blood, British version of Tiffany & Co. without the seriously big-time jewels, although they certainly do have jewels.

They have a store in New York, with prices to match—so if you're looking for an elegant gift, Asprey is the place to go while in London. Even if you buy zip, go just to gawk.

Since any gift you buy from Asprey has a high-status message, you may do very well here for the kind of business gifts that have to look like money, but you hope to get a good buy on. On a recent visit, I found something that might fall into this category: a small magnifying glass that rotates in and out of its own leather case (£30).

Alfred Dunhill
30 Duke Street, SW1 (Tube: Piccadilly Circus).

This is the largest and most extensive collection of Dunhill products in what I would call the mother store, but with the heavy-duty masculine image of the store, I guess I have to call it the father store.

The shop actually looks a little more like a Dunhill museum than a retail store. Nevertheless, the merchandise is absolutely top-of-the-line as far as quality goes. Note that people in Britain (and continental Europe) still smoke, so those wonderful Dunhill lighters are still quite an item. Americans have been concentrating on pens instead. There's also a complete line of ready-to-wear goods and leathergoods and, of course, cigars.

In fact, Dunhill is probably most famous as a tobacconist. Once again, the quality is aimed at the top of the market. The cigars are stored in a climate-controlled room to ensure freshness; pipe tobaccos are available for sampling. Dunhill also has a beautiful line of humidors, or will convert your prized antique box into one for you. *Remember*: It is illegal to bring Cuban cigars into the U.S.

General Trading Company
144 Sloane Street, SW1 (Tube: Sloane Square).

I guess this is a department store, but it doesn't sell clothes and it's actually more like a treasure chest than a real store and although it's a British institution, it is very un-British in feel.

GTC is more an old-fashioned emporium—it sells a little of everything in a series of townhouses that are strung together into one big funhouse dedicated to the art of whimsy. You go up and down sets of stairs here and there as you wander in and out of connected salons, finding cute gifts and some souvenirs, imports from Bali, silk flowers, botanical-print wastepaper baskets, pretty umbrellas, etc. The store has anything and everything, including a bridal registry and an interesting tabletop department.

Princess Diana did indeed register here; you have a good memory. This store, by the way, is not in the Sloane Street grouping of big-name boutique branches—don't let the street address throw you—it is very close to **Peter Jones**, a great department store, and King's Road. You may also have breakfast or lunch here.

THE IRISH LINEN COMPANY
35-36 Burlington Arcade, W1 (Tube: Piccadilly Circus).

In business in London since 1875, this is the perfect little shop for those in search of visual traditions. It's in the Burlington Arcade, and the windows are draped with tablecloths and place mats. Everything reeks of tradition, high tea, and *grand-mère*. While they aren't giving away the stuff, the prices are rather moderate.

OBJETS EXTRAORDINAIRES
79 Walton Street, SW3 (Tube: South Kensington).

This little shop specializes in embroidered pillows with witty sayings on them like: Born to Shop. They have a window at The Dorchester and a store in the heart of Walton Street as well as a catalog that lists all the phrases available. I was looking for "You have to kiss a lot of frogs before you find a prince" for a French friend of mine, but found several other gems including the usual shopping jokes.

160 BASIC LONDON RESOURCES—A–Z

Halcyon Days
14 Brook Street, W1 (Tube: Bond Street).

For all you collectors of fine English enamels, it's time to go crazy. The Halcyon Days shop in London is small, but loaded. You can find both antique English enamels and contemporary designs that include "paintings," clocks, picture frames, cuff links, music boxes, sewing accessories, pens, etc. The prices are less expensive than in the U.S. and mail order is a cinch.

Best of all, once you buy an item, for years afterward you'll be on the mailing list, and gorgeous brochures will come to you a few times a year—all with the London prices.

Swaine, Adeney, Brigg & Sons
185 Piccadilly, W1 (Tube: Piccadilly Circus).

If you are looking for one shop in all of England that represents the upper crust, then this has to be it. It's more of a museum than a shop—you come here for your hunting, riding, and fishing supplies as well as the perfectly crafted brolly (umbrella), your tweeds, sweaters, Shetlands, and other day-to-day needs. There are business clothes, leathergoods, and women's things as well.

A virtual mini–department store for a way of life to which only a small percentage of the world can still afford to subscribe. The firm holds several royal warrants, has a branch store in San Francisco, and has been in business since the 1700s. This is the real thing, folks.

HAIR SALONS & HAIR PRODUCTS

I've always thought that having my hair done in London was not only a convenience, but a chance to feel smart, with-it, and plugged into British style. Being in London is celebration enough to splurge on an experience you won't quickly forget. Unless it rains.

Hair Salons & Hair Products

MICHAELJOHN
23a Albemarle Street, W1 (Tube: Green Park).

I guess it's no secret that I've been going to Michaeljohn for more years than I have been writing the *Born to Shop* books. It's especially great for me to now have John's daughter Kate do my hair whenever I am in London. Not only does she do a great job, but I have the pleasure of feeling as proud as a mother whenever I see her.

Since you might not feel the family connection at Michaeljohn that I enjoy, you may wonder why I chose this salon over the other well-known shops, why you should plunk down what is a pretty price to have your hair done.

I have one simple answer: royals.

Michaeljohn is at once chic and casual; it's the kind of place where old friends meet and everyone gets to know you. And everyone looks over at the mirrors to catch the passing of a royal personage on an almost daily basis—there is a small private room in the center of the salon where you may see Princess Anne, the Duchess of Kent, or just the Julie Andrews kind of royalty. Americans, please note, you need not bow or curtsy to British royalty. Only British subjects do this. You may not offer your hand, introduce yourself, or talk to them, however. You must wait for a royal to address you.

Now then, the price here is steep, but you get top talent, you get royals, and, in actuality, the prices are the same as in New York. Other big-name London salons actually charge more.

For the basics:

- It's best to call or fax ahead for an appointment. A cut, shampoo, and dry with the heads of the house (Michael, Frank, or John) comes to about $100 for a woman (less for a man), which is decidedly less than many big-name salons in New York. Kate is about $50. Call 171-491-4401 or fax 171-495-0152 (direct calls or faxes to the attention of John Prothero); the salon will confirm your appointment with a return fax. First appointment of the day is at 8:30 A.M.; last appointment is 5:30 P.M.

- If you order tea or coffee, you will pay for it on the spot or it will be added to your bill. Refreshments are not free as they are in the U.S. Coffee costs £1.
- Men and women co-mingle in the salon. Men are big on treatments in London, so don't be surprised to find male customers on the floor or downstairs in the men's treatment area. Ian comes here for a haircut every now and then, but dotes on the skin treatments, the aromatherapy, and whatever it is that they do to his feet that he can't stop talking about. He usually books in after a big trip to help combat jet lag.
- Tip is at your discretion. The norm for a wash and blow-dry, however, is to tip the shampoo guy £1.50, and then give the change from a £5 note (£3.50) to the stylist.

Michaeljohn products, as well as many other hair products, are sold at the front desk.

NICKY CLARKE
130 Mount Street, W1 (Tube: Green Park).

Clarke is famous as a hot talent who made his mark by cutting the Duchess of York's hair from long to short when she was still the Duchess of York. Or actively the Duchess of York. Or something. Other clients are big-name models, movie stars, and rock and rollers—men and women.

The salon is low-key, with magazine covers framed on the walls of the Berkeley Square salon. The prices are not particularly low-key: Clarke himself charges £150 for a cut and blow-dry. There is a five- to six-week waiting list. Phone 171-491-4700 for an appointment. Their four lines of hair products are sold at **Tesco Metro**.

Molton Brown
58 South Molton Street, W1 (Tube: Bond Street).

I come to this salon to buy their products. I've never had my hair done here, but the salon is so famous that if I didn't have a regular place of my own, I would give this a try. Call 171-629-1872 for an appointment.

Vidal Sassoon
11 Floral Street, WC2 (Tube: Covent Garden).

If the only name you trust in British hairstylists is Vidal Sassoon, there is a salon convenient to Covent Garden, and it's attached to a gym and spa called The Sanctuary. Prices at Sassoon are slightly higher than at **Michaeljohn** for women. There are several salons dotted around London. To phone the Covent Garden salon for an appointment, call 171-240-6635. Hair products at the salon or **Boots**; also available in the U.S.

HATS

Hats may mean more to the British than Ascot; they are that much of a tradition. Women—in London especially—really do wear hats. You need a hat each spring at the beginning of The Season. You need a hat each fall/winter, when hats keep the head warm. How *many* hats you have tells the world how well-off you are.

Few pleasures are greater than spending half an hour on the street floor of **Harvey Nichols** trying on hat after hat. If you get more serious than that, try some of these resources. Don't ignore markets as a resource for less expensive hats—there are some talented hatmakers at both Covent Garden's **Apple Market** and several markets in Greenwich.

Also remember that the best way to wear a real hat is with as little hair showing around the face as possible. If you have long hair, keep an elastic in your handbag for trying on hats. Hat prices begin around £20 for a straw nothing; you'll pay £80 for a nice designer hat; it's going to cost £200–500 for one of those extravagant things you see in fashion magazines.

The Season officially begins in the middle of June so that hats begin to show up in shops around Easter time but get truly serious *after* Easter, around the first of May, because the weather won't change until some time in May (at least that's the hope). Many stores hold promotions to show their hats; Harrods traditionally has Hat Week during the first week of May. This is a time when hat designers have special shows and you can come over and have the designer twist and turn and fluff and fool with your hair and hat and head. Heaven. For details, you can phone the millinery department: 171-730-1234, extension 3433.

If you are planning to go to a wedding in Britain (and you are a woman), it is expected that you will wear a hat. Rent *Four Weddings and a Funeral* to get the drift. And yes, of course, every hat you buy should come with a hat box. Don't dare travel with an important hat out of its hat box.

JOHN BOYD
16 Beauchamp Place, SW3 (Tube: Knightsbridge).

My goal in life has been fulfilled; I now own a John Boyd hat. (See cover.) I bought it secondhand, but these days, that's okay. It's still a John Boyd hat. And I feel rich and famous in it. I feel like a princess in it. I probably look like a fool, but I *feel* more chic than Princess Anne.

Mr. Boyd has been making hats for the Royal Family for many, many, many years. What is wonderful about John Boyd is that he doesn't just produce one look. Princess Anne and Margaret Thatcher are obviously different looks. Can you imagine them in each other's hats? Mr. Boyd will add or subtract bows, veils, and feathers depending on your taste and needs.

The newish Beauchamp Place shop is not forbiddingly *haute*, so don't be frightened—saunter in and sit in front of a mirror for a spell. Prices get real at £100.

🛍 THE HAT SHOP
58 Neal Street, WC2 (Tube: Covent Garden or Leicester Square).

South Molton Street, W1 (Tube: Bond Street).

This shop gets so crowded on weekends that people have to wait in line to get in. It's also worth it.

Prices are in the moderate range, although little is under £25. Styles range from high fashion to somewhat funky. I went absolutely bonkers for a straw version of the Mad Hatter's Hat from *Alice in Wonderland*, a mere £25. This shop is right down the street from Covent Garden; open on Sundays!

Their newer branch, on South Molton, is a little more spacious. I could stand here and try on hats for an hour. The last one I fell in love with, this time for £85, was a copper velvet number that I knew I would never wear. Regret lingers.

JAMES LOCK & CO.
6 St. James's Street, SW1 (Tube: Green Park).

One of the most famous hatmakers in London, Lock has an old-fashioned shop amid a street of old-fashioned shops that makes shopping here like being in a history book. Prices here begin quite moderately and go right up to expensive, but you might find what you want for $50. Hats for both men and women are sold here; the color of the hat box differs for each gender.

RACHEL TREVOR-MORGAN
18 Crown Passage, SW1 (Tube: Green Park).

Her tiny shop is right behind James Lock & Co.; she does their made-to-measure for ladies and will dye straw or fabric to match your suit.

STEPHEN JONES
29 Heddon Street, W1 (Tube: Oxford Circus).

By appointment only; call 171-734-9666. Be prepared to spend £100–200 and wait three weeks until your creation is ready. Stand by for two fittings and you'll feel ready for a trip to Ascot. Witty and brazen hats are the specialty. Frequented by royal clients and Sloane Rangers, Jones is one of the "in" talents at the top of the heap. Men and women are welcome clients.

PHILIP TREACY
67 Elizabeth Street, SW1 (Tube: Sloane Square).

Perhaps the biggest of the "name" mad hatters, Treacy makes those fabulous toppers you see in all the fashion layouts right before the beginning of The Season. Now that I've got my John Boyd, this could be my next goal. Prices begin at £120. But let's face it; the really extravagant super stuff begins around £250.

Treacy supplies most of the hot London designers with the hats for their collections. You need a strong sense of yourself to wear one of his creations, but you'll never be forgotten if you carry it off.

SOPHIE HENDERSON
30 Brunswick Gardens, W8 (Tube: Notting Hill).

Chic and socially acceptable without being, dare I say it: over the top? The hats all have names, of course, and they begin around $80, which is really a bargain. If it's close to The Season, ring for an appointment: 171-229-7493.

HERBERT JOHNSON
30 New Bond Street, W1 (Tube: Bond Street).

Men's and women's hats in a vein so traditional you may think you are the Queen Mum; Johnson holds several royal warrants. The quality of these hats is so extraordinary that even if you buy a boring one, there is tremendous comfort in knowing it has class; it will last forever and no matter what you paid for it—it was worth it.

THE HATMAKERS
Apple Market, Covent Garden, WC2 (Tube: Covent Garden).

If price is an issue, but you still have £15–25 to spend on a fun, fashionable, and slightly funky hat, this is a great choice—among the vendors at Covent Garden Market.

HORSE & RIDER

If you're into the horsey set, and won't find your trip to London complete without a sniff of saddle soap, you'll find the horse trail of retailing to be marvelously old-fashioned. It's the old England, steeped in dark-grained wood and tradition and foxtails. Is your Hermès scarf tied in a knot around your waxed leather handbag? I certainly hope so.

J.A. ALLEN
1 Lower Grosvenor Place, SW1 (Tube: Victoria).

If you have a horse-crazy daughter, perhaps she'd like a book from J.A. Allen, the foremost equestrian bookstore and publisher. You name it, and they've got it here. If you just want to soak up horse vibes, this is the place to do it. The sales help is most helpful, and they never say "neigh."

Henry Maxwell
11 Savile Row, W1 (Tube: Piccadilly Circus).

Once you've got a leg up on horse lore, you'll need boots. So trot on over to Maxwell (in the basement), where you will be glad you're close to ground zero when you see the prices. (That was the last riding pun, I swear.) We are talking heavy-duty royalty and polo-playing playboys for customers, and well over $1,000 for a pair of polo boots. A Maxwell boot is le dernier cri to those in the know, so if you've got it—flaunt it. If you're planning on crashing Virginia fox-hunting society, Maxwell will start you on the right foot. Bespoke shoes and boots.

Tricker's
67 Jermyn Street, SW1 (Tube: Piccadilly Circus).

If you find Henry Maxwell a tad pricey, but don't mind spending $1,000 or more for a pair of riding boots, try Tricker's. Shoes start at £300.

James Lock & Co.
6 St. James's Street, SW1 (Tube: Green Park or Piccadilly).

If you need the right hat for the fox hunt, you'll pay about $200 for a very proper bowler at a firm that has been in business since the mid-1700s and knows a lot about crowning glory; silks here, too. Lock sells all sorts of hats, by the way, and they hold a royal warrant.

J. Dedge & Sons
16 Clifford Street, W1 (Tube: Piccadilly Circus).

For traditional riding garb, try J. Dedge & Sons, which specializes in garments for showmen and hunters; they will fit you in London and then send your order within two months. Dressage heaven.

Gidden
15d Clifford Street, W1 (Tube: Green Park).

This saddlemaker gave up their fashionable shop in the Burlington Arcade; you can track them down to their not inconvenient Mayfair shop for a saddle or a handbag. As chic and properly British as **Mulberry,** but a little bit less nouveau. The look is colored leather with natural trim; this is sort of a sophisticated version of Dooney & Burke with even more horse-and-rider country style.

They will also make you a saddle as they have done for the Royal Family for years. And years. Riding habits, boots, and the needed repairs, etc.

JEWELRY

Costume

Fior
31 New Bond Street, W1 (Tube: Bond Street).

While I was waiting for Ken Lane to get the rights back to his name and reopen, I discovered Fior for fabulous fakes. One of the things I like best about this store is how honest they are. I asked if I could wear a certain ring in the bathtub or shower and they said "no way!" All sorts of copies in glitz and enamel.

Butler & Wilson
189 Fulham Road, SW3 (Tube: South Kensington).

20 South Molton Street, W1 (Tube: Bond Street).

If you are a fan of authentic or reproduction Art Deco or Chanel-style jewelry, or just love chunky costume "glitz," these shops are a must. Princess Diana wears it; so do most movie queens. There's a desk shop in **Harrods** (and in **Selfridges**) on the street floor—but go to one of the boutiques for more selection and a better deal on your VAT refund. Chic and hot and dynamite.

Expect to pay £25 for earrings or a simple pin; the bejeweled cross on a cord (not a chain) that I was in love with cost £99. They also sell sunglasses, hair clips and other hair doodads, and T-shirts.

There are shops in London Heathrow at Terminal One and Terminal Three.

Cobra & Bellamy
149 Sloane Street, SW3 (Tube: Sloane Square).

Another source and local legend for repro important works that range from simply fun to simply stunning. For costume jewelry, it can get pricey—I fell for a multistrand faux pearl twisted choker at £213! They also sell vintage costume jewelry.

Arabesk
156 Walton Street, SW3 (Tube: South Kensington).

Inventive, creative, somewhat outrageous, very dynamic, and more. I actually felt like a fool for having little Cs on my earrings when everything here had so much class and true style. Earrings begin at £25.

Erik Van Peterson
117 Walton Street, SW3 (Tube: South Kensington).

Attention, trendies! Here's a new source for you, where new work is inspired by the 1920s and is to die for. Jewelry, accessories, and watches. Vintage and repro. Fab, fab, fab. Also a showroom across the street.

Farah Lister
137 Fulham Road, SW6 (Tube: South Kensington).

Expensive, exciting, and costumey. Everything looks important without being a copy. The gray glass beaded piece I flipped for costs £245 for a multi-strand choker, just so you get my drift. Big with the fashion editor set. Very tiny shop.

Merola
178 Walton Street, SW3 (Tube: Knightsbridge or South Kensington).

Specialists in 20th-century costume jewelry and reproductions of older pieces with a special eye toward the work of Miriam Haskell. Located in the heart of the best costume jewelry district in London, this is a prime source. Prices are not low but are competitive.

Important Jewelry

There are enough royal jewelers and purveyors of pearl, diamond, and sapphire in Mayfair to choke a princess. Try **Garrad** or **Colingwood** if you need to get the point. And don't forget about **Tiffany & Co.**, located at 25 Old Bond Street, W1 (Tube: Bond Street). I've opted for the fun stuff.

Elizabeth Gage
20 Albemarle Street, W1 (Tube: Green Park).

A big-time society jeweler with a salon filled with banquettes, ruffled pillows, and necklaces that are a cross between the elegant hippie look and Bulgari. Each piece is made of the finest metals and gemstones, but is unique in a way that jewelry should be; this is expensive and important stuff, not silly glitz. Much has a Greco antiquities influence.

Kiki McDonough
77c Walton Street, SW3 (Tube: South Kensington).

Next time I open my wallet and find a spare £595, I'm rushing out to buy Kiki's 18K, gold-link bracelet with colored stones set here and there. You may think I'm kidding—I'm not! Located on a street that already has numerous jewelers, this one not only has inventive things, but also some traditional-looking designs that, on second glance, turn out to be witty or special. Clients include Princess you-know-who and the Duchess of York.

LEATHER GOODS

This section covers the major players who began in leather goods and are not now full-fledged fashion houses. Of course, many of them now sell clothing and a full range of accessories. I've also included Hermès, a fashion house that became famous as a leather goods resource—whether those leather goods were saddles or platform shoes for movie stars. Prada, which began life as a leather goods firm but now sells very cutting edge fashion (thank you, MiuMiu), is also here, and Louis Vuitton has never budged from leather goods. Go figure.

Many of these names are American or continental European suppliers, so I have written only a limited amount about them. If you are looking for a handbag that is like none other seen in America, you'll want to concentrate on styles that aren't exported or firms without stores in the U.S. (Like Loewe, the Spanish firm.)

From a price point of view, once you have a VAT refund, you may save a smidgen. Don't expect big savings in Britain (understatement is my middle name) but you can still be proud of yourself if you don't rack up huge bills due to Uncle Sam when you return to the U.S.

Remember that London prices are basically high; the local cultural tradition is to have a few handbags of excellent quality and wear them to death. Some of the resale shops sell recycled handbags, but beware of fakes. In some of these shops, some fake Chanel is often tossed in with the authentic. If you don't know your stuff, tread carefully. Finally, the hot new status *Le Brit* handbag is from Coach. I don't need to tell you that Americans should buy American made products in the U.S., or even at American outlet stores (Coach has gorgeous outlet stores).

I have not listed all globally famous designer names which sell handbags (such as Chanel) below. Ditto Burberry and the British status symbols. One final thought: a **Filofax** is technically a leather goods item (even though they also come in plastics these days). See page 191 for details about the Filofax system, which costs much less in the U.K. than the U.S.

British Hot Shots

MULBERRY
40-41 Old Bond Street, W1 (Tube: Bond Street).

Mulberry leads the pack with the newest story in retail. This heretofore almost cult company has finally made the big leap into a flagship store on a major shopping street and is ready to take its place as the most famous name in English leather goods. The look is sort of countryish—a local Ralph Lauren if you will. With a touch of Hermès. I saw a blue backpack that I've never gotten over. Can't forget the price, either. Oh, well. There is a factory outlet store.

Mulberry has expanded past leather goods to home decor and clothing for men and women. There is also a new line, London Look, which was created to be sold from the Bond Street store only. Don't miss the chance to check out this very British yet still very chic lifestyle line which will inspire you to become rich and famous and casual. Smart casual, as the Brits say.

Selina Blow
42 Elizabeth Street, SW1 (Tube: Sloane Square or Knightsbridge).

For those Sloane Shoppers who have an *A to Z* guide in their handbags, check the map to find this discreet little fashion street and its most famous tenant, a shop selling specially created handbags—as well as some clothes and other accessories—by the most up-to-date names to roll off the floppy diskettes of Britain's fashion editors. Check out the Rose Basket—a tiny bag that looks like a small duffle topped off with silk flowers. At £200 it tells the world you are a trendie.

The International Names

Fendi
37 Sloane Street, SW1 (Tube: Knightsbridge).

Branch of the famed Italian leather goods firm selling more than those little Fs. Luggage as well as handbags and accessories.

Gucci
33 Old Bond Street, W1 (Tube: Bond Street).

17-18 Sloane Street, SW1 (Tube: Knightsbridge).

Even with the departure of Dawn Mello, Gucci has seen the future and is hanging onto it. So incredibly chic you may want to blow it all on just the right bag with bamboo toggles.

Hermès
155 New Bond Street, W1 (Tube: Bond Street).

179 Sloane Street, SW1 (Tube: Knightsbridge).

The Bond Street store is larger and has better light. All the better to see the silks, the ties, the enamel bracelets, the to-die-for (in all senses of the word) ashtrays and the total line. Give yourself a spritz while contemplating the handbags. So how much is the infamous Kelly bag? Actually, you can get a nice one for about $3,000. Crocodile brings the tab up to about $10,000. If you consider that your Kelly will last 20 years (or longer) and if you ordinarily spend $500 on each of your handbags, you may see that one good Kelly bag is worth its weight in gold.

LOEWE
130 Old Bond Street, W1 (Tube: Bond Street).

Since Loewe has closed its U.S. stores, you may not be familiar with this Spanish leather goods firm which offers quality that is competitive with Hermès at prices that are much lower. We're not talking inexpensive, but you can certainly walk away happy for less than $1,000. Very smart and chic. Pronounced: "Lou-eh-vay."

PRADA
44 Sloane Street, SW1 (Tube: Knightsbridge).

This Italian leather goods firm branched into the new millennium in the last few years when the granddaughter of the founder made her way into fashion and every fashion editor in America decided that nylon was chic and that pared down clothing was chicer still. Handbags come in leather or nylon and average approximately $500.

TRUSSARDI
50 South Molten Street, W1 (Tube: Bond Street).

This Italian leathergoods firm is best known for their innovative color story in leather goods and totes.

LOUIS VUITTON
149 New Bond Street, W1 (Tube: Bond Street).

198 Sloane Street, SW1 (Tube: Knightsbridge).

In my middle age I am beginning to think Louis Vuitton is worth the price. It simply is indestructible. The investment more than pays for itself in wear.

LINGERIE, SOCKS & STOCKINGS

Fogal
36 New Bond Street, W1 (Tube: Bond Street).

Fogal may be the most expensive pantyhose in the world but I've got a secret. Each season they stick the weird colors and not so popular sizes in a bin in the back of their London shop. Items here cost £2–£8 (£8 is for cashmere).

Knickerbox
189 Regent Street, W1 (Tube: Oxford Circus).

The Knickerbox business is one of the major success stories in recent retail history: The underwear buyers from **Marks & Spencer**—famous throughout the land—went out on their own and opened Knickerbox. Almost immediately, it became a gigantic multiple with shops in every mall, kiosks in every train station, and even high-street stores in high-rent districts. The underwear (bras, panties, camisoles, etc.) comes in cotton and silken varieties and in jazzy and even risqué styles. Prices are not dirt cheap.

Janet Reger
2 Beauchamp Place, SW3 (Tube: South Kensington).

If you've ever wondered what the True Brit woman wears under her rather safe and standard clothing, you might be shocked to discover how frilly and fancy her underthings can be. Janet Reger is the Victoria's Secret of the British underwear crowd: more sophisticated than many (and more expensive), but not so pricey and fancy that it's totally out of your range.

The Sock Shop
Charing Cross Station, WC2 (Tube: Charing Cross).

There is not a train station, underground station, or high street in the U.K. that does not have a branch of The Sock Shop. Despite the popularity of these stores (selling socks and pantyhose, and sometimes underwear and umbrellas), I remain baffled. Yes, the styles are incredibly cute, but there are no bargains.

MAKEUP

If you think British women have such incredible skin they don't need makeup, you're wrong. They do have incredible skin, but they are as interested in product as the next woman. A lot of British women adore Estee Lauder products. All department stores sell the usual international brands (see "Department Stores" on page 138), but I have listed a few secrets that may interest specialists here.

These are brands, with retail sources.

No. 7
Boots the Chemist, various locations.

A relatively new line, No. 7 is packaged exactly like Chanel makeup and Chanel products and is a spoof on the No. 5. The line is inexpensive and meant for teens on up. We're talking £3 for a nail polish. Their self-tan fade away cream is the rave of my London girlfriends. Sold at **Boots**.

🛍 BOURJOIS
Boots the Chemist, various locations.

This is another Chanel product but this one is no take-off; this is the real thing. Bourjois is made in factories in France owned by the family that also owns the Chanel name for perfume and makeup. The products are not identical but there are numerous similarities. The line is moderately priced. In France, it is a dime-store brand. It is the U.K. as well, but at £4 for an eye shadow it is not as cheap

178 BASIC LONDON RESOURCES—A–Z

as what you might buy in your grocery store at home. But then again, you can't buy Chanel in your grocery store at home either. Sold in **Boots.**

Mary Quant
3 Ives Court, SW1 (Tube: South Kensington).

Are you too young to know who Mary Quant is? Shame on you. I came of age to the tune of Mary Quant and the mod, mod years. If you didn't, then you should know that she went out of business, had a makeup line that was sold in **Boots,** but then it disappeared and there was no Mary Quant for a while. Now, as all good things should, Miss Mary is back in business with her own teeny shop a block from Walcott Street and selling just her own brand of makeup. (My editor Erica's favorite summer lipstick color is Ribbon Tickle.)

Shu Uemura
NK Space, 41 Earlham Street, WC 2 (Tube: Covent Garden).

This Japanese makeup guru is a legend in his own time and is sold in all international cities; he has his own freestanding stores in a few—like Paris. In London, you buy at Liberty, Harvey Knicks, or Space NK—a very with-it shop in the Thomas Neals minimall in Neal Yarμd.

Santa Maria Novella
117 Walton, SW3 (Tube: Knightsbridge or South Kensington).

Actually, this isn't a makeup line; it's a range of treatment and skin products from the famed *farmacia* in Florence, but they have opened up in London on Walton Street, of course, for the Sloane Rangers who haven't had a chance to stock up while on holiday.

MENSWEAR

This topic couldn't be broader unless I simply called it "Men" but, as we all know, that's just way too big a category to generalize about. So, some basic rules:

- Women should shop for themselves in men's clothing stores. Sorry, guys, as politically correct as the reverse may be, you're on your own.
- Bespoke is a huge business in London still but the number of clients using this book who actually use bespoke services is so small that I have not listed Saville Row tailors or the shoemakers who make shoes for £1,500.
- Most of the big resale shops (see page 194) do sell a few pieces of handsome menswear. Seek and ye shall find.
- Menswear goes on sale in January and July just like women's wear does. This is when the $200 Hildith & Key dress shirts go for $100 and are considered a true bargain. Stock up. Do note that the better shirt houses have a minimum order, so be prepared if you are having custom-made shirts made.
- Most of the big designers who have global representatives have branched into an assortment of items in order to expand their markets—this means that they often have menswear on one floor of the store you think only sells womenswear. Even the not hoity or toity have menswear, like French Connection.
- Shabby chic is quite acceptable for gents, especially for weekend and country wear. Vintage abounds. Jumble sales are socially acceptable. Anything that looks new, especially in the countryside, is an embarrassment to a true Brit. If not careful, you could look American.
- The basic men's business uniform is more conservative than in Continental Europe and the U.S.; there is indeed a certain look. See page 67 for

The Look. Even in the area of tie choice, where the businessman has the most room to be creative, British gentlemen tend to wear school ties (a major no-no if you did not go to that school, Americans!) or simple styles from conservative British stylemakers. Wearing an Hermès tie signals you are an international player or hotelier.

- All department stores sell goods for men. All the British men I know who use off-the-peg sources actually shop at **Marks & Spencer**, where you can get a silk tie for £6 and a suit for £200. Tuxedos are also sold. Note that M&S has a variety of grades of goods and you can see the difference in quality as the price goes up. M&S prices are not dirt cheap by British standards, they are fair.
- British men's specialty stores sell the basics; they are old-fashioned haberdashers. In other words, **Alfred Dunhill** is just one of many.
- Jermyn Street is menswear row. Almost every shop on this two-to-three-block-long small street sells toiletries, shirts, or ties. Simply walk from one end of the street to the other; it's really fabulous. More fabulous during sale season.
- There is a British street fashion scene for men; its stores are mostly in Soho although Camden Locks is the market of choice for the younger no-tie set.
- There is an American preppy look in casual dress for men in London. If you are American, forget about buying it in the U.K., where prices are too high for Ralph Lauren/Polo and for The Gap.
- Shop in America.

SOME VEDDY, VEDDY BRITISH MENSWEAR

HACKETT
137 Sloane Street, SW1 (Tube: Knightsbridge).

Hackett made its name as the "in" store in which to buy high-quality used clothes years ago, but now they sell their own very new, very proper preppie,

Some Veddy, Veddy British Menswear 181

quite "U" clothing. Ian tells me that the reference to anything being "U" or "Non-U" is from the 1970s and really dates me. So *excusez-moi*, but to me the differentiation is very British and says it all.

Now then, years ago, Sloane Rangers flocked here in droves to buy the discarded remnants of nobility and the kind of slightly frayed look that the British find so endearing. Hackett became hot. Nowadays, Hackett has gone upscale and has opened a few shops that sell new clothes with the same kind of retro look. *De rigueur* if you plan to fit in; owned by Alfred Dunhill.

You can buy everything from the country look to the Witty Britty look to more staid, traditional togs. Much unisex clothing. But then, they also sell bespoke suits at a bargain price—about £900.

The new shop on Sloane Street is an attempt to make Brooks Brothers work in London in the Hackett frame of mind. They plan to open in the U.S. as well. Mail order available.

SIMPSON
203 Piccadilly, W1 (Tube: Piccadilly Circus).

A specialty store for men, with some women's things, known for its traditional look and its dedication to the Daks line, a veddy, veddy British traditional line on which Brooks Brothers is based. Prices are high, but this is the place for the solid British look, and the six floors of almost department-store nature make this a one-stop-for-the-works kind of place.

If you are invited to do The Season, this is a solid choice (boring but safe) for him and for her. The ladies' floor is now advertised as "a debutante's delight"—try that on an American audience. They also claim that this store is a great place to meet the right kind of men. Let me know how it goes.

PAUL SMITH
41 Floral Street, WC2 (Tube: Covent Garden).

Paul Smith Femme
40 Floral Street, WC2 (Tube: Covent Garden).

Paul Smith Jeans
Langley Court, Covent Garden, WC2 (Tube: Covent Garden).

Paul Smith Sale Shop
23 Avery Row, W1 (Tube: Bond Street).

One of the kingpins of Covent Garden retail, Paul Smith is also one of the purveyors of the Witty Britty look in menswear. What makes these conservative clothes work so well is the marvelous array of colors they are made in. You can find a great selection of tweed suits, sports coats, corduroy pants, and shoes. Prices are moderate to high; the freestanding store in Manhattan pales when compared to the wonders of Londers. There's also women's clothes and jeans for all.

Smith has a new store specializing in jeans for men and women—it's a stark, modern space. This is considered a flagship store and will be spun out to branches all over the world.

The sale shop may not be permanent; call first before you venture forth: 171-493-1287.

Other Resources

High & Mighty
83 Knightsbridge, SW1 (Tube: Knightsbridge).

Okay, so it's an American firm. But for large size and tall men, it's a godsend.

Rochester Big & Tall
90 Brompton Road, SW3 (Tube: Knightsbridge).

Again, if you fall into this category, you'll be glad to know about this source down the street from High & Mighty, closer to Harrods.

Shirts

A well-made tailored shirt is essential for the look for both men and women; many of the tailors create a woman's shirt to allow for a woman's body but the right proper thing is for a woman to wear a man's shirt.

Please note that there is a price discrepancy between off-the-peg shirts (ready made) and bespoke shirts. Not only do bespoke cost more, but each house has a minimum order—which is usually six. It is possible that the price difference between off the peg and bespoke may be slight, as is the case at several of the finer firms, thus encouraging you to become a member of the bespoke club.

Once you become a regular, you can fill in as needed, but shirts are most often ordered annually as they wear out. And the British really wear them before they wear out. Most fine shirtmakers will replace a frayed cuff before they ask you to bury a shirt.

Because **Turnbull & Asser** has such a strange policy with sleeve lengths (all off the peg shirts have the same arm length), many other shirt tailors go out of their way to offer a range of sleeve lengths.

HILDITCH & KEY
37 & 73 Jermyn Street, SW1 (Tube: Piccadilly Circus).

One of several very proper men's shirtmakers on Jermyn Street, Hilditch & Key has two different shops selling the famous men's shirt as well as women's ready-to-wear—in keeping with the look. All the shops look like Old World gems. Please note that there is a full inch of shirt fabric under the cuff, so should the sleeve need to be lengthened, the fabric is readily available. Shirts can be fixed in a day or two if the standard size does not fit you.

Pick from made-to-measure (six-shirt minimum) or a special stock shirt, which is not quite as expensive and means the sleeves are made to measure, but the body is not. Expect to pay at least £100 per shirt. If you want a private visit made to your hotel room, call 171-930-5336 to make an appointment, or fax: 171-321-0216.

TURNBULL & ASSER
71 & 69 (women's). Jermyn Street, SW1 (Tube: Green Park).

Known basically as a shirtmaker, Turnbull & Asser has become one of the most famous names in British menswear. Prince Charles buys his pj's here. He also buys his shirts, as do many other famous and not-so-famous men who just love the finest cotton and tailoring that money can buy. Although—let's get small here—the word on the street is that when times are tough, there are cutbacks even at places like Turnbull & Asser. Many a man is complaining that his old shirt stays don't fit into the new, narrower gussets, that the buttons aren't of the same quality.

Still, for the thrill of it all, a stop by Turnbull & Asser is quite an experience. The main store is on two levels, with the ready-to-wear shirts, bathrobes, and underwear downstairs, and ties, sweaters, and accessories upstairs. One door down Jermyn Street is the Churchill Room, which houses the bespoke department for shirts and the ready-to-wear suits. Entering the shop is like going back in time to the days (1885) when Reginald Turnbull and Ernest Asser first began making hunting gear for the nobility. The walls are wood-paneled and the atmosphere is hushed. However, the sales help is quite helpful and will tell you that if you have time to be fitted, a bespoke shirt will not cost you much more than a ready-to-wear one.

The Turnbull & Asser staff travels to New York and Los Angeles twice a year to see their clients. They take up residence in a hotel suite and make appointments with their longtime customers. When you are in the London shop, ask to be put on their list.

Turnbull & Asser is carried in the U.S. through Bergdorf Goodman in New York and Neiman Marcus in other cities. The popularity of the Turnbull & Asser shirts is so great that when Bergdorf has its once-a-year sale before Christmas, the lines begin to form at 7 A.M.

Turnbull & Asser makes their ready-made shirts with only one sleeve length; if you are tall, have long arms, or are a chimpanzee, you may be out of luck. But don't panic; my friend Barry, who is easily 6'3" and therefore not what you'd call tiny, fits perfectly into a Turnbull ready-made. If your arms are shorter than their shirts, you will be fitted accordingly at the store and the sleeve will be shortened to your measurements. But if you're going to this much trouble to begin with, why not get a custom-made shirt? It is actually cheaper to buy a custom-made shirt in a hotel in the U.S. from the Turnbull & Asser representative than it is to walk into Bergdorf or Neiman and buy a shirt that will have to be altered.

If you buy in London, expect to pay £150 per shirt. But the shirt will probably last a lifetime with proper care and, possibly, new cuffs.

THOMAS PINK
85 Jermyn Street, SW1 (Tube: Green Park).

If he wants to try something a little more exciting than a **Turnbull & Asser** shirt but still be in the pink, he may want to ring up Thomas Pink—a firm which became famous by offering more for the money to the very "U" students who were (and always are) broke, but needed bespoke (or almost bespoke). Mr. Pink's shirts have their own logo, a pink square of fabric, sewn into the shirttail.

The original Thomas Pink was the guy who coined the phrase "in the pink"; they have a catalogue and two tax free shops at LHR (Terminal One and Terminal Three); sleeves are available in a variety of lengths and yes, there is a woman's line.

The basic two-fold poplin shirt costs £45, which makes it less expensive than some of the other big names. There are also very acceptable silk ties for £27.50. For mail order service, phone 171-498-3882 or fax 171-622-2803. There is a flat charge of £12 for overseas delivery no matter how much you order.

Silk knot cuff links, my passion, cost £5.

Harvie & Hudson
97 & 77 Jermyn Street, SW1 (Tube: Green Park or Piccadilly Circus).

This is one of my favorites, just because I never hear anyone talk about them—but they strike me as just as much fun, if not more so, than the bigger names. Little shops; very old-fashioned. I love it here. Same old stripes but great British charm.

MULTIPLES

A few successful chain stores dominate British retail. There's one of these shops on every high street, in every main shopping neighborhood, or even in the next new mall. That's why they call them multiples. In the British business press, these stores are referred to as "high-street multiples," because they are usually found on the high street of every town.

Some stores have a hundred (or more) branches; those listed below are either my favorite branch of the store or the ones in the most frequently shopped neighborhoods. There is some crossover between British Big Names and this category; obviously **Laura Ashley** is a high-street multiple. I've tried not to duplicate any listings, but there is a thin line between these two categories of merchandise and stores. Also, please note that this section only contains listings of multiples that sell clothing. There are a number of large British multiples that specialize in toiletries and other health and beauty products, such as **The Body Shop** and **Culpeper the Herbalist.** See pages 111–114 for listings of these multiples.

Austin Reed
103-113 Regent Street, W1 (Tube: Piccadilly Circus).

A chain of stores selling men's and women's traditional (read: boring) British clothing from the big makers—this is the place to shop if the Brit Look—in its most conservative incarnation—is your need. Branch stores tend to be in need of renovation. All the sturdy and steadfast British big names are sold through these stores; you can sometimes bump into something fashionable.

If you have been invited to partake in The Season, if you are going to a social or business function in which you must look British, this is an excellent resource—you can't go wrong. You will find clothing here that you will enjoy wearing and which will help you "fit in."

Please note that some branches of Austin Reed open early in the morning for the business crowd running an errand or two on the way to the office.

French Connection
249 Regent Street, W1 (Tube: Oxford Circus).

I spent years thinking this was a French firm, so sophisticates beware—this line is not only British but is made by the same firm that owns designer Nicole Farhi. Furthermore, they have now opened a flagship store right on Regent Street.

The line specializes in wearable fashions that have a touch of trendy around the edges, but are not over the top in any way. Prices are meant to be midrange but in the U.K., that means they start out high. Sale prices may be more impressive.

The store carries men's and women's clothing.

188 BASIC LONDON RESOURCES—A–Z

Jigsaw
21 Long Acre, Covent Garden, WC2 (Tube: Covent Garden).

65 Kensington High Street, W8 (Tube: Kensington High Street).

449 The Strand, WC2 (Tube: Charing Cross).

124 Kings Road, SW3 (Tube: Sloane Square).

31 Brompton Road, SW3 (Tube: Knightsbridge).

One of the best examples of what a British multiple can be, Jigsaw is a fashion chain selling hip-but-wearable fashion for women. The line is such that a lot of merchandise is on the cutting edge (which means good, frequent sales) and much of it is for women under forty. Prices are moderate; the stores are always high-tech chic; there's always something to see and be impressed with—even if you are just sizing up the hot looks. This chain is just beginning to move into the international market. Don't leave Britain without checking out at least one of these stores. They also do a men's range.

Karen Millen
46 South Molton Street, W1 (Tube: Bond Street).

34 Great Marlborough, W1 (Tube: Oxford Circus).

59 King's Road, SW3 (Tube: Sloane Square).

I am carefully enthusiastic. The clothes are usually made in light and/or neutral colors, have a comfortable droop to them, and say fashion without saying fashion victim. There are a handful of stores in London's best trading areas; the one behind **Liberty** is on Great Marlborough—this is a wonderful street that connects to Carnaby Street.

Miss Selfridge
40 Duke Street, W1 (Tube: Bond Street).

There is a Miss Selfridge department in the main **Selfridges** store, but there are numerous free-standing Miss Selfridge stores all over London. Their specialty is the young, kicky look at inexpensive prices—this is a find for teens or those who want to dabble in a trendy look without spending too much money. I could go on at great length about this store. You haven't shopped London until you've seen these clothes.

Monsoon
67 South Molton Street, W1 (Tube: Bond Street).

A chain of low-to-moderate-priced women's fashions made in India in current styles but of fabrics inspired by the mother country (India), and therefore gauzy, colorful, sometimes ethnic (but not always), and very distinctive. The look is very popular in the 'tweens-through-twenties set. The business is so gigantic, and so popular during hard times, that there are now spinoffs such as a chain of small stores selling only accessories called **Accessorize** and a small chain for dress-up clothes named, appropriately, **Twilight.**

I usually love this line, although some seasons are better than others. I also find some of their items well priced and others way too high. I adore their new perfume called, gee, Monsoon.

There are branches in all major trading areas including Covent Garden; there's one right behind Liberty as well.

Next
160 Regent Street, W1 (Tube: Piccadilly Circus).

Every city in Britain has a handful of Next shops—some sell women's clothes; some sell men's clothes; some sell home furnishings; some sell kids' clothes; and some sell accessories to go with the above. Next is a force for the yuppie consumer, selling a total-lifestyle look that is modern, as opposed to the Laura Ashley sweet-flowers routine.

If you want to look like a British yuppie in perfectly safe clothing with a neutral but classic style, this is your source.

Don't miss their X stores for the teenage set; very avant-garde and hip, with sort of wild architecture. Okay, it's not Lloyd's of London, but it's architecturally interesting.

DOROTHY PERKINS
311 Oxford Street, W1 (Tube: Oxford Circus).

Petite clothes are sold in specialty parts of some of the major department stores, but this high-street multiple is devoted to the smaller sizes and sells clothes for the professional woman at low-to-moderate prices (for Britain, anyway). They've changed the range slightly to include some street fashions as well.

PRINCIPLES
The Plaza, Oxford Street, W1 (Tube: Oxford Circus).

Hot, with-it fashions at low (for Britain) prices, with plenty of designer knockoffs and in-step accessories. Many of the stores look—from the outside—like Next; don't be confused, because the looks inside are definitely different.

RACING GREEN
193 Regent Street, W1 (Tube: Piccadilly).

Perhaps locals cheered when this store opened recently—I was not amused. The line comes straight from its mail order catalog. I categorize it as an imitation Polo and horse/rider look. You might like it, but I find it too preppy and too cheap for my taste.

WHISTLES
Covent Garden, WC2 (Tube: Covent Garden).

An on-the-edge chain with high-fashion looks and prices that are too high for the young people who can wear these clothes. The prices are even too high for me, even though I may be a little old for some of this stuff. When droopy is in, they do droopy. When wrinkled is in, they do wrinkled. Very L.A. clothes that actually work in fashion circles in London. I once saw a pink plush chubbie with black stencils of Minnie Mouse. That's the kind of place it is.

Susan Woolf
9-13 Brompton Road, SW3 (Tube: Knightsbridge).

70 New Bond Street, W1 (Tube: Bond Street).

I'm not sure if this is a multiple-in-the-making or just a designer store with several branches like **Nicole Farhi**, but Susan Woolf has fashions for career women as well as for those who like a casual, clean line and simple elegance that's not overblown, overly young, or matronly either. The clothes are not inexpensive but they aren't unaffordable—maybe £200 or so for a blazer. I just bought a jacket on sale for £80 that I consider the steal of the day.

Dressier than Ann Taylor but not quite Calvin Klein. A fine choice if you need to fit into British style but still want to be comfortable and chic.

PAPER GOODS & FILO FACTS

Filofax
21 Conduit Street, W1 (Tube: Bond Street).

This is a freestanding Filofax boutique, not a stationery store that sells the stuff. It's rather fancy, considering the neighborhood and the clientele, and is replete with pages, inserts, and various notebooks in the many sizes. Prices are still half of what they are in the U.S., and they have sales and closeouts. I always have a ball here. Note that they begin to sell calendars for the upcoming year about eight or nine months before you need them, so don't be shy, even if it's July.

Paperchase
213 Tottenham Court Road, W1 (Tube: Goodge Street).

167 Fulham Road, SW3 (Tube: Fulham Broadway).

The "in" place for paper goods, Paperchase offers a wide range of products—everything from greeting cards, stationery, Filofax pages, and party items to a variety of materials for the serious artist. I often buy my Christmas cards here; part of the proceeds go to charity.

Smythson
44 New Bond Street, W1 (Tube: Bond Street).

If you're looking for stationery fit for a queen, stop by this very elegant shop, which has been producing top-quality paper since the turn of the century. If you buy your writing papers at Cartier in New York, or at any of America's finest paper shops, you'll see some old friends here in London. Aside from the selection of writing papers, there's a wide variety of leather-bound goods, including address books and notebooks, diaries, and lovely desktop accessories. This is an old-fashioned, blue-blooded, very regal kind of place, a bit expensive, but cheaper than in the U.S. for the same goods.

They do not make Jewish New Year's cards. You should have seen the salesman's face when I asked.

There is a tiny branch store on Sloane Square but you don't get the feel of the power of their prestige there.

Italian Paper Shop
Brompton Arcade, SW3 (Tube: Knightsbridge).

If you love that swirly, marbleized, antique-Italian-paper look, you may want to poke into the Italian Paper Shop, which is in an arcade right between **Harrods** and **Harvey Nichols**. Prices are higher than in Italy and lower than in the U.S. The store lacks the charm of similar shops in Venice or Florence, but the goods are the same. The pencils, at about $1 each, make smashing gift items.

Mirabilia Italiae
16 Royal Arcade, Old Bond Street, W1 (Tube: Green Park).

Very different from the Italian paper shop with its swirly Venetian papers, this tiny shop sells the English version of Italian paper goods complete with the Pineider line—the most prestigious name in fine writing papergoods in Florence and Rome.

Morgan's
168 Drury Lane, WC2 (Tube: Covent Garden).

This is a stationery shop with several branches to serve locals, but they have a stupendous selection of Filofax materials. Even their business card is printed as an insert.

American Retro
35 Old Compton Street, W1 (Tube: Leicester Square).

A fabulous store for all kinds of neat used clothes, and a fine introduction to what's happening in Soho, but I am sending you here for the latest in Filofax inserts. You may buy the SafeFax here—a leather page with specially sized slots that store condoms.

It costs almost $40, but what price safe sex? If you like, you can write the manufacturer and order yours directly and discreetly: SafeFax Ltd., Suite C, 52/53 Dean Street, London W1.

RESALE SHOPS

About the only way I can afford to wear **Chanel** is if I buy it used. Many women must feel the same way because London is abloom with resale shops, called dress agencies. There's an entire block of them across the street and around the corner from Harrods.

🛍 PANDORA
16-22 Cheval Place, SW7 (Tube: Knightsbridge).

Grandmother of all dress agencies; the one that made Cheval Place what it is today—this is where I buy my Chanel. Locals call this a dress agency; I call it heaven. I'll also call it the future, especially in London, where more and more people are buying secondhand and aren't afraid to admit it. I'm talking $50 for a YSL blouse, $38 for an Hermès scarf. Armani jackets go for a mere $200. (Well, it's mere to some people.) Used clothes are no more than six months old.

The store is fairly large; there is a dressing room in the back. They have a strange system with automatic markdowns which is explained on handwritten signs with a color code.

There's a wide range of types of clothing and sizes; some handbags and a few accessories. I paid £295 for a Chanel cashmere sweater with clover leaf buttons and think I got the steal of the century.

I sent my friend Marie here; she trotted over looking for a discount house selling Chanel. She swears I neglected to tell her the clothing was used. "Gently worn," she sniffs, "is not an expression the British know. I do not want a Chanel suit that Lady Who Ha has sweated in." Nonetheless, Marie made off with the Hermès Kelly bag of her dreams for £120.

Hours are 10 A.M. to 5 P.M., Monday to Saturday. They take plastic.

RENATE
4 Cheval Place, SW7 (Tube: Knightsbridge).

The first of the chain of resale shops—so fancy you pass by, intimidated. Don't be.

SALOU
6 Cheval Place, SW7 (Tube: Knightsbridge).

A Chanel handbag marked "copy" for £145 makes me a tad nervous but there were Hermès scarves and plenty of Chanel suits in the £350–450 range.

THE DRESS BOX
8 Cheval Place, SW7 (Tube: Knightsbridge).

Yet another. In fact, this one was here way before Pandora relocated around the corner. It's a staple.

STRELIOS
10 Cheval Place, SW7 (Tube: Knightsbridge).

One of the many resale shops in a row on Cheval Place, Strelios is small but stuffed with the very best clothes. I tried on my first Chanel couture gown here. I couldn't buy it because I knew it would ruin my life—it was so well made that it made everything else I own look disgusting. Price for a Chanel suit averages about £450; the gown I tried on was £1,400.

PAMELA'S
16 Beauchamp Place (Tube: Knightsbridge).

Pamela's has moved to a basement level on Beauchamp Place and while its new location is convenient to your regular shopping haunts, I can't get you into a sweat over it. Last time I was there, it was worse than boring. Because I have had great good luck here previously, I wish you a better time.

DYNASTY
63 Kensington Church Street, W8 (Tube: Kensington High Street).

This is the kind of shop you pop into because you're in the neighborhood; not to make a special trip, please. Dynasty is a resale shop although the day I was there recently, the only items that interested me were hats at £40, which I decided was too high. Still, it's in the middle of Kensington Church Street.

DESIGNS
60 Rosslyn Hill, NW3 (Tube: Hampstead).

Closed on Sundays when much of the Hampstead retail scene is hopping, so decide early on if you want to get a look at some slightly used designer duds. Prices are basically one-third the original price.

SHOES

For the most part, shoes are expensive in London and only make sense if there is a sale, if you are shopping for a brand that cannot be found in the U.S. (**Charles Jourdan** has virtually disappeared in the U.S.), or if the dollar is good and you can qualify for a VAT refund. For example, I buy the "Tuxedo" style of **Ferragamo** shoes on a regular basis in London. They cost about $165 in New York plus tax. If the pound is trading at $1.50 and the shoes cost £100 and I get a VAT refund, I can save money.

I have listed only the local names for special, traditional or unusual shoes. Americans can be found at **Joan & David** at 151 Bond Street (the rage with English ladies), but since their shoes cost less in the U.S., do you really need to stop in?

Shoes

BERTIES
Covent Garden, WC2 (Tube: Covent Garden).

A famous London shoe resource at the moderate-price level, Berties has shops all over London, as well as branches and department-store distribution in the U.S. They are famous for high style at moderate prices.

MANOLO BLAHNIK
49-51 Old Church Street, SW3 (Tube: South Kensington).

Okay, so maybe the average reader can't pronounce his name or afford his shoes. But those truly in the know know Blahnik.

Manolo is one of the leading designers of expensive, creative shoes with vamp for the vamps of the world. They do not come cheap (in either case). He has a few stores dotted here and there in the shopping capitals of the world. The London shop is run by his sister, which makes it a must-do if you have a foot fetish. Ivana Trump is a regular.

CHURCH'S SHOES
163 New Bond Street, W1 (Tube: Bond Street).

What did you come to London for, if not to buy Church's shoes for him? These are traditional wing tips and slip-ons at high prices; otherwise enjoy this tiny shop with the typical "well-worn" English interior. Actually, there are branches in the U.S.; the prices in London are usually equal to U.S. prices—but, get this, the U.S. has outlet stores.

PATRICK COX
8 Symons Street, SW3 (Tube: Sloane Square).

The single hottest new name in British foot fashions has already opened a small shop on Manhattan's Madison Avenue and made waves in the international world of fashion with his pink (and orange) patent leather loafers on lug soles. The Wannabe line is almost affordable (under £100); others may cost £200 per pair. The store is small and can be hard to find. If the Sloane Square tube station is to your rear and you are facing the department store **Peter Jones**, King's Road is on your left and Symons is the small street on your right, immediately beside the department store. Cox's store is right behind Peter Jones on Symons Street.

GINA
42 Sloane Street, SW1 (Tube: Knightsbridge).

Every single British fashion magazine I read has been raving about Gina as a source for the well-heeled. It's got a cute little purple storefront and a fancy address, but frankly I have no idea what all the fuss is about.

The designer is named Emma Hope and she is considered the last word in vamps. The shoes are high-fashion, expensive, and sometimes innovative. I think this is a good store, but not the last word. Let me know what you think, or what I'm missing here. Yes, the Princess of Wales does shop here.

There's another store across the street to provide more space for the expanding line.

HOBBS
Covent Garden, WC2 (Tube: Covent Garden).

An excellent shoe chain for well-made, sporty, and dressy shoes at the top end of the moderate price range, but not so over-the-top that you can't afford them. Always reliable for fashionable, but not overly chic, footwear. Also handbags.

PIED À TERRE
19 South Molton Street, W1 (Tube: Bond Street).

Another chain, far more upscale than **Berties**, but not so out of line price-wise that you'll wince.

Various designer names are here, some of whom are more famous in Europe and Britain (like **Michel Perry**) than in America. They stock many inventive styles as well as staples. Shops are located everywhere; this is almost a high-street multiple.

F. PINET
47 New Bond Street, W1 (Tube: Bond Street).

This store is rather a Bond Street institution and is the kind of store I pass constantly in my regular Mayfair shopping rounds. That means you, too, will find yourself going right by. This is where I spend time musing at the stock in the windows and wondering if I can ever wear "that kind of shoe" and where I never shop. Locals count on this resource for special occasion shoes—dress up shoes, colored leather shoes, creative, inventive designs, catch me catch me shoes, etc. They do carry flats as well as heels but I am always attracted to the high heels in green snakeskin. Not for the horse and rider set.

RUSSELL & BROMELY
24-25 New Bond Street, W1 (Tube: Bond Street).

If you are looking for your favorite European designer shoe, such as Bruno Magli, Walter Steiger, or Charles Jourdan, stop by this very fashionable shop. There are several locations throughout London, but this elegant store serves social London, for those who want one-stop shopping with lots of brand choice; for men and women.

SHELLY'S
270-66 Regent Street, W1 (Tube: Oxford Circus).

159 Oxford Street, W1 (Tube: Bond Street).

14 Neal Street, WC2 (Tube: Covent Garden).

44-45 Carnaby Street, W1 (Tube: Oxford Circus).

40 Kensington High Street, W8 (Tube: Kensington High Street).

124 King's Road, SW3 (Tube: Sloane Square).

Shelly's has been the purveyor of shoes for the hot London foot for years; **Doc Martens** were probably born here. They carry many other brands as well. Truth is, I kind of liked the platform, granny lace-up in pale turquoise (£40). The chartreuse clogs were £43. They simply sell a high-fashion shoe for a very reasonable price. Bring your teens and 'tweens; otherwise stop by just to convince yourself you've seen it all.

Oh yes, if your kids are younger, don't panic: Shelly's also sells the **Buckle My Shoe** line, which has some freestanding stores. This is the same look, but for tots.

Furthermore, you can buy normal styles here, too. Prices are quite low—like £40! They offer overnight delivery in the U.K.; call 181-450-0066.

SHOOTING & FISHING

Few enthusiasts take their sport more seriously than the British; hunting and shooting (not the same sport) and fishing are serious pursuits. Your ability in these areas has social ramifications, as does the equipment you use. While **Orvis**, the American fly-fisher's mecca, is here (27 Sackville Street, W1), wouldn't you rather shop where the English have for generations? A royal warrant is always a fine indication of where to begin to shop among these sources. Also note that many of these shops serve as quasi social services: at Holland & Holland, come September, you can book a ticket to a shoot at their range in Ruislip. This is a catered event (of course) and costs about $200 per person. I promise not to make any bad jokes about party games. Or game parties.

James Purdey & Sons Ltd.
57 South Audley Street, W1 (Tube: Green Park or Marble Arch).

Gun and rifle makers; three royal warrants. Keep their catalog on your coffee table merely for the fun of it. Take your kids, as if you were in a museum. Pretend you are going on safari with Clark Gable, or going shooting with David (King Edward VIII). Don't miss it. This store is right behind **The Dorchester.**

Holland & Holland
31-33 Bruton Street, W1 (Tube: Green Park or Oxford Circus).

While the latest trend in British retail is for Americans and French to open up in London, here's an example of the opposite trend—a venerable British firm expanding to foreign shores. They have opened on rue Victor Hugo in Paris (#29) and will be opening in Manhattan shortly. Go figure.

For those who don't shoot on weekends and possibly don't know, Holland & Holland is a gunmaker. We are not talking bang-bang-you're-dead but shooting guns and presentation guns and important collectibles and prices that can easily reach to £250,000. A new gun takes perhaps a thousand man hours to create (more than a Saville Row suit) and costs about £10,000.

Hardy Brothers
61 Pall Mall, W1 (Tube: Green Park).

They made Queen Victoria's fishing rod. Need I say more?

SWEATERS

The perfect sweater requires three ingredients: chilly weather, homegrown wool, and long winter nights.

Actually, sweaters date back about 2,000 years and were found in Egyptian tombs. Sweaters as we know them grew up in medieval times, when men were the knitters and guilds specified that this was not women's work. Their business went the way of the Industrial Revolution and became the knitting industry we know and love. Women adapted to the cottage side of the industry and began to knit at home, by the fire, when it was too dark to do much else.

Today's sweater's value is based on who made it and how. A hand-knit sweater is more valuable and will always cost more than a machine-knit sweater; sweaters made with synthetics have the least value, while those made with wool or cashmere (or any other natural fiber, such as cotton, silk, or linen) have far more value.

Cashmere sweaters are valued by the number of plies or strands in the yarn—from one to four is common. The higher the number of plies, the heavier the sweater, and the more expensive it is. Cashmere sweaters are sold year-round in the many cashmere shops London is famous for; they are only a seasonal item at **Marks & Spencer** and are only sold at the Marble Arch store.

Traditional Sweaters

Traditional sweaters are in solid colors and come in crewneck or V-neck styles, in either pullover or cardigan—men's and women's versions. They are sized for the small European body and have not changed in style in decades; if you are looking for a big, sweatshirt look or extra fullness, you will not find

The Cashmere Crisis

If the sole purpose of your trip to London was to load up on cashmere sweaters and save a fortune, you are about to get a shocking piece of news: There are very few cashmere bargains these days. In fact, the world of sweaters has been in a cashmere crisis for years and most of the cashmere that comes to market these days is from the Orient.

While English cashmere sweaters are traditionally from Scotland, China also got into the cashmere sweater business in a big way as they gathered steam and faced capitalism and the *garmentos* of New York. Cashmere goods coming out of China could be had at bargain prices, and the demand for cashmere soared. Scotland, although pressured by the Chinese, refused to lower prices and slogged along—often losing the sale to private-label brands sold in giant lots through U.S. department stores. Then the Chinese realized the value of cashmere and raised the prices. The rest is history. The Scottish also raised their prices; both makers lowered production. You might consider buying a sweater made of platinum.

The best way to capitalize on the cashmere crisis is to plan ahead. Watch prices in the U.S., read the fine print in ads, and pay attention to where goods have been manufactured. Cashmere is in high demand, not only for sweaters, but for other items of clothing, and prices are sky-high. Yet there are still big promotional sales.

Price everything in the U.S. before you get to London, then spend some time pricing in regular London sweater stores. After you know the going prices—if you are still standing despite the shock of it—head for the few discounters in London (**Portobello China & Woollens, Westaway & Westaway**) who have factory overruns, seconds, and discontinued colors. These stores don't usually have a large selection, but they do have the best prices you'll find these days.

> While it is still possible to buy discounted cashmere sweaters in Scotland, the prices there may not be any less expensive than at the discount sources in London. The selection in the Borders' towns (especially Hawick) will be far superior to what you can find in London, but there will not be a price break—unless you hit some kind of lucky deal. If you're heading for Scotland, take a peek at *Born to Shop Great Britain* for a full tour of all the sweater factories in the Borders.
>
> Cashmere is at a premium these days. You do not need to pay $500 for a simple V-neck sweater, but you may be asked to pay that by some stores. Just smile politely and then run. You might want to run to a discounter, or you might just want to run home.
>
> One final thought: Try some of the resale shops, page 194. Granted, a woman tends to keep her cashmeres forever—that is the point after all—but if it's fashion cashmere, it just may go to a dress agency. I bought a marvelous Chanel cashmere sweater for £295, which is not inexpensive, but is a bargain for what I bought. Give it a thought.
>
> Also, note the difference in quality between Scottish cashmere and Chinese. Scottish is better. Don't buy inferior cashmere just because it's cheap.

it in a traditional sweater (although women can buy men's sweaters and add shoulder pads). For best selection of these types of sweaters in London, try **Westaway & Westaway** (see page 209).

Traditional Sweaters in Fashion Styles

A solid-color sweater, especially in cashmere, that fits into today's fashion styles—such as a sweatshirt cut, a tunic, a double pocket at the hip, or whatever—is extremely difficult to find in England, and will cost a lot of money. **N. Peal** (page 207) specializes in this look.

Shetland Sweaters

Shetland is a type of wool that has a slight nap to it; when woven into a garment, the nap is apparent. Shetlands are mostly seen in crewneck styles, in stripes or solids. While most Shetlands are in standard colors, a few shops sell them in brights and fashion shades.

Argyle Sweaters

Argyles are diamond patterns that are knitted into sweaters (or socks) in contrasting colors. **Scotch House** stocks them.

Fair Isle Sweaters

Fair Isle patterns are lines of zigzag colors that are laid in either at the yoke of a sweater or across the central body, in contrasting colors. Because of the intricacy of these designs, look for higher price tags—especially if the sweater is hand-knit. Try **Westaway & Westaway**.

Engineered Prints

Fairly new to the world of sweaters, engineered prints are designs created by computers or creators on small knitting machines; they produce rows of identical designs—usually animals. The Princess Di sweater with the rows of white sheep and the one black sheep is an engineered design. You'll see these with rows of rabbits, frogs, bears, etc. This is the look **Warm and Wonderful** made famous; or try **Sally's Own** at the Covent Garden market.

Aran Sweaters

The Aran Islands, on Ireland's western coast, were the home of an isolated group of fishermen. The women knit sweaters in a certain pattern so men lost at sea could be identified and brought home to rest. Today that pattern is so well-known it is called a "fisherman's sweater," and comes in cream or "natural" wool.

Twin Sets

Twin sets have come back into style; to British women they never went out of style.

Twin sets come in cotton, cashmere, and lamb's wool; I've seen great lamb's wool sets at **Marks & Spencer**. My single best source for cashmere twin sets is a factory in the Borders of Scotland (see *Born to Shop Great Britain*), but you can find them in London in traditional places like **N. Peal**, etc. They cost more than in the Borders—a lot more.

Art Sweaters

Some of these are works of art; some of them cost as much as works of art. London is in the middle of a crafts revival led by a small group of big-name knitting superstars. Look for work by Kaffe Fassett, Jessi & Jamie Seaton, and Susan Duckworth. I think **Anne Higgins's** work, while in a different category, is also art.

Shawls

There is this very chic movement toward wearing an enormous shawl, preferably in cashmere and more chicly, with a ruffle. Without a ruffle is socially acceptable, especially if the knit is of two different colors on either side of the shawl. Trimmed with fringe (but not fur tails) is okay, as is trimmed with satin.

Such shawls are expensive, especially in cashmere, where you may be asked to pay £800 for such a beauty. I buy mine in lamb's wool. In fact, truth be told, I buy mine in Rome for about $100 each, and those are the expensive ones—the cheap ones cost $50 or so and come from the market in Florence. I mention this because a lamb's wool shawl in England, even if you get a good deal, even if perhaps you buy from a factory in the Borders, will still be over £200.

Sweaters and Knitted Goods

Since sweaters are so expensive, look to street markets and fairs if cost is a factor. Covent Garden—both **Apple** and **Jubilee Markets**—always has good buys. **Sally's Own** and **Colinette** are two famous dealers in the Apple Market; you'll find your own favorites as well.

N. PEAL
Burlington Arcade, W1 (Tube: Piccadilly Circus).

192 Piccadilly, W1 (Tube: Piccadilly Circus).

For the quality- and convenience-conscious, N. Peal offers quite a variety of wools and cashmeres in a multitude of colors and styles. They are top-of-the-line in the business, but frankly, I could faint from the prices.

That's retail, of course. I don't have a source for N. Peal at wholesale, but I have noticed that they have a lot of sales. I've always noticed that they run numerous promotions. In November last year, just before Christmas (Dear Santa), N. Peal offered a cashmere roll neck for £149. This item is regularly priced at £179; so there's a handy $50 savings just for reading the newspaper. Add to that the fact that they do free mail order within the U.K. Phone to ask if they have any new promotions: 171-493-9220.

N. Peal is in the Burlington Arcade, in two different shops. Both shops look small, but they have underground levels. As other merchants in the arcade go out of business, Peal moves into their space as well, so don't worry about lack of stock. Then there's a whole other medium-sized shop on Piccadilly, near **Hatchards.**

Peal is the kind of shop you swear you won't patronize because of the high prices, but then you go back after you've been to every discount resource in London. While you can get traditional sweaters in any number of places and at a variety of prices, Peal is one of the few outlets that sells fashion merchandise made out of cashmere. Notice that their sweaters are entirely different from the look-alikes you'll see everywhere else. They do have twin sets, they have bodysuits (called a "body" in British), and they have blends of cashmere and silk or even just plain old-fashioned wool. The color palette will leave you drooling. The quality puts cheap cashmere to shame. And look at that shawl with the little ruffle.

Pringle
93 New Bond Street, W1 (Tube: Bond Street).

Not as fashion conscious as N. Peal, but ever so lovable (royal warrants and all), Pringle is great for classics. Now, they've added the missing ingredient: washable cashmere. I don't mean handwashable (that's how I've always done mine), but machine washable. Sweaters cost about $200 and actually seem a relative bargain.

Scotch House
84 Regent Street, W1 (Tube: Piccadilly Circus).

191 Regent Street, W1 (Tube: Oxford Circus).

2 Brompton Road, SW1 (Tube: Knightsbridge).

7 Marble Arch, W1 (Tube: Marble Arch).

187 Oxford Street, W1 (Tube: Bond Street).

A must-stop for the lover of those classic Scottish tartans and kilts, for sweater lovers, for lovers of grand wooden staircases and stores that look like stores should look. The store on Brompton Road in Knightsbridge is the nicer, but Regent Street is very convenient.

They carry all the major brands and have matching sweaters and jackets for many styles. This also is a wonderful place to purchase scarves in the traditional tartans or in more subtle colors to take home as gifts for your family. Remember when you were six and Mommy brought you back a kilt of your own? (You always lost the pin, too, didn't you?) This is where you can return the favor for someone on your gift list. The kids' department is excellent; don't miss their chart of tartans and clans.

Shirin Cashmere
12 Beauchamp Place, SW3 (Tube: Knightsbridge).

You've got the money, you're ready to pay, but you're desperate to escape shabby-chic classics and find something wild and wacky or just lush and plush? Step this way. Shirin sells high-fashion looks in cashmere. Very chic, very now, very expensive.

Cashmere by Design
64 Neal Street, WC2 (Tube: Covent Garden).

Very simple lifestyle shop where all your basics are cashmere. Colors change with the seasons; prices are awfully reasonable . . . considering.

Westaway & Westaway
62-65 Great Russell Street, WC1 (Tube: Holborn).

92 Great Russell Street, WC1 (Tube: Holborn).

If you can't stand wondering who has the cheapest sweaters and the best selection, take my word for it and head to Westaway & Westaway. It's located across the street from the British Museum, and you are guaranteed to find any sweater in any color and style that might be desired.

There are two shops, which carry a large selection of knitted garments from Scotland and Ireland, as well as the classic cashmere and lamb's wool favorites. They have slightly discounted Burberrys and Aquascutum items, kilts, shawls, and yardgoods in one shop, and then sweaters, sweaters, sweaters in the other shop.

In both shops notice there are rooms upstairs and downstairs as well as a back, back room that you might have trouble finding if you don't know it's there. Please note that men's sweaters cost less than women's.

Don't forget to look at the sale merchandise on the lower shelves in the downstairs rooms. There also is a more fashion-oriented shop one block away.

To order, call toll-free in the U.S.: 800-345-3219—this phone rings in London so do use GMT when you phone. If you reach the office after hours, you can leave your order information after the recording.

PORTOBELLO CHINA & WOOLLENS
89 Portobello Road, W11 (Tube: Notting Hill Gate).

If you love crazy fun, this one's for you. This is Bargain Sweater City. Sweaters that elsewhere cost $100 are $75 here. Sweaters that cost $150 elsewhere cost $100 here.

There are seconds; some of the merchandise is big-name without labels, but the help will tell you what it is. It is worse than mobbed on Saturday, and you have to be the kind who likes this kind of stuff to endure it.

The service is top-notch. The last time I was there, they pulled out zillions of sweaters for me, searched for cashmere twin sets for me, and were most helpful and polite, considering I didn't buy a thing and the shop was jam-packed. Prices here are among the best in London—probably in all England.

There is not a big selection. But if you give up on a sweater, you can always buy a teapot.

TARTANS & TWEEDS

Americans have so mangled British English over the centuries that there is now some confusion as to the difference between a tartan and a plaid—a difference that will get you into deep water when you come to buy one or the other. A *tartan* is a pattern of fabric, with alternate colors in the warp and the weft in which the colors repeat themselves in a set order. A *plaid* is a piece of clothing worn as part of a Scottish dress uniform. In the U.S., the term *plaid* does refer to a pattern of alternating colors set in a sequence, but in England a plaid is not a tartan. Or vice versa.

Tartans signify the great families of the Highlands, each family having its own special way of weaving its colors and stripes into a particular sequence which no one else can copy. There is usually a battle tartan and a dress tartan for each family or clan. The men who fought for a certain clan all wore the same pattern, and certain areas of the Highlands became known for these patterns.

Now then, if you want to get all gussied up in proper Highland attire, you will probably want to wear the right tartan. You may easily discover the right one for you either by using a chart for your last name or by using a map and finding the village your family came from. In London and Edinburgh, retailers have these lists right on hand, and will gladly help you. Of course, a lot of people just pick what they like best.

Scotch House in London (2 Brompton Road and 191 Regent Street) has the best charts of the clans; all the shops in Edinburgh (except maybe **Kinloch Anderson**, where your bloodline must be worn on your sleeve) have brochures and charts to lend you or sell you.

A *tweed* has nothing to do with a tartan, and the two are rarely worn together. Tweed fabric is named for the River Tweed, and is a blend of various colors of wool so that a pattern emerges. Many tweeds are named for the places that created them, such as the Harris tweed. Tweeds are often nubby with a rough hand. They are 100% wool and can be bought by the meter or as ready-made garments. Men's tweed jackets can sometimes be much less expensive in the U.K. than in the U.S.

Tweed fabric bought off the bolt will be considerably cheaper—expect a 50% savings. If you're really into saving money, you'll buy the fabric in Scotland and then take it to Hong Kong to have the tailoring done there. Even if you're not Hong Kong–bound this year, you may think about the plan. The best thing about tweeds is that they never go out of style. Hang on to the fabric, get a classic suit made, and it will last 20 years—or longer.

TEENS & 'TWEENS

Dr. Martens Department Store
1-4 King Street, Covent Garden, WC2 (Tube: Covent Garden).

You know that you are old if you do not know what Doc Martens are. You know that you are old if you think that Doc Marten is a doctor. You know that you're old when you don't know if you should write Dr. or Doc because the correct name is written "Dr.," but it is pronounced in street vernacular as "Doc." Professor Higgins, please.

Now then, middle-age moms, lend me your ears.

Doc Marten is a brand of shoe, now a brand of clothes, now a cult statement worshipped by 13-year-olds around the world. The store, opened right in the heart of Covent Garden, is one of those "you just have to see it to believe it" kind of places. They call it a department store because it contains five floors of things that teens want to spend money on and think they really want to own.

The merchandise is only part of the phenom; seeing the kids "hang" is the other part. I'd consider bringing the videocam. Hang out yourself, eavesdrop, and you'll dine out on the experience for a week. Cooool.

Prices are very expensive, but no one seems to care. I found gift items on the first floor—like notepads and wax candles in the shape of a shoe. There were a variety of items for a few pounds—wallets ($10), notebooks ($3)—but the candle was quite over-priced ($18). I'm the only one who seems to have noticed. I later saw $10 items on sale in France for $20!

About the street address: don't let it throw you. This building is right across the street from Covent Garden marketplace. You can't miss it.

Sign of the Times
15 Shorts Gardens, Covent Garden, WC2 (Tube: Covent Garden).

Sign of the Times has become an established name in street fashion. It began as a stall in Kensington Market, opened another stall in Hyper Hyper, and now has its first freestanding shop in Covent Garden—it's considered the kind of place where with-it fashion nobs must pay homage.

Whatever it is that the motorcycle and pierced nose crowd is wearing, you'll find it translated here—babydoll to vintage. Prices begin at £25.

Workers For Freedom
4 Lower John Street, W1 (Tube: Piccadilly Circus).

Although they have a reputation as the wild kids on the block, this Soho house actually makes very chic and wearable clothes that are not cheap. They may be on the cutting edge, but they are not too outré to be worn well by middle-aged matrons wanting to make a fashion statement. After all, the designers Graham Fraser and Richard Nott used to work for **Valentino**. This is not particularly a teen resource; the prices are very high. I think it's more for movie and rock stars.

RED OR DEAD
36 Kensington High Street, W8 (Tube: High Street Kensington).

33 Neal Street, WC2 (Tube: Covent Garden).

186 Camden High Street, NW1 (Tube: Camden Town).

This is a teen and 'tween resource and is so popular that it's on the way to becoming a multiple. They also influence other designers with their contribution to street fashion. My 16-year-old friend Serena, queen of a Manhattan prep school, used to send to Red or Dead for her Doc Martens before they were available in New York.

Red or Dead has a range of expensive to inexpensive clothes that are considered on the cutting edge. The Kensington High Street shop is virtually next door to **Hyper Hyper** and across from **Kensington Market**, making this the only place in town you need bring your teen or 'tween. Actually, all store locations are in precisely the right place for the market—there's one near Covent Garden and another near my least favorite place in London, Camden Town. Shoes, accessories, and items that kids call clothes. Ahem.

As befits alternative retail, they have slightly alternative hours. The stores open at 10:30 A.M. Monday through Friday, 10 A.M. on Saturdays, and at 12:30 P.M. on Sundays.

STIRLING COOPER
West One Mall, Oxford Street, W1 (Tube: Bond Street).

This is a cheapie multiple, but they sell top-dog looks for teens with prices that are conducive to throw-away fashion. Lots of black leather and studs. A little more mainstream than **Red or Dead.**

🛍 Hennes & Mauritz (H&M)
261-271 Regent Street (Tube: Oxford Circus).

I have loathed Hennes in London for as long as I can remember (whereas I love it in Sweden, where the chain originates); I've always considered it a shop that sells cheap junk. My opinion changed on my last visit when I spotted a copy of a Todd Oldham T-shirt through the doorway. I walked in, spent some time in the store, and left absolutely smitten with how much trendiness can be yours for so few pounds. There are none so pious as the recently converted.

You see, I bought this Todd Oldham shirt at Henri Bendel for $250 before I came to my senses and returned it the next day. I bought the copy at Hennes for less than £20 and am still congratulating myself. Furthermore, I saw the Hennes T-shirt featured in an editorial in French *Elle* as the look of the moment. Am I good or what?

Even if you buy nothing here, you've got to wander around listening to the young girls talking to each other about the clothes and their lives. Many of these sweet young things are American.

Will somebody please open up a branch store in my local mall?

🛍 Hyper Hyper
26-40 Kensington High Street, W8 (Tube: High Street Kensington).

Whether you like avant-garde fashion or not, this is like a trip to a museum of visual delights on Mars. Take teens and adolescents with you . . . and your camera. Street fashion is blooming in London and is rapidly being absorbed into American mainstream fashion. The big New York department stores estimate that over 50% of their merchandise comes from London now.

The best buys in London are on unknown designer goods. Many of these unknowns sell their work for $500 a pop—so not everything is a steal. But if you are the kind of person who seeks a unique design before a well-known brand name, check out some of the up-and-coming stars and get yourself over to Hyper Hyper.

These clothes are not just for 20-year-olds, by the way. I saw plenty of things suitable for people like me.

X
189 Oxford Street, W1 (Tube: Oxford Circus).

Sometimes referred to as Department X, this store is best recognized by the big X in a circle on the front window . . . which might not be that easy to spot because so much else is going on in the front window. Never fear. Your teens will pick up the vibes from down the block and march you right in the door. This is a member of the Next chain, and there are a few of these 'tweenage stores around the U.K.; whether or not you or yours wear these clothes, you owe it to history to take a look. This is the hip video look par excellence, and it is truly fabulous, in a sort of rock-and-roll way. Don't miss it.

ACADEMY
188A King's Road, SW3 (Tube: Sloane Square).

15 Newburgh Street, W1 (Tube: Oxford Circus).

One of the best shops on King's Road is Academy, which isn't large but does have a wide selection of up-and-coming English designer fashions. There's also a Soho branch.

RITVA WESTENIUS
153 Fulham Road, SW3 (Tube: Fulham Broadway).

Perhaps she should win a prize for her unusual name as well as for her unusual wedding designs. If you are looking to become Cinderella in your next life or are planning the wedding to end all weddings, you'll find old-fashioned elegance as well as poufs of net attached to satin tops in a look that no one back home can duplicate. The clothes offer tiers of skirts with fairy-tale embroideries and details. I find these clothes too sophisticated for a teenager; you need to be a middle-aged teenager to really appreciate them.

David Fielden
137 King's Road, SW3 (Tube: Sloane Square).

If you have been ambivalent about a trip to see the hotshot designers of King's Road, but you crave the best and the brightest, hop right on the tube and repeat after me: David Fielden, David Fielden, David Fielden. The shop is small, but his talent is huge.

Fielden does wild clothes and swirling hand-painted nonsense in high-fashioned statements that will make your jaw drop open. Not for your mother or the Queen Mother.

TOILETRIES (ENGLISH BRANDS)

France has the big discounts, not London, but local brands are famous and make good gifts. Prices are usually moderate. Also note that the new European fragrances are introduced in France first, then the Continent, then London, and then the U.S., so you may be able to find a new scent that is not yet available in the U.S.

D.R. Harris & Co.
29 St. James's Street, SW1 (Tube: Piccadilly or Green Park).

This is one of my best secret London finds, although I sort of owe it to a Jilly Cooper novel. This old-fashioned apothecary sells its own lines of goods; Skin Food is the cream that I learned about in the novel. There are also men's colognes and shave products, quill toothpicks, and almond oil moisturizers.

CROWN PERFUMERY
Grosvenor House Hotel, 35 Park Lane, W1 (Tube: Hyde Park Corner or Marble Arch).

Where have you been that you've never heard of this one? Now, now, don't fret. The crown has been closed for sixty years. But nostalgia is more than it used to be—the shop has reopened, many Victorian scents have been revived (and renamed), and the headquarters is following a new London trend; Crown Perfumery is in a hotel lobby, just like Daniele Ryman. The line is quite exclusive and you can buy your own Baccarrat perfume bottle and have it filled and then refilled. Of course, it'll cost a king's ransom, but what's money for?

J. FLORIS LTD.
89 Jermyn Street, SW1 (Tube: Piccadilly Circus).

London has two leading local perfumers; Floris is one of them. Special floral perfumes include Roses, Lilies, Lavender, and on and on. They are so classically English. The firm was begun in 1730 and kind of looks and feels the same: true Brit style and old-fashioned vibes. Even the packaging is fabulous. Royal warrant.

PENHALIGON'S
41 Wellington Street, WC2 (Tube: Covent Garden).

110A New Bond Street, W1 (Tube: Bond Street).

Burlington Arcade, W1 (Piccadilly Circus).

The other leading perfumer. Especially well-known for their toilet water and soap that men adore,

Penhaligon's also holds a royal warrant. Their products are produced according to the original formulas of William Penhaligon, who began his business as a barbershop in 1841. It's very olde England in here, and fun to sniff around. Kids seem to like it here, too.

JAMES BODENHAM & CO.
88 Jermyn Street, SW1 (Tube: Green Park).

Related to the Floris family by marriage, James Bodenham is a Victoriana kind of shop with gift items as well as potpourri and smell-good items and fragrances. There are many food items (jams and spices, as well as teas) and fragrances, but it's the apothecary nature of the store that makes it so much fun.

CZECH & SPEAKE
39c Jermyn Street, SW1 (Tube: Piccadilly Circus).

Trendy Italian and old-fashioned English in the same breath, this bath shop specializes in brushes and bath-time accessories, as well as its own brand of fragrances. The shop is all gray and black and brass; the packaging is very special in a high-tech-traditional manner. One of the most interesting shops in London, with a product that not too many Americans know about. The ideal gift for the person who has everything.

JO MALONE
154 Walton Street, SW3 (Tube: Knightsbridge or South Kensington).

Jo Malone is a perfumer, but she is also an aromatherapist and a local legend, so I really wasn't certain where to list her in these pages. Her foray into retail is unusual because she only opened her shop a year ago when she became too booked to ever take a new client again. Now you can wander into the tiny shop on Walton Street—the best shopping street in London perhaps—and discover the products for yourself. Yes, there is perfume, but there is much more.

Models and movie stars are clients, yes . . . royals, too. Orange and geranium cream is the product of choice but I like grapefruit and ginger body lotion. Then there's lime, basil & mandarin cologne: a unisex winner that is very Sloane Ranger.

Don't miss it.

MOLTON BROWN
58 South Molton Street, W1 (Tube: Bond Street).

Molton Brown is a very chic Mayfair beauty parlor. They sell their own hair products (**Harrods** also has the line), which are made from old-fashioned natural recipes. I still use the seaweed setting lotion whenever I set my hair in rollers.

The line comes in amber plastic bottles which look like old-fashioned apothecary bottles with Victorian-style labels. Don't forget the Molton-Browners, big pipe cleaners for rolling your hair.

The makeup line is carried in New York at Barneys. I don't happen to use this salon as my local hairdresser (it's famous—you certainly might want to give it a try), but I do love their products—and they make great gifts.

TOYS & KID STUFF

Whether you are traveling with children or looking for gifts to bring home, you'll find a few resources in London that are very special. The day my son outgrew Hamley's, I could have wept.

Do remember that girls, beginning around age 11 or so, really have teenage interests and that many of the aromatherapy and bath-soap shops will interest them as much as Hamleys. When my friend Serena (now 16) went to London when she was 12, all she wanted to do was buy shoes—Dr. Martens, of course. See page 196 for more on shoes and page 212 for the hip and hot stores who cater to teenagers of all ages.

Bear in mind as well that kids of all ages can be wild about comic books, CDs, and, even though the prices may make you wince, collectible toy soldiers, dolls, and other expensive toys. See Chapter 10, "Antiques, Used Books & Collectibles" for listings on where to buy these items.

Kids will also like the various street markets, Covent Garden for its shopping, its atmosphere, and its performance diversions and some of the naf souvenir shops on Oxford Street where they have wind-up toys that do all sorts of obscene things.

THE DISNEY STORE
140 Regent Street, W1 (Tube: Oxford Circus or Piccadilly Circus).

Give me a break.

HAMLEY'S
200 Regent Street, W1 (Tube: Oxford Circus)

Pussycat, pussycat, where have you been? To Hamley's, of course; then later, to the Queen. Whether you have children or not, Hamley's deserves attention.

If you are beginning to find yourself feeling dizzy, you will be relieved to find a snack bar in the basement. Prices will not make you dizzy—although American toys are more expensive here—but Corgi toys are a bargain. If you're looking for that unusual toy not readily available in the U.S., Hamley's is a must. The gift shop on the street level is the best (and easiest) place I know of to buy gifts for all your friends and neighbors.

If your child collects dolls, you will have a tough time making a final decision. There's also a huge array of Britains, the small metal British Regiment Guard soldiers for all the collectors in your family.

If you are wondering how you will get your packages home, Hamley's will ship them to your door. The paperwork takes about twenty minutes but is well worth the time. Make sure, of course, that you are sending home an unsolicited gift valued at less than $50. Otherwise, you will pay duty.

I like the fact that Hamley's also sells puzzles and brain teasers; these can be good gifts for older children or adults and nice little travel rewards for train journeys or transatlantic flights.

Even if you don't have children, don't know any children, and don't even like children, if you are interested in retail—go out of your way to visit this London masterpiece theater.

There is a tiny branch of Hamley's at Unit 3 of Covent Garden; it's so small it just seems to be a zoo of stuffed animals; there's also a branch of Hamley's at LHR. You deserve the mother store.

HARRODS
Knightsbridge, SW1 (Tube: Knightsbridge).

Fabulous toy department; possibly as good as **Hamley's**. There's a sample of every toy imaginable and the kids can play, ride, climb, bite, or torture the toys and each other. Fourth floor.

TROTTERS
34 King's Road, SW3 (Tube: Sloane Square).

Buy your franchise now and open up in an American mall—get rich quick! Trotters is a children's shop with a great formula and a lot of energy. They have toys, clothes, and a play area—all of it so cute you'll find it impossible to resist. The shopping bag, with the big fat pig, is one of the best bags in London. There's another pig outside, to mark the store.

WARNER STUDIO STORE
174 Regent Street, W1 (Tube: Piccadilly).

I mean, really.

Chapter Nine

HOME FURNISHINGS & DESIGN RESOURCES

THE AMERICAN REVOLUTION

The war for freedom from the motherland may have begun in Boston Harbor but it didn't end when George Washington became president and it's surely not over now. Only these days, it's the Americans who are taking Britain by storm with their retail therapy.

Ralph Lauren and Tiffany & Co. have been Bond Street fixtures for years. What about:

- **Jerry's Home Store** (163 Fulham Road SW3) is more Pottery Barn meets Crate & Barrel than anything Sir Terence or anyone at Habitat (Sir Terence no longer owns Habitat) could come up with.
- **The Shaker Shop** (322 Kings Road, SW3) is a regularly featured, leading design resource for all the British home furnishings magazines.
- **Kaffe Fassett,** the American knitting sweater king, is also now designing for **Designer's Guild**. And he ain't designing sweaters.

223

You may be off to Britain for cabbage roses, paisleys, and creeping ivy, but the real design scene is a multilayered, multinational cake.

ENGLISH DECOR

And despite **Jerry's Home Store**, we Americans have not come to London to look at cheap glassware. (No offense, Jerry.) Some of us are here for the swag. In fact, more of us should be here for the swag. While a large number of the tourists who go to London to shop are seeking raincoats with zip-out linings and matching kilts for the kids, I'm going to attempt to redirect your thinking. Or some of your thoughts. This is the shopping police: Have you thought about your living room today?

Ralph Lauren has proved quite handsomely (and expensively) that Americans want the olde English, shabby-chic, hounds-and-horses, cabbage-roses-and-faded-fringes look of yesterday. Maybe I can't get it for you wholesale, but I sure know a lot of places to shop for this kind of look in London, places with cheaper prices than in the U.S. Not everything (especially Ralph Lauren) is going to cost less in London, but there are a lot of buys out there and many more choices at prices that are competitive to the U.S. Furthermore, shabby has never looked as good as it does in London, so get with the team and buy it where it originated. Why have the copy when you can get the real thing?

ENGLISH DESIGN

After all, the real thing has taken generations to develop. However, fear not. Thanks to the foresight of a group of designers, antiques dealers, and fabric manufacturers, and having nothing whatsoever to

English Design 225

do with Pamela Harriman, the English Look has been packaged and is for sale in London.

You can actually wander throughout certain areas of London and see showroom after showroom, each with a different—but totally acceptable—version of The Look.

Many Americans give Laura Ashley credit for popularizing the use of English patterns and actually sprucing up the colors to appeal to a worldwide audience. Truth is, Laura Ashley popularized a bastardized version of Country Chic with tiny flowers and a dense repeat.

The use of authentic Country English style actually goes back to the beginnings of Colefax & Fowler over 50 years ago; there is no question that John Fowler is the grandfather of The Look as we know it now. And having Colefax & Fowler prints in your home is a status symbol.

It's been said that the British national character is one that resists change, has tremendous respect for tradition, and likes to do things the way they have always been done in generations past. So it is with English decorating: the themes show a slow transition as generation after generation adds only a small mark to the whole look.

While the British have a healthy respect for eccentrics, English style has touches of eccentricism woven into the traditional art forms. Even Vanessa Bell's Charleston House with its 1930s Arts and Crafts revival wackiness is considered a classic British take.

Eccentrics have always been appreciated (try buying a piece of Clarice Cliff pottery these days without flinching), but period continuity is what Americans count on as part of the base of goods available to them. With that come the essentials of the English lifestyle that Americans seek to absorb, emulate, or simply mimic: dog, horse, garden. Flowers and more flowers.

I mean sure, there has been a yuppie movement toward the affordable in London; not everyone inherits a fully furnished castle. But when Americans come to Britain to buy design, they pretty much want The Look.

You don't need a taxi to Jerry's after all.

FRENCH DESIGN

While many middle-class French people think that **Habitat** offers fine French design, and I don't want to begin to disagree with them, there are a few French multiples that have taken on in London. After years, **Souleiado** has gone out—but that's a financial problem that has to do with their parent firm, not the wonderful Provençal prints. **Les Olivades** is still great, and still in business on Walton Street.

My favorite newcomer that has really taken London tabletop by its forks is **Genevieve Lethu** (132 Brompton Road, SW3—Tube: Knightsbridge), who has opened up a small shop right across the street from Harrods. This already takes guts. How can you not like her?

Real English stylists who want French buy it in France.

SHOPPING THE SOURCES

There are a few rules of which you ought to be aware when buying in London:

- Have plenty of business cards on hand—if you are working as a member of the trade, introduce yourself when you enter a shop; ask upfront what trade discount or courtesies are offered.
- It is proper etiquette for dealers to identify themselves; they usually give themselves away by their knowledge anyway, but go ahead, tell 'em who you are. If you've brought along an expert for a second opinion, don't be shy. Introduce.
- British decorating and design houses are not in the business of reducing prices unless you are an

established client with an open account. Be prepared to show that you are indeed a professional, that you have a credit rating, etc. It's best to have at least three references from big U.S. firms where you hold open accounts. It's not a bad idea to have U.S. showrooms write, call, or fax ahead to a London showroom before you arrive.
- Very often, English design firms will not take personal orders from out-of-towners. This is especially true if the firm has an agency in the country where you wish the goods to be shipped. They will not compete with their own overseas agents.
- Unlike U.S. design firms, British design firms will sell goods directly from their London showrooms to anyone. You don't even need to pretend you are a member of the trade.
- Be prepared to handle your own shipping.

In flea markets and at fairs:

- When shopping in a market such as **Bermondsey,** or on **Portobello Road,** expect to bargain. If you pay the price as marked, you will be overpaying. In this kind of circumstance, having a knowledgeable local at your side can be beneficial. As a member of "the trade" you are expected to know the proper value and negotiate accordingly. At least know the U.S. price for a similar item.
- Deal with cash when possible. Often a store will offer a discount for cash transactions because then they do not have to deal with credit-card fees. In the markets, only cash is accepted. Many stalls will not even take traveler's checks. If the store does not offer a discount for cash, ask to see the owner and make your point.

While you're there:

- When you are in the fabric house, ask if there are any close-out bins. Quite often, fabrics are

discontinued or half rolls are sold and the showroom cannot sell the pieces left. There just might be some wonderful leftovers that are perfect for your home or for a piece of furniture you hadn't thought of re-covering.
- When buying wallpaper, ask about the life expectancy of the paper. Once again, printing processes differ, and the wallpaper you are dying for could in fact be printed on a paper that is not as sturdy as your needs. Many of the **Laura Ashley** papers are wonderful, but have a life expectancy of only four to five years. Some are not coated, and they absorb dirt at a rapid rate. These are considerations that every designer worries about when

---

Measure for Measure

English fabrics are sold by the meter or the yard. Ask.

Wallpaper rolls are very often double rolls, not single rolls. That is to say, one single British roll measures almost as long as two American-sized rolls. Ask.

Always verify the width of the fabrics (most American fabrics are 54 inches wide) and the size of the repeat, as both will affect the amount you need to purchase. If you are buying for a particular piece of furniture, take the measurements of the piece and a photo with you. Most fabric houses have trained staff who will help you determine how much fabric is necessary for your job. If there is any question, buy extra. Yes, you might be able to find the same fabric at home, but the dye lot will be completely different and your two pieces will never match. You are safer having the extra for pillows, if you don't need it for your job.

Allow for the repeat. If you have no idea what I am talking about, you should reconsider your abilities as an interior designer.

doing a design job. Since you will be doing it yourself, you, too, must be aware! There are Laura Ashley vinyl wallpapers, but there are two types: British vinyl and American-made vinyl from a different company. Not all patterns are made by both houses.
- If you are buying fabrics that need trimmings to match, buy them at the same time and with the fabrics in hand. The English trimmings (fringes, ropes, tassels, etc.) are designed and colored to match the fabrics. Do note that in Britspeak, the word "fringe" refers to the bangs of a hairstyle. Use the word "trim." These trimmings are not cheap, but they can be much, much less in England than in the U.S. Also, the London selection is superior to what you'll find in the U.S.

Other tips:

- If you are planning to buy a lot of furniture, make arrangements with a shipper before you start your spree (see page 236). Very often the fabric houses will ship for you, but the furniture dealers prefer that you make your own arrangements. If you are buying antiques valued at over £2,000, you will need to have an export license from the British Customs offices. A good shipper will also help arrange this for you. It is easier to have all your goods arrive in one container than in dispersed shipments. Ask your shipper if they will pick up from a variety of sources and if there is any charge for this extra service. Be sure to get the best insurance possible on your goods. Don't save money on shipping. Shop the options, but buy the best.
- When buying at auction be aware that you will be bidding against dealers who know their goods and what they are worth. Do a very careful inspection of the auction items the day before and check carefully for repairs and/or replacement of parts. The technology of furniture repair has made

it possible to repair and/or replace damaged parts of a piece of furniture without the untrained eye being able to see the work. If you are not buying to collect but only to enjoy, this won't matter. However, if you are collecting Georgian antiques, every repair changes the value of the piece. If the dealers are not bidding, take their cue that something is wrong. If you want a piece badly enough, however, you can very often outbid the dealers. They need to resell the piece to make a profit and therefore need to stop well under the street value for that piece. This is where you will have the advantage. You can save money and get a valuable piece of furniture/art/carpet or collectible while having the fun of beating the dealer.

- When buying period pieces, whether at auction, through a dealer, or at a stall, remember to get papers of authenticity. Any item 100 years old or older is free of U.S. Customs duties. However, you will be asked for proof of age by officials. They are on to tricks in this area, so don't try to pass off a new tea service as antique. However, this is also a gray area in British law. If you buy a chair that is Georgian but has had some parts replaced, this would be considered a reasonable restoration and would be fine. But if more than half of the chair has been restored so that most of the parts are new, the law is not clear, and your chair may not be considered duty free.

- Don't expect to be able to buy a national treasure. Important pieces must be approved for export by the country of origin before they are granted an export license. If you are bidding against a museum in an auction, it is quite possible that the work will be awarded to the museum even though you can outbid them. All countries are unwilling to let go of their finest works of art and furniture.

- If the work of art or piece of furniture is not wanted by the museum, be sure that the price you are paying is not more expensive (taking shipping, insurance, etc., into account) than it would be to buy a similar piece through a dealer in the U.S.

BOOKING ENGLISH STYLE: PART 1

If you're as interested in English style and decor as much as I am, you'll have a ball with all the magazines your news agent can sell you. Go to several different news agents, because even the biggies in the train stations don't always have the full range.

BOOKING ENGLISH STYLE: PART 2

British publishing has far more choices in the subjects of design, architecture, style, crafts, and reference for buying antiques. Alas, British book prices are also outrageously high. Make sure there is no American edition to a book you are planning to buy before you go hog wild at your nearest **Hatchards** or **Dillon's**.

Also, note that if you buy price guides, prices will be in pounds sterling pegged to local values; many items are more (or less) valuable across the pond.

For an almost staggering selection of books on design—not just British—be sure to visit the **Design Centre of London,** which has a huge book-selling space divided into many categories of the arts, including architecture.

DESIGN CENTRE OF LONDON
28 Haymarket, SW1 (Tube: Piccadilly Circus).

DESIGN ON SALE

Not only do showrooms have sales, but there are big social sale events held once or twice a year—usually to raise funds for charity—where designer furnishings are sold off. The Grand Sale is an annual event sponsored by *House & Garden* and held in a huge hall for maximum fun; it's usually in the fall—ask your hotel concierge or watch for ads in the magazine's pages.

Also pick up brochures in design showrooms; frequently they announce sale events.

CHELSEA DESIGN WEEK

This is an event for the trade: it includes complimentary chauffeur-driven cars to whisk you to various participating showrooms, where they lay it on thick. Only the big names play. One day is open to the public. The event is usually in March; write Chelsea Design Week, The Basement, 4 Charlwood Place, London SW1V 2LU.

AUCTIONS

The designer's best secret is the London auction, where more and more people are hoping to get a deal. Because prices are set at auctions and then determined for similar items throughout the art and furniture world, you may not find a bargain at all. Naturally, the London auction scene is the big time, whereas country auctions are easier to deal with and may offer better prices. I must admit, with a warning, that we went to a country auction and found that the furniture was desirable and well-priced, but the cost of shipping it back to the U.S. did not justify buying anything.

Nevertheless, auctions are a tremendous amount of fun and should be considered for pure entertainment's sake. In London, however, there are certain auctions that are quite serious and important and, while fun, are taken without much of a sense of humor. If you attend a big auction at a prestigious house, ask around about proper wardrobe.

Ladies should plan on simple suits or silks for day. Evening auctions can be black-tie events—they are seldom white-tie. Viewings are almost always during the day, as are the majority of auctions. Proper business clothes are essential, even if one isn't bidding.

Like all major cities, London has an auction season: October to May. Country auctions are often held in the summer, but fancy auctions are held only at auction houses in the city during the season. Occasionally auctions are closed to the public—like the fur auctions in St. Petersburg, where pelts are sold to furriers in lots—but usually you can be admitted to an auction by catalog or for free. Weekly auction programs are published in *The Times* on Tuesday and in *The Daily Telegraph* on Monday. Some houses sell certain types of works on specific days of the week, like china on Monday and European oil paintings on Friday—or something like that. In season, there will be about a hundred auctions a month in London alone.

It would be a mistake to assume that everything you buy in an auction is a bargain. Or real, for that matter. You have seen that James Bond movie about the Faberge Easter Egg, haven't you?

Various auctions have various functions in their respective fields; often it is to set the prices for the rest of the world. On the other hand, you should not be intimidated. You may indeed get a real "steal," or you may be shopping in a country where the market price for an item you are interested in is considerably less than in the U.S.

Please note that there is no VAT on antiques.

Do be wary of fakes at auctions, particularly from the less famous houses. If you buy an item because you love it, and if it doesn't matter whether it's real or not, that's one thing. But, if you are buying for investment, name-dropping, or status-seeking purposes, use a house expert or, better yet, a private expert as a consultant. The better houses will not intentionally sell you a forgery or a fake; small-time auctioneers may not care what's in the lots, as long as they move them out. A house may even admit they don't know if a piece is authentic. **Sotheby's** uses the full name of an artist in the catalog listing when they know the work is authentic, but only the initials of the artist if they have some doubt as to the provenance of the work.

The experts at the big auction houses are trained to not only know their stuff, but also to be informative and polite. If you want to bone up on a point of curiosity or just pick someone's brain, wander into a good auction house and speak to someone at the front desk. They well may give you information you never knew or turn you on to a free and expert opinion.

The most famous auction houses in London are **Sotheby's** and **Christie's**, but don't underestimate **Phillips** or **Bonham's**, which have been around since 1793.

BONHAM'S CHELSEA
65-69 Lots Road, SW10 (Tube: Take a taxi!).

BONHAM'S KNIGHTSBRIDGE
Montpelier Street, SW7 (Tube: Knightsbridge).

CHRISTIE'S
8 King Street, St. James's, SW1 (Tube: Piccadilly Circus or Green Park).

South Kensington, 85 Old Brompton Road, SW7 (Tube: Earl's Court).

PHILLIPS
101 New Bond Street, W1 (Tube: Bond Street).

10 Salem Road, WC2 (Tube: Bayswater).

SOTHEBY'S
34-35 New Bond Street, W1 (Tube: Bond Street).

There are also stamp and coin auctions. **Harmer's** (91 New Bond Street, W1; Tube: Bond Street) is the leading stamp auction house; **Stanley Gibbons**, another famous house, has an auction about six times a year, 399 The Strand, WC2 (Tube: Charing Cross). Don't forget country auctions that you may find on a weekend outing, which usually are charming—but if they had something truly important to sell, it would have gone to a big house in a major city to command a big price. So enjoy. At a country auction, expect to pay cash for your purchase. Be prepared to have to make your own shipping arrangements (see page 236).

When you shop at an auction of any kind, remember:

- The house is not responsible for the authenticity of the article.
- There is a house commission charged to the seller, but the buyer will have to pay taxes. Some houses also commission the buyer—ask, as this can raise the price of your item by another 10%. This is called the buyers premium. There's a recent trend, in order to reel in the big auctions, for the house to cut the commission but up the premium. Know your terms and ask questions.
- You are entitled to know the price a similar item went for in previous years and the price the house expects the item to go for at the current auction. Often these prices are posted at the viewing or may be published in the catalog. The house's expectation of what something will go for at auction proves meaningless several times a year, but it is a beginning.
- Find out before you bid what currency you must pay in. International houses often accept many currencies, and you may do better with your dollar converting to one rather than another. This can pay off with a large purchase.
- If bidding is not in U.S. dollars, keep a calculator in your hand during the bidding to know what the prices are; remember to do your figure at the current American Express rate of exchange rather than the bank rate. The bank rate will be more favorable than the one you will actually

be paying, so don't cheat yourself from an accurate conversion of what you will truly be paying.
- Expect to pay tax on the item when you call for it. Find out the tax ahead of time. VAT is not paid on antiques.
- The auction house may pack and ship your purchase for you, but it may be cheaper to do it yourself, or ask your hotel concierge to handle it for you.
- Make sure that the item you are about to buy may leave the country! Some countries won't let you out with what they consider to be items of their heritage. Conversely, make sure you can get it into the U.S. You will not be reimbursed if the government confiscates any of your property. If the item is an antique, get the papers that verify its age. According to Customs, an antique is any item 100 years old or more.
- Don't bid against Bill Gates.

SHIPPING

The good news: You've just found the most wonderful, gorgeous, fabulous, chic, and inexpensive sideboard. You've longed for one for years, know it will be the envy of all who see it.

The bad news: It certainly won't fit into your suitcase.

Whether the item is as cumbersome as a sideboard, as small as a few bottles of perfume, or as fragile as dinner plates, you can arrange to ship it home. All it takes is a little time and a little more money.

You will want to know enough about shipping costs to be able to make a smart decision about the added cost of your purchase. To make shipping pay, the item—with the additional cost of shipping, duty, and insurance (and Customs agent, etc., if need be)—still should cost less than it would at home, or be so totally unavailable at home that any price makes it a worthwhile purchase. If it's truly unavailable (and isn't an antique or a one-of-a-kind art item) at home, ask yourself why. There may be a good reason—such as it's illegal to bring such an item into the country! If you are indeed looking for a certain type of thing, be very familiar with American prices. If it's an item of furniture, even an antique, can a decorator get it for you with a 20% rather than a 40% markup? Have you checked out all the savings angles first?

There are basically two types of shipping: surface and air. Air can be broken down two ways: unaccompanied baggage and regular airfreight.

Surface mail is the cheaper of the two. Surface mail may mean through the regular mail channels—i.e., a small package of perfume would be sent through parcel post—or it may require your filling an entire shipping container, or at least paying the price for use of an entire container. Many people make the mistake of assuming that only the weight of an item will matter in the shipping. While weight matters, there may be a 500-pound difference per price bracket!

A piano may weigh more than two Queen Anne chairs, but they may cost the same to ship. Surface mail may take three months, but we've had delivery in three weeks. Allow three months to be safe, longer if so advised by the dealer.

If you are shipping books (antique or otherwise), note that there are special surface rates and no U.S. duties.

Generally speaking, rates are per cubic foot and include:

- Picking up the purchase.
- Packing the goods (crating may be extra).
- Handling export documents.
- Sea-freight charges.
- Customs clearance on the U.S. end.

If you want to save money, ask about groupage services. Your goods will be held until a shipping container is filled. The container will then go to the U.S., to only one of four ports of entry (Los Angeles, New York, San Francisco, or New Orleans), where you can meet the container at the dock, be there when your items are unpacked, and then pay the duties due. A full container is 1,100 cubic feet of space (or 8', 6" by 8', 6" by 20' long—or big enough for about one hundred pieces of furniture) and will not be delivered to your door (no matter how much you smile). A container to New York will cost you £3,000, which includes wrapping, shipping, and London paperwork. U.S. collections and bills of lading usually add £100 to the bill. Insurance costs 1-1/2 of the total value of the goods.

Air freight is several times more expensive than surface, but has the assurance of quick delivery. You can air-freight small items up to 50 pounds (in weight, not price) through traditional business services such as DHL and Federal Express. Or you can use freight services which will air-freight larger-sized packages and even furniture.

If your purchase was so delicate and so important as to need to be flown, it might indeed need an international courier, who is a person who hand-carries the item for you. (This is often done with pieces of art or valuable papers.)

You can find a list of shippers and packers in the back of the book *Guide to the Antique Shops in Britain* (dated), published by Antiques Collectors Club.

Among the most famous names in the trade:

- **Lockson Services Ltd.**, 29 Bloomfield St., E1 (Telephone 171-515-8600; fax 171-515-4043).
- **Fentons**, Beachy Road, Old Ford, E3 (Telephone: 181-533-2711; fax:181-985-6032).
- **Featherston Shipping**, 24 Hampton House, 15-17 Ingate Place, SW8 (Telephone: 171-720-0422; fax: 171-720-6330).

- **Gander & White,** 21 Lillie Road, SW6 (Telephone: 171-381-0571; fax: 171-381-5428).
- **Davies Turner,** Overseas House, Stewarts Road, SW8 (Telephone: 171-622-4393; fax 171-720-3897).

When you choose a shipper, ask for a buying kit.

INSURANCE

Insurance usually is sold by the package by your shipper. Do not assume that it is included in the price of delivery, because it isn't. There are several different types of insurance, with deductibles or all-risk (with no deductible), so you'll have to make a personal choice based on the value of what you are shipping. Remember when figuring the value of the item for insurance purposes to include the price of the shipping.

If you bought a desk for $1,000 and it costs $500 to ship it home, the value for insurance purposes is $1,500. If you have the replacement-cost type of insurance, you should probably double the price, since that is approximately what it would cost you to replace the item in the U.S.

CHINA, CRYSTAL & SILVER RESOURCES

The British are blessed with a crazy location in the sea of geography: they've got coal and they've got clay. As a result, they have a centuries-old tradition of producing bone china. You can visit the china factories in the countryside (see *Born to Shop Great Britain*), or you can visit all the china stores in London.

- Most china stores in London sell only first-quality. The prices are usually 30% less than in the U.S., but if the dollar is bad, that saving may shrink. During sales, especially in January, you may discover a 50% savings. During sales, some of the biggies (like **Harrods** and **Lawley's**, for example) do truck in seconds, which are so marked.

- The problem with really saving big on china comes with the shipping. China must be packed, crated, insured, and—in some cases—you must pay duty on it (not if it comes home in parcels worth under $50 and marked "unsolicited gift"). Even with VAT refunds, you will still raise the cost of your purchase appreciably. But, that doesn't mean you shouldn't consider a big haul. It just means you need to mentally register the landed price, not the asking price.

- Prices on the same items are supposed to be the same in each retail outlet, but may vary by as much as £2 per place setting. If a retailer is overstocked with a certain pattern, he may deal on the price of a large order.

- If you want to buy seconds, consider a trip to Stoke-on-Trent; if not, come to London for the January and June/July sales, or even order by telephone during a sale period. **Harrods** has a toll-free phone number during the January sale, to make it even easier.

- Silver, even silver plate, is getting more and more expensive each year, but is still a good bet when bought secondhand. Avoid the fancy stores and stick to street markets, such as **Bermondsey** or the famous **The London Silver Vaults** (page 244). By law, silver must be marked—look for marks, or ask. To bring silver (or plate) into the U.S. tax-free, it must be over 100 years old. Get a receipt that says so from the dealer at the time of purchase.

- England is also famous for its lead crystal, although the most famous brands come from Ireland or Scotland. You can buy crystal during the big sale periods when you buy china, or head for the factory-outlet stores, which usually feature the best prices on discontinued patterns. If you are filling in an existing pattern, you may want to buy at the airport either in London or Shannon.

CHINACRAFT
98 The Strand, WC2 (Tube: Charing Cross).

Chinacraft offers stock on all the biggies—Spode, Minton, Royal Crown Derby, Wedgwood, Aynsley, Coalport, and Royal Worcester. Quite a selection of crystal is available, including patterns from Waterford and Baccarat.

Oh, yes, and here's a little secret or two for you about Chinacraft: If you buy a lot (over $500), see if you can politely negotiate a discount. The salespeople are used to big spenders who will come in and order half a million pounds' worth of delectables, but you can buy less and still get a discount—if you are nice. Discounts vary on stock—if they have a lot of something they want to move out, they will discount it up front. Anyone walking in may ask about a pattern, and they may tell you that they'll take 15% off on that pattern. On another pattern—perhaps one that is out of stock and has to be ordered for you—a discount would be impossible. It's all very flexible.

A catalog with prices in dollars costs $5, but best news of all, Chinacraft comes to the U.S. and takes hotel space to show their goodies in major U.S. cities. You may go for tea and order your goods at London prices. You also may phone. You are guaranteed safe delivery.

People often wonder why one would shop here rather than at **Reject China Shop** (see page 243). So here goes: The two offer entirely different attitudes and shopping experiences. Please note that prices may not vary significantly! Chinacraft is a somewhat elegant store selling masses of fancy merchandise; Reject China is a mass store selling fancy merchandise as if it was discounted, which it often is not. Chinacraft gives you the personal attention

Thomas Goode
19 South Audley Street, W1 (Tube: Green Park or Hyde Park Corner).

If you're looking for the ultimate shopping experience for your selection of china, glassware, silver, or exquisite accessory pieces, this elegant shop is a must. In fact, if you were looking to pick one simple, very London, very elegant shopping experience that epitomizes why you travel, why you have to shop in foreign cities, and what can be gained by educating your eye in the world's best cities, well, Thomas Goode just might be your best choice.

The store is almost the size of a city block and rambles through a variety of salons; don't miss any of them—including the far back where the antique knickknacks are sold, or the far side where there is now a tea room (with very high prices).

Don't bring your children. Do bring your credit cards. And possibly your camera. Don't bring Ian.

Goode carries all the top European brands of china and crystal and has monogram services available on the premises. They have a number of innovative designs for tabletop and a lot of expensive doodads that you can also find at a plebeian place such as **Harrods,** but which are much more pleasing to the eye in the surroundings of Thomas Goode. The sales help is incredibly well-bred and nice.

No bargains here. Well, maybe that's not totally true. I bought a set of Jasperware cups and saucers on request by my friend Polly. They weren't in stock, so I ordered them. I then found the identical cups at the Reject China Shop—at the exact same price as at Thomas Goode.

Friends have told me there is a mark-up at Goode that you won't suffer elsewhere; the one time I tested that theory, it fell flat. I happen to think that £25 for a Wedgwood Jasperware cup that isn't yet available in America is a bargain.

Lawley's
154 Regent Street, W1 (Tube: Piccadilly Circus).

I love Lawley's because of the contrast in styles: its blue carpets and velvet cases and department-store elegance during the year, and its plank tables of bins of seconds during the sale periods. The selection is vast; the prices are fixed—as are everyone else's.

The sales are advertised in the regular newspapers (such as *The Times*, not *The Sun*) and are called midwinter and midsummer sales. That means the January sale is in the second to third week in January; ditto the summer sale—it's in the middle of June. Don't assume that all London summer sales are in July.

During the sale period, you will get factory prices right there in downtown London, on Regent Street, no less.

Plate collectors please note that Lawley's caters to the collector's set for all categories of china.

Reject China Shop
134 Regent Street, W1 (Tube: Piccadilly Circus).

33-35 Beauchamp Place, SW3 (Tube: Knightsbridge).

56-57 Beauchamp Place, SW3 (Tube: Knightsbridge).

Covent Garden, WC2 (Tube: Covent Garden).

After many years of shopping Regent Street and the wonders of London, I've about given up the thrill of this branch store. I just can't figure out where the bargains are, and I get overwhelmed by the stock and the tiny print on the price lists and the feeling that I can't find the bargain.

244 HOME FURNISHINGS & DESIGN RESOURCES

The last time I priced something at this great "bargain" source, it cost exactly the same amount as at Thomas Goode!

Still, the stores are convenient to the tourist trade and are stocked to make you think you've found rock-bottom prices. On Beauchamp Place, not far from the museums on Cromwell Road, there are three small stores with differing stock, which I actually find fun to browse, although frankly I haven't bought from this store in many years, because I think they infer a bargain without really delivering one.

The Covent Garden store is tiny and specializes in mass-market teapots with a few pieces of Portmerion and some blue-and-white; all at the going bargain price you can find around town. No bargains, but the store is tiny and crowded and cute and definitely part of the fun of shopping Covent Garden.

There is also a large store on Regent Street; most of the action is downstairs.

They are used to tourists and will ship for you with ease. Catalogs/mail-order/telephone orders with credit cards. Prices on some items are 20% less than the fixed prices; you can deal on big orders. Discuss the VAT refund and shipping prices carefully and make sure everything is clear to you. It helps to come with a price list of your pattern from the U.S. if you are after real savings. Firsts are often priced exactly the same as in non-discount stores; "bargains" may or may not be better than anyone else's bargains.

This is a good place to shop, but don't fool yourself into thinking it's the best place in town.

THE LONDON SILVER VAULTS
53-64 Chancery Lane, WC2 (Tube: Chancery Lane).

Originally founded in 1882 as a large safety-deposit box and now in the Holborn section of London, the Silver Vaults comprise 35 shops selling a variety of large and small items at all prices. Only one shop is at street level; the rest are underground. Expect to find everything from silver buckets to Faberge jewelry.

ENGLISH MODERNE

Contemporary looks are frequently combined with old-fashioned architectural styles in London; the look has moved through the 1960s and come out the other end with clean lines and moderate prices.

Heals
198 Tottenham Court Road, WC (Tube: Tottenham Court Road).

Heals is the mother of English Modern Design and the source of Terence Conran's inspiration. Heals is a furniture and lifestyle department store in the real-people part of London now far from Regent Street (it takes some degree of purpose to get there). It is expensive and offers similar looks to all modern housewares stores but better quality and therefore higher prices. You'll find the squishy sofa of your dreams here (hardly a tourist item) and plenty of yummy bedlinen and tabletop. Convenient to the store is a branch of practically everything else as well so that you can see the same looks established by Heals and then copied at Habitat and Pier One imports. They have great sales.

Habitat
196 Tottenham Court Road, W1 (Tube: Goodge Street).

206 King's Road, SW3 (Tube: Sloane Square).

Habitat made British home-furnishings history, although not in the same way as Mr. Chippendale. After the spare Scandinavian look came the modern British look—an update of Scandinavian chic with a touch of high tech. It was all begun by Terence

Conran, who was later knighted for his contribution to the world. Habitat, although no longer owned by Sir Terence, is still a glorious place to shop, even if the look isn't the newest look and you can see a lot of this stuff at home in the U.S.

Note that there is a difference between Habitat shops and **The Conran Shop** in Michelin House in London.

THE CONRAN SHOP
81 Fulham Road, SW3 (Tube: South Kensington).

The Conran Shop should not be confused with the now defunct Conran's in the U.S. The rehabbed Michelin House with its Deco tiles and hoopla welcomes you first into a cafe, and then a store of mini-showrooms with modern yuppie furniture. Go downstairs for a less stark and more moderately priced version of the first floor—here's where you'll find the fun: baskets, gifts, dried flowers, china, toys, books, foodstuffs, coffees, luggage, umbrellas . . . everything.

NEXT
160 Regent Street, W1 (Tube: Piccadilly Circus or Oxford Circus).

The bigger Next shops have small decorating/home-furnishing areas where you can buy table arts, gifts, and usually fabrics, sheets, etc. The style is another version of what you're probably already familiar with from Conran's Habitat or the Pottery Barn, but prices are modern and the look is competitive with whatever else is hot in the design trends.

FABRICS, FURNITURE & OBJETS D'ART

It is hard to separate the fabrics, furniture, and collectibles sources from each other. Most often a fabric showroom will also carry a line of furniture,

Fabrics, Furniture & Objets d'Art 247

and a furniture dealer will have an exclusive line of fabrics. Many of the showrooms make individual items out of their fabrics—cosmetics bags, novelty gifts, etc.

DESIGNER'S GUILD
267-271 and 277 King's Road, SW3 (Tube: Sloane Square).

Tricia Guild has been going for a long time with her Designer's Guild, one of the best-known sources in town for all the pieces you need to put together a look. She has prospered because she has been able to change that look and not grow stale. She also brings on board others to help out and create a fresh face—hence the current line by **Kaffe Fassett.**

The effect is stupendous. If you're tired of the old Country English look, you'll revel in all this color and excitement. There are two shops, a few doors apart. Don't miss either. Even if you aren't going to buy so much as a meter of fabric, come in and absorb all the trends. This is hot. Warehouse sales are advertised annually. Open to the public.

JOHN STEFANIDIS
253 Fulham Road, SW3 (Tube: Fulham Broadway).

One of the big-time hotshots of British interiors with his own books and his own following, Stefanidis offers a more modern version of John Colefax, without a look over the shoulder to the English manor house: no big cabbage roses to blind you. The small showroom offers two floors of things to look at, including wallpaper, fabric, furniture, and some gift items. We're talking about $50 for a roll of wallpaper—but an English roll of wallpaper is double the size of an American one. The shop is in a wonderful location near a string of other design showrooms and antiques shops; anyone may browse and buy.

Anna French
343 King's Road, SW3 (Tube: Sloane Square).

Although Anna French features a lot of lace and lacy looks, her design showroom offers a complete range of all the items necessary to the Country English post-modern look: marbleized wallpapers, faux finishes, swags of lace, fabrics printed with big flowers that aren't cabbage roses. The look would coordinate well with many **Jane Churchill** or **Designer's Guild** choices; there's a lot of Arts and Crafts inspiration in current works. But more classical possibilities are also available. Open to the public.

Jane Churchill
81 Pimlico Road, SW1 (Tube: Sloane Square).
135 Sloane Street, SW1 (Tube: Sloane Square).

The line designed by Jane Churchill is English in feeling (it goes with her last name), but international in scope. It's higher in cost than **Laura Ashley**, but with a younger look than **Colefax & Fowler**. The look is very packaged and is positioned a few rungs up from Laura Ashley. The line and look have expanded to various forms of Cutie Pie; I find the dancing veggies a bit much but at least the woman is not vegetating. Quite affordable and worth looking at.

Trade operates a separate business; the shops provide regular retail for the general public.

Nicholas Haslam
12 Holbein Place, SW1 (Tube: Sloane Square).

To show you are "in," please refer to this man as "Nicky" and act like you know him and his famous touch: his handmade kilim shoes. The shop is on a small street that intersects Pimlico Road and Sloane Square. His showroom is a wonderful collection of every period and style, with preference to none. The truth is that Nicky Haslam is one of London's more sought-after designers, with a very versatile design

Nina Campbell
9 Walton Street, SW3 (Tube: South Kensington).

One of the most famous names in London design, Ms. Campbell became well-known to Americans when she stepped in to rescue the Duke and Duchess of York from their American design team. Turns out her career lasted longer than the Duchess of York's.

Obviously, you work with her personally to design your estate, but her small shop does have some gifts and things to drool over; there is also a boutique in **Harvey Nichols** with more of the same merchandise. I bought a fabric-covered "bulletin board" (the chicest bulletin board ever created, I might add) for a wedding present—it was £35, but so sophisticated you could die for it.

Valerie Wade
108 Fulham Road, SW6 (Tube: South Kensington).

My friend Marie tells me I have to shop here every time I come to London. Last trip I really did try, but I couldn't find it . . . it didn't help that I wrote the address incorrectly. Marie says the shop is small, but not that small. She buys needlepoint rugs and various accessories here each trip over and since I trust Marie's taste impeccably, I wish you the best of luck in finding Valerie. Tell her I'm on my way.

ENGLISH FABRICS

Osborne & Little
304 King's Road, SW3 (Tube: Sloane Square).

Along with **Colefax & Fowler**, Osborne & Little reigns as top of the line for The Look. The firm began as antiquarian booksellers, with a sideline of hand-printed wallpapers. However, when Sir Peter Osborne and his brother-in-law Anthony Little won the Council of Industrial Design Award for their first wallpaper collection in 1968, they began a revolution in the interior design and manufacturing business. Shortly after, the firm gave up the interior design aspect of the business to concentrate on the design and production of fine English wallpapers and fabrics.

Osborne & Little designs are wonderful because they are always based in history but not limited by it. A charming English botanical print might be reinterpreted in bolder colors. A whole line of wallpapers reflects the paint effects of marbleizing and stippling found in old Italian villas. Because they are now machine-produced, the fabrics and wallpapers are even affordable. The showroom is quiet and dignified, just the kind of place where you might like to have high tea.

Anyone may browse and buy.

COLEFAX & FOWLER
39 Brook Street, W1 (Tube: Bond Street).

110 Fulham Road, SW3 (Tube: South Kensington).

151 Sloane Street, SW3 (Tube: Sloane Square).

The king of English chic is located, appropriately, near South Molton Street and Old Bond Street, home to all the best designers. Entering the Colefax & Fowler showrooms is like taking a step into an English country home. The building was built in 1766 by Sir Jeffrey Wyattville and is clearly being held together with chintz. Inside, the rooms are the size of small sitting rooms, the carpet is worn, and the furnishings are old. However, this is all part of the mystique. Upstairs houses the most magnificent collection of English chintzes ever to be desired by an Anglophile. Every year their designers bring out a new collection of fabrics and wallpapers more beautiful than the previous year's—assuming you like the look, of course.

Anyone may browse and buy.

WARNER & SONS LTD.
7-11 Noel Street, W1 (Tube: Oxford Circus).

I keep a swatch of Warner fabric on my bulletin board, awaiting the day I can reupholster the living-room furniture. I'm not the only Warner fan; they hold a royal warrant.

Benjamin Warner began the firm in 1870 as a silk-weaving company. As a matter of fact, Warner & Sons still uses the original silk-weaving Jacquard hand looms for some of its work. The archives document over 30,000 fabrics by name of designer, year designed, and a sample of the fabric whenever possible. Warner will reproduce any of the designs in their archives for a minimum order of 120 meters per colorway. They will also custom-design a fabric for your job if a reproduction is not to your liking. Trade preferred.

ARTHUR SANDERSON & SONS LTD.
112-20 Brompton Road (Tube: Knightsbridge).

Okay, okay, the truth first. I know where one of the Sanderson factory-outlet stores is (it's in Manchester; see *Born to Shop Great Britain*) and I buy my Sanderson glazed chintzes for £5 a yard and brocades for £3! Indeed, Sanderson is one of Britain's most famous fabric houses; they celebrated their 125th anniversary in 1985.

If you can't make it to Manchester, there's an awfully nice showroom across from Harrods and you can buy gift items, bed linen, wallpaper, and all sorts of things . . . including modern made prints from William Morris originals. Prices are much better than in the U.S.

Chapter Ten

ANTIQUES, USED BOOKS & COLLECTIBLES

LONDON, QUEEN OF IT ALL

It isn't possible to write a chapter that completely covers the antiques and collectibles scene in London. There's just too much to it: the specialty dealers, the collectibles, the books and musical recordings—not to mention the fun you can have every minute of every day—even Sunday—shopping these sources!

My husband, Mike, has taken to the streets to help, but please note that with the brisk pace at which real estate is still changing hands these days, there are constant changes.

We've listed what we consider to be the best and the brightest in all the categories that comprise antiques and collectibles in London. This is not a complete directory to all of London's shops, sources, and dealers. It should provide enough sources to satisfy the novice shopper and to give the accomplished shopper (or dealer) a more than adequate overview, however. We hope that even if all you take away is ideas, you'll leave emotionally and visually satisfied by London's exciting antiques and collectibles scene.

The best thing for an American to remember about shopping for used items in London is that all prices are possible. While a lot of people pooh-pooh Portobello Road and say the bargains are gone, I disagree strongly. In fact, I have two things to say about Portobello, but they offer an entire overview of the antiques and collectibles scene in London:

- It ain't 1969 anymore.
- There's still plenty to buy.

The 1990s have their own language of value. There are plenty of bargains to be found on Portobello Road—if you know what you are doing. In fact, if you have only one day for antiques shopping in London and your budget is limited, I'd happily send you to Portobello Road. It's more fun on a Saturday, but during the week you'll find it calmer and more open to serious business.

I do not own museum-quality belongings; I am not particularly interested in what the trade calls "important" pieces—those that cost thousands of pounds and are collected by the rich and richer-still set.

We have a limited budget and want to have some fun with what we buy. I like to look in the showrooms and get ideas (Mike doesn't); I buy a lot of junk and rehab it.

When you shop London, try to get a mix of everything when you shop, and remember: You cannot get a good price until you know what the going price is; you cannot get a "bargain" until you know exactly what you are buying. Only by studying the finest examples can you decide if an item is a fake, a copy, a handsome repro, or a deal.

You can easily spend all your time in London seeing and learning. Ask a lot of questions; take a lot of time. After all, most of this stuff has been around for a hundred years or more. It'll keep.

BOOKING ANTIQUES

The London and Provincial Antique Dealers Association (LAPADA) publishes a paperback book called *Buying Antiques in Britain*, which is filled with advice, tips, resources, and advertising. Most of the ads have pictures. This is an invaluable little guide for those just getting started. You can buy it at antiques markets or through the association at 535 King's Road, London SW10.

There are also several collectors' magazines sold on newsstands; they have information on fairs and auctions and editorials about collecting. They usually cost about £2–3 an issue, but you'll enjoy them heartily. Try the *Antique Dealer and Collector's Guide* (U.S. subscriptions cost $50 a year), *Antique and Collectors' Fayre*, a more low-end collectors' magazine, and *Antique Collector*, published by the National Magazine Company and our favorite of the bunch (U.S. subscriptions cost $30). *The Collector* is a small-sized freebie published by Barrington Publications that is often given away in shops and includes maps of London's antiques areas, as well as the usual advertising and lists. A new consumer magazine called *Miller's Magazine* (£2), published by the famous couple, is the talk of the trade; BBC also has their own antiques magazine, price guide, and editorial based on their Roadshow experiences.

Most important to the trade is a tabloid newspaper called *Antiques Trade Gazette*, published each Wednesday by Metropress Ltd., 17 Whitcomb Street, London WC2. You can buy a single copy at some West End news agents or kiosks, or apply for an American subscription through Joyce Golden & Associates, 551 Fifth Avenue, New York, NY 10176.

DEFINING ANTIQUES

The U.S. government has been defining an antique as any object that is 100 years old, or older. There is some discussion that this rule will be changed to use the beginning of the 20th century as the new cutoff point. If you are sweating it out, ask before you leave home.

If your purchase does not meet this definition, it is merely "used," and you must pay duty on it at the regular rate.

ANTIQUES FAIRS

One of the best ways of learning something about the London antiques market is to attend a few antiques fairs. Antiques fairs come in several categories; most of the London ones are *vetted* (a committee certifies that all goods are genuine) and cost several pounds for admission. They may be associated with a charity or fancy-dress ball on opening night. Some fairs are vetted but less formal, and others are just plain old country fairs where anyone can show. By and large the antiques fair scene in London is serious, and normally the country shows are held in the country. In the city it's strictly the big time.

While goods are sold at these fairs, I certainly don't buy them. In fact, I use these big-name fairs merely as an educational device to learn about quality; I cannot begin to afford to buy at these fairs. To be quite honest about it all, I sometimes find the price of admission to such an event more than I can bear—the thought of actually buying an item is almost obscene.

Learning to establish fair prices on authentic items is imperative if you are going to shop in non-vetted markets or fairs; otherwise you can expect to be cheated. Use museums, auction houses, and high-quality fairs as your educational stomping grounds to bone up on the best of Britain.

To get dates of fairs, check *Miller's Magazine* or the trade periodicals (see page 254), ask your concierge or the British Tourist Authority, or check out our list of the standing events. There are usually four fairs a month, although most of these are not famous. You can also write to the fair organizers for more information (see below).

Also, note that each fair has its own rep, its own crowd, and its own fame. Some fairs are fancy-shmancy (the month of June is chockablock with these events, which are almost part of The Season), while some are ragtag affairs. Anything at Alexandra Palace is my kind of fair; anything at the Grosvenor House is not. Although, I do appreciate that Grosvenor House is about the social season first and antiques are just a means to an end, so I do get the picture. I'm just not part of the picture.

Only you know what's inside your wallet and your living room.

Olympia Decorative Arts and Antiques Fair

Earls Court Exhibition Centre, SW5, is an international fair; several hundred dealers participate. Stands are most often arranged as room sets. The date of the event is often piggybacked with another big fair so that people can plan to attend both. Olympia is usually considered a less expensive fair than some of the other high-end ones, but it is not a jumble sale. It is a vetted event. Call 181-385-1200 for more information, or contact Philbeach Events Ltd., Earls Court Exhibition Centre, London SW5. (Tube: Kensington Olympia)

The Little Chelsea Antiques Fair

Chelsea Old Town Hall, King's Road, SW3, is held twice a year with less than a hundred participating dealers, and should not be confused with the **Chelsea Antiques Fair,** a bigger and fancier show (see page 258). Both are vetted. (Tube: Sloane Square)

West London Antiques Fair

Kensington Town Hall off Kensington High Street, W8, is one of two fairs run by the Penman Antiques Fairs Company, the other one being the **Chelsea Antiques Fair** (see page 258). This fair, like the Chelsea, is held twice yearly (August is the second time) and attracts good-quality dealers. (Tube: High Street Kensington)

Grosvenor House Antiques Fair

Grosvenor House Hotel, Park Lane, W1, is one of the best antiques fairs held in London and is timed each year to run after the Derby (say "Darby," darling) and before Ascot and Wimbledon. This is The Season, my dears. The top antiques dealers from all over Britain are invited to exhibit their best pieces, and everything except paintings has to be over 100 years old. A committee reviews all items for authenticity. This is also one of the top social events of the season, and watching the crowds is as much fun as examining the antiquities—some are the same vintage. There is a preview night before opening; it's a formal gala at £500 a pop. (Tube: Hyde Park Corner)

International Ceramics Fair

Held at the Dorchester Hotel, Park Lane, W1, this has become an annual event with a substantial following. The fair usually coincides with the

Grosvenor House Antiques Fair (see above), because they complement each other. Some of the antique glass pieces on exhibit here are so delicate that the technique of getting them from the fair to your home would pose an interesting problem. All forms of ceramic-ware are on exhibit, including those from other countries. (Tube: Marble Arch or Hyde Park)

Antiquarian Book Fair

Park Lane, Piccadilly, W1, does not have much to do with furnishings; however, no good library would be complete without a rare book or two in its collection. Collectors and dealers swap stories and collection items, including book illustrations and prints. (Tube: Green Park or Hyde Park)

Chelsea Antiques Fair

Chelsea Old Town Hall, King's Road, SW3, is held twice yearly, in March and September. Our favorite time to go is September, because the weather usually is wonderful and most of the tourists have left town. However, the March fair is not as crowded, and better deals might be made then. This fair has been going on for over 60 years and probably will continue for another 260. Note that this venue is near several King's Road antiques galleries. (Tube: Sloane Square)

The British Antique Dealers' Association Fair

The Duke of York's Headquarters, SW3, is another Chelsea fair held in early May. It usually kicks off with a big charity gala. (Tube: Sloane Square)

STREET MARKETS

In London, many market areas are so famous that they have no specific street address. It's usually enough to name the market to a cabbie, but ask your concierge if you need more in the way of directions. Buses usually service market areas, as may the tube. There are markets that have everything from clothing to jewelry to books and art. Some specialize in antiques; see page 255 for more on serious antiques markets, and page 265 for the antiques supermarkets.

APPLE MARKET
Covent Garden, WC2 (Tube: Covent Garden or Charing Cross).

The Apple Market is the official name of the marketplace held under the rooftops of Covent Garden in the courtyard space between the brick lanes of stores. This is a rotating affair which usually houses craftspeople, so this is the part where you get out the highlight pen: antiques are sold on Mondays *only*, in order to coordinate with the antiques goings-on across the way at the **Jubilee Market.**

There are three markets at Covent Garden, within a sneeze of each other, so if you care to know where you are, please pay attention. There is a map on page 87.

It's easiest to understand what Apple Market is in contrast to the Jubilee Market. Jubilee is often junky; Apple is always classy. And it offers some of the best prices on British crafts.

The courtyard space is filled with vendors who set up little stalls and pin their wares to backdrops; sometimes boxes of loot are under the tables. The market is vetted, so the participants must apply for permission to sell and be granted an official space and day. If they show up on other days—which many do—they set up in stalls other than their regular one. Thus you can prowl the market on two different days of the week (ignore Mondays for this example) and see the same people in different places, with a few new faces interspersed. Mondays are more formal because this is the sole antiques day. Any day is a good day for the Apple Market.

Many vendors take plastic; some will bargain if you buy a lot. They don't get set up before 10 A.M., and many are still setting up at 11 A.M. They do stay there until dark, which is later in summers than winters.

JUBILEE MARKET
Covent Garden, WC2 (Tube: Covent Garden or Charing Cross).

It's not fair to compare the Jubilee Market to Bermondsey or even to Greenwich, because it's a small-time affair. Hell, it's not even fair to compare the Jubilee Market to the **Apple Market**, a few hundred yards away. Jubilee Market is basically a very touristy, teen-oriented, crass marketplace at the back of Covent Garden. However, on Mondays all the dealers (about 25 of 'em) are antiques dealers and the market is much more fun. It never turns high-end, but it is affordable and is very much worth a look.

Jubilee Market gets going earliest on Mondays: There are people there at 8 A.M., but since nothing else is open at that hour, you may find yourself high and dry and bored. The Apple Market dealers don't set up until about 10 A.M., so consider 9:30 A.M. as a good time to begin prowling Jubilee Market.

OPERA MARKET
Covent Garden, WC2 (Tube: Covent Garden).

This is the King Street market to Covent Garden and it is the junkiest market. It, too, sells antiques on Mondays; crafts and imports and cheap towels on other days of the week. This is not my favorite market in London. But while you're there, it shouldn't be a total loss. Oh yes? Guess I must confess that I bought a large Mickey Mouse at this market once; it cost £15 and was a gift for a business acquaintance at Disney. It was the size of a two- year-old child, in good shape, but without a tail. It was not easy to get it home from London or to Orlando, but when I did my friend called me with total delight—the gift was worth a fortune and if it had a tail would have been worth a serious fortune. Junky markets can pay off.

BERMONDSEY MARKET
Corner of Long Lane and Bermondsey Street at Bermondsey Square, SE1 (Tube: London Bridge, then cab it).

Also known as the **New Caledonian Market**. Open Friday only from 7 A.M. until 2 P.M. Go early for the best deals. Take a torch (flashlight) and elbow the dealers who are there to buy it all. Many of the deals are done out of the trunks of cars, or in the indoor cafe across the street. The dealers who are buying arrive as early as 5 A.M. and leave early too. The official market opens at 7 A.M., but by this time the good pieces will have left, only to appear the next day on **Portobello Road** or in **Camden Passage**.

There is also a covered market building across the street called the **Bermondsey Antiques Market and Warehouse**, which is run by the London Borough of Southwark (say "Suthack") as a commercial retail operation. There are around a hundred stalls. In this building you will find a bureaux de change and a cafe (entrance from the outside of the building).

Now then, this is one of the points on which Ian and I fight at least once a year: he says you must be at Bermondsey Market before noon because the dealers start to pack up by then; he says he knows better than I do because he not only lives in London, but lives near Bermondsey Market and passes there frequently in his motor car.

I say that I've been there at 2 P.M. when the dealers start to pack up and that it's not over until 3 P.M.

Either way, go early in the morning and then you won't have to worry about which one of us is right.

Should you get there any time after noon, do send us a postcard and let us know your opinion.

🛍 PORTOBELLO ROAD
Portobello Road, W11 (Tube: Notting Hill Gate).

Saturday in London means Portobello Road; Sunday means Greenwich. That's the way I love my London weekends, no matter what time of the year . . . even in slight drizzle.

I buy every time I'm in town. Not only antiques, but new items like hand-knit sweaters and cashmeres, dishes, reproductions of expensive botanicals that look great when framed, old linens, buttons, and more, more, more.

Here's the skinny: the people with the stands and tables and stalls are just there on Saturday. The shops behind them are also open on Saturday, but do not sell the stuff you see in the streets, so don't get your vendors mixed up. If you are a more serious antiques shopper, come back during the week and explore the three or four dozen serious shops (see page 274).

The street market is open from 6 A.M. to 4 P.M. on Saturday only. Some businesses open just Friday and Saturday; no one is open at all on Sunday. Don't forget to explore the shops on Pembridge Road and Westbourne Grove after you've shopped the full range of Portobello Road.

🛍 CAMDEN PASSAGE
Upper Street, Islington, N1 (Tube: Angel).

There are over 200 antiques stores open every day, and on Wednesday and Saturday the area becomes crowded, with hundreds of stalls selling just about everything imaginable. The more permanent shops have a good collection of fine-quality antiques; this is more upscale than **Portobello Road**. Open Monday, Tuesday, Thursday, and Friday from 10 A.M. to 5 P.M.; Wednesday and Saturday from 8 A.M. to 4 P.M.

Camden Lock
Camden High Street, NW1 (Tube: Camden Town).

This is definitely the lower end. Located in the Regents Canal section of Camden, where canals once provided a practical means to transport goods from the docks in the East to the main canal that carried on to Birmingham. However, the area around the Camden Lock has become the home of black-leather fashions and cheap old clothes. This is really a teenage vintage clothing neighborhood more than anything else; this is really a scene that may not be your cup of tea if you are over 40 and wash your hands regularly. Open Saturday and Sunday from 10 A.M. to 5:30 P.M.

Piccadilly Market
St. James's Church, Piccadilly, W1 (Tube: Piccadilly Circus).

For 15 years now the craftsmen and hippies have been meeting on Fridays and Saturdays in the churchyard right on Piccadilly to sell a less-than-perfect-but-still-fun selection of sweaters, imports, and knickknacks. There are too many imports for me to feel great about this market, but you can't fault the location or the fun. I've been buying vintage clothing from the dealer in the far right-hand corner (if you are facing the church from the street); there are Aran sweaters and kilts and other touristy items, as well as the usual incense burners from Nepal. The market is not very big or even very good, but I love it and think it's worth a browse.

GREENWICH MARKETS

I stand very loud and very firm on this fact: There is simply no better Sunday than the one you will spend in Greenwich, SE10. I've outlined the way that I do it as a tour (see page 310). Since the town is small and the weekend markets dominate, you can probably figure it all out on your own. The markets are held both Saturday and Sunday. I have been on a Saturday and find that I slightly prefer the vendors on Sunday (they are elsewhere on Saturdays), but if you can't get here on a Sunday, a Saturday will help convince you that Greenwich is an essential part of the shopper's London.

There are several markets in Greenwich, so the idea is to spend the day going from one to the next. The fact that Greenwich houses museums, ships, and sights of historical interest means little to me, even if there's no time like Mean Time. If you want to combine culture and shopping, arrange your schedule accordingly.

Crafts Market

The Crafts Market is held under a covered roof in the center of "downtown" and consists of rows of stalls selling merchandise much like at Covent Garden. The prices are slightly less than London.

Bosun's Yard

Around the corner from the Crafts Market, right at the waterfront, Bosun's Yard holds the overflow from the Crafts Market. It's a little too much for me: these are the dealers who just came back from Tibet and think they have something to sell, but it's a cute place and you can get an ice cream cone here.

Canopy Antiques Market

The scene of another one of Ian's and my many fights. He said, "You don't want to go to that market; it's very junky."

I said, "I know; it's my favorite market. I love junk."

You will not like this market if you don't like junk. This is of less standard quality than your average flea market or jumble sale. But I love it. The market sprawls for quite some bit; I enter at the far end—not where the truck says, "Beigels [sic] Sold Here."

The reason I enter from the far end is that this is where the jumble is; if you enter the first gateway, you have regular market stalls with new goods. I don't like these as much. The dealers in the back specialize in vintage clothing (there's an entire shed of it), home decor from the 1950s, costume jewelry, and then junk.

Greenwich Antiques Market

Believe it or not, none of the above are the antiques market for which Greenwich is famous! The one that started all the fuss is on the high street, which means it's the first market you reach if you arrive by train, or the last market you reach if you arrive by boat and return by train.

This market is not huge, but it's packed with fun. The dealers farthest from the street specialize in vintage clothing. The quality of the merchandise here cannot be classified as junk; there may even be a few true antiques.

Take BritRail from Charing Cross Station any Saturday or Sunday for a town filled with markets.

ANTIQUES & COLLECTIBLES SUPERMARKETS

Antiques supermarkets have been created to give the smaller but established dealers a permanent place to set up and display their wares. They are covered shopping centers for antiques, collectibles, and junk. The fun is figuring out which is which. Very often the dealer stalls change, especially in these hard times; therefore I'm not really pointing out faves. Since the buildings are not going anywhere fast, I suggest you plow through. Don't forget that if you catch a rainy day in London town, an antiques gallery or supermarket can keep you busy for hours. The other advantage to shopping at a covered market is that very often other services are offered: There are repair shops at **Grays**, bureaus de change at **Antiquarius** and **Grays,** and places to eat at all of them.

Grays
1-7 Davies Mews, 58 Davies Street, W1 (Tube: Bond Street).

These two buildings, located on the opposite ends of the same block, house over 300 antiques stalls containing every variety of item, large and small. Davies Street conveniently intersects South Molton Street at one end and Brook Street at the other, placing it directly in the heart of the big-name-designer section of London.

When you need a break from fashion, it is easy to breeze over to Grays and rest your eyes on some breathtaking antique jewelry, bound to coordinate with any purchase you have made on Bond Street. Don't miss the river tributary that runs decoratively through the basement of the Davies Mews building. The shops are open Monday to Friday from 10 A.M. to 6 P.M. only. They are not open on Saturday or Sunday.

You can grab a bite in the cute cafe on the lowest floor.

Alfie's Antiques Market
13-25 Church Street, NW8 (Tube: Edgware Road or Marylebone).

Alfie's is under the same ownership as **Grays** and houses another 150 stalls. It's a series of blue townhouses now joined together higgledly-piggledly, so you weave around a lot when you shop. This is well worth the trip; prices are moderate and dealers will deal. Because the location is a tad offbeat, the dealers tend to be a little more funky, so you get high quality and some value. This is perhaps one of the best supermarkets for seeing a lot and feeling that you're getting good value. And if anyone can get that dealer down on the green glass 1950s necklace, I'm willing to pay £15, but not a tuppence more. Not far from The Landmark Hotel. Closed Sunday and Monday. Open Tuesday through Saturday from 10 A.M. to 5:30 P.M.

ANTIQUARIUS
135-141 King's Road, SW3 (Tube: Sloane Square).

Located right on King's Road in Chelsea in the thick of several antiques venues, Antiquarius could be mistaken for a theater from the outside. In actuality it was constructed in an old snooker hall building dating way back when. With over 200 stalls, Antiquarius has gained a reputation for being the place to go for Art Nouveau and Art Deco pieces of every variety, from jewelry to furniture. There's also a very famous dealer (Sue Norman) for blue-and-white porcelain. Open Monday to Saturday from 10 A.M. to 6 P.M.

CHENIL GALLERIES
181-183 King's Road, SW3 (Tube: Sloane Square).

Chenil Galleries is more of a shopping arcade with a long thin thrust to the floor pattern and a swell chance to browse in good merchandise that is not intimidating. They have an art gallery and are known for being a good place to look for antique medical instruments, as well as 17th- and 18th-century paintings and smaller items. There's a sensational dealer for costume jewelry. Another one of the Chelsea galleries, this one should be combined with your visit to **Antiquarius**. Open Monday to Saturday from 10 A.M. to 6 P.M.

BOND STREET ANTIQUES CENTRE
124 New Bond Street, W1 (Tube: Bond Street).

Like **Grays**, the Bond Street Antiques Centre is located amid the finest in fashion and specializes in the finest of miniatures, porcelain, jewelry, silver, and paintings. This one is a tad fancy for my taste. Open Monday to Friday from 10 A.M. to 5:30 P.M.

OLD CINEMA
160 Chiswick High Road, W4 (Tube: Turnham Green).

From Bond Street to Chiswick High Road is a long way, I think Margaret Thatcher can tell you that, but if you're into a little more funky fun and want furniture, this is a department store turned warehouse. Open seven days a week with tons of stuff. Yes, you can get there on the tube—exit the station and turn left, get to the next road, turn left again, and there it is.

THE OLD CINEMA
157 Tower Bridge Road, SE1 (Tube: Tower Bridge).

Okay, so they've got two warehouses. This one is near Tower Bridge; I haven't been yet but I would combine it with a trip to Bermondsey Market. Although this market is open every day of the week and Bermondsey is only on Fridays.

ANTIQUES NEIGHBORHOODS

The best thing about antiques neighborhoods is that the good shops stay for a long while and they attract other shops, so that if one should close or move, another comes in, and an area stays stable, more or less. High rents plague London, like any big city, but these neighborhoods are nuggets where you can just wander and gawk.

Mayfair & Mount Streets (W1)

This is the most expensive part of London; the prices in the antiques shops reflect the rents and the unwritten law that objects displayed in windows must be dripping with ormolu. New Bond Street is the main source, but don't forget side streets such as Conduit Street, Old Bond Street, Vigo Street, and Jermyn Street. Mayfair is also headquarters for several auction houses, decorating firms, and big-time dealers. If you're just looking, make sure you're dressed to kill. If you're serious, you should probably have an appointment or a letter of introduction, or both. (Tube: Bond Street or Green Park)

If you like a fancy but good market, don't miss **Gray's**, the market (see page 266). If you like hoity with your toity, don't miss:

- S.J. Phillips Ltd., 139 New Bond Street
- Mallett & Son, 141 New Bond Street
- Wartski, 14 Grafton Street

Then there's Mount Street, which is a neighborhood unto itself although it is part of W1 and uses the same tube stops. This street begins, appropriately enough, with an **American Express** office (No. 89), where you will undoubtedly have to go for more cash. As a shopping destination, Mount Street is easy to miss because it's set back a little bit. It's sort of a two-block job, stretching from behind The Dorchester right to Berkeley Square, a sneeze from Bond Street.

Here you can find a group of excellent antiques shops; my favorites on this street include **Stair & Co.** (No. 14). Then you pass the Connaught to connect to more of Mount Street and **Blairman and Sons** (No. 119), and **John Sparks Limited** (No. 128).

Church Street/Marylebone (NW8)

Don't confuse this area with Kensington Church Street, which is an antiques area on the way to Portobello Road and is also in the same postal code.

This antiques area on the way to **Alfie's Antiques Market** is not comparable to Portobello Road, but is fun nonetheless, and pretty much affordable. Forget it on Monday. Aside from Alfie's, there's the **Gallery Of Antique Costume & Textiles** (2 Church Street), as well as **Simon Tracy** (No. 18), **Beverley** (No. 32), **Bizarre** (No. 24), **Risky Business** (two shops at Nos. 34 and 46), and **Pillows** (No. 48). This is kind of a funky neighborhood where you can wear casual clothes and not have to worry about the posh. (Tube: Edgware or Marylebone)

Covent Garden (WC2)

The neighborhoods surrounding Covent Garden, from Charing Cross to The Strand and over to Leicester Square, are known as important haunts for those interested in antique books, used books, stamps, records, and also ephemera. There are some famous antiques stores sprinkled in here, and many vintage clothing shops, but it's mostly a papergoods neighborhood.

But wait: On Mondays, there are three markets at Covent Garden, **Apple Market**, **Opera Market**, and **Jubilee Market**, which is about 100 yards away from Apple Market. At Apple Market the stalls (which are normally devoted to craftspeople) are taken over by rather high-end antiques dealers. Jubilee Market is more open—many price ranges are available and there's more room for bargaining and fun. You may also find local publications about other markets and fairs at some of the dealers at Jubilee. I'm not talking hoity-toity antiques here, but you can have fun anyway. (Tube: Covent Garden)

King's Road (SW3)

Don't ask me why transportation to King's Road is so difficult. The only way to get to all of the shops is to walk and walk some more. Or to keep flagging down the bus. The most interesting part of King's Road actually starts right at Sloane Square, but goes on and on to shops with numbers up in the high 500s. **Furniture Cave** is the farthest away (No. 533), while **Designer's Guild** (No. 277) is right in the thick of the chichi decorator part. If you take the tube to Fulham Broadway, you have to walk a good bit and you come out at the high end in the 500 block near **Furniture Cave.**

The better part for upscale shoppers is the middle 200–300 range of King's Road. There are several antiques malls here, and lots of showrooms. In terms of visual stimulation and the possibility of affording something nice, this neighborhood may offer the best combination of the right things. Other neighborhoods are cheaper, but this has a trendiness that can't be ignored... even in antiques.

Whatever you do, check out **Steinberg & Tolkein,** 193 King's Road, extraordinary dealers in vintage costume jewelry (and the like) with two floors of space and drool-over pieces, including old Chanel. (Tube: Fulham Broadway)

Fulham Road

This is another way to get to the upper King's Road area, then the Fulham Road area, and then over toward Brompton Cross, depending on which way you want to walk. Look at a map!

There's lots of stuff in the Fulham area between the Gloucester Road tube stop and Brompton Cross, but within a special block or two of Fulham Road you'll find either an antiques shop or a decorator showroom behind every door. Look in at **Peter**

272 ANTIQUES, USED BOOKS & COLLECTIBLES

Lipiteh (No. 120), **Today's Interiors** (No. 122), **Michael Foster** (No. 118), **Christophe Gollut** (No. 116), **Colefax & Fowler** (No. 110), **John Stefanidis** (No. 253), and **Clifford Wright** (Nos. 104–106). If you keep walking you'll hit **Souleiado** (No. 171) and several other shops, and then Michelin House, which is where **The Conran Shop** has made history (No. 81). (Tube: Fulham Broadway or South Kensington)

Lower Sloane (SW3)

I call the area including Pimlico Road, Ebury Road, and Lower Sloane Street simply Lower Sloane. It is an extension of Sloane Street, after you pass Sloane Square. Most of the dealers here are fancy, as is the clientele, but everyone is a tad more approachable than the high-end, don't-touch crowd. There are a lot of showrooms here, as well as antiques shops. If you're on Sloane Street, instead of turning to the right to get to King's Road, you walk straight and follow Lower Sloane Street to Pimlico Road. Convenient for cutting back to King's Road and Chelsea antiques shops. (Tube: Sloane Square)

Kensington Church Street (W8)

Shoppers, please note that few of these stores are open all day—if at all—on Saturday, so despite the fact that you're a stone's throw from Portobello Road, Saturday is not really the day to combine these neighborhoods.

Of course, a lot of serious Portobello Road dealers are open during the week (without the stalls and stands of Saturdays), and you can combine the two neighborhoods that way. The best way to do so is to exit the tube at Kensington High Street, cross the street at the light, and head slightly to your right before you zig up Kensington Church Street.

You'll pass **Lancer's Square** (an American-style mall), on the right side of the street; Church Street will bend to the left as you go up the hill.

A zillion shops and a small gallery line Kensington Church Street. Many of the stores are the small fancy kind that make you nervous to even press your nose to the glass. The closer you get to Notting Hill Gate (at the top of the hill you are climbing), the more funky the stores get.

The month of June can be tricky for shopping this area, as most of the good stores exhibit at the important shows and close up shop.

Oliver Sutton (34 Kensington Church Street) sells only Staffordshire figurines; pressing your nose to the glass may suffice, as you can see quite a selection from the street. At No. 58 is a small gallery with very serious dealers in their tiny glass cubbyholes. **Jonathan Horne** (No. 66) is another famous dealer for pottery, tiles, and ceramics—also very serious. **Simon Spero** (No. 109) has more pottery. For a slight change of pottery pace, pop in at **New Century**, a gallery that sells new art pottery that is hoped will become collectible (No. 69).

Don't miss three little dealers in a row along Peel Street, who have Kensington Church Street addresses (it's a corner junction)—among them **Hope & Glory** (No. 131A), which specializes in royal porcelain memorabilia.

The **Kensingon Church Street Antiques Centre** is not large, nor much to drool over, but there is a fistful of fine dealers here, and its worth a half hour of your time. If you fall in love, you can spend the day. There's a dealer in majolica there, Nicolaus Boston (is that a fabulous name or what?), who will take your breath away with his collection. (Tube: Kensington High Street or Notting Hill)

Portobello Road (W11)

I just love this Saturday market event (page 262), but don't think this is just a flea market scene or that Saturdays are the only day. Saturdays are the main event, but during the week, especially on Friday, the regular shops are open without the

Saturday circus atmosphere. And yep, there is a ton to see, even on a weekday. Warning, a few arcades or galleries open Fridays 12 P.M.–4 P.M. as well as Saturdays, but are not otherwise open.

There are a few antiques markets here, with many stalls and dealers, as well as some freestanding shops on Portobello Road and on Westbourne Grove. Get there via Pembridge Road to check out a few more shops (especially strong for vintage clothing), or by walking up the hill via Kensington Church Street, where there are a few more dealers. See above. Note a change in postal codes; this is nothing to be alarmed about. (Tube: Notting Hill or Kensington High Street)

Without the Saturday circus, the main action on Portobello Road is the number of galleries packed with dealers. These galleries are often called arcades. Check out:

- Chelsea Galleries, No. 67
- Alice's, No. 77
- Geoffrey Van, No. 105
- Portobello Antique Arcade, No. 139
- Lipka Arcade, 284 Westbourne Grove

ANTIQUARIAN BOOKS, MAPS & AUTOGRAPHS

If you collect first editions or antiquarian books or even if you're just seeking a title that's currently out of print, flip this way. Below are listings of the best antiquarian and used booksellers in London. If you're looking for the latest Martin Amis or Jeffrey Archer to read on the plane home, turn to the contemporary bookseller listings in Chapter 8.

In addition to perusing these listings, collectors of antiquarian books should also consult two new magazines devoted to the topic—*Driff's* and *Slightly*

Antiquarian Books, Maps & Autographs **275**

Soiled—which are available at **Sotheran's of Sackville Street** and the Cecil Court stores. Both carry news of auctions, sales, and book fairs, not to mention gossip about booksellers.

The West End

MAGGS BROTHERS LTD.
50 Berkeley Square, W1 (Tube: Green Park).

Don't believe those ghost stories you hear about Maggs.

While it had been rumored for years that the Maggs mansion, built in 1740, was haunted, no ghosts were spotted during World War II, when firewatch rules required at least one Maggs employee to sleep on the premises each night. Of course, the house next door was completely destroyed, and the one across Berkeley Square suffered heavy damage.... But there are no ghosts.

The only remaining mystery at Maggs is just how many books they have on hand. They've been accumulating since Uriah Maggs founded the firm in 1857, and not even their insurance company has been able to come up with a correct figure.

Such eccentricities are allowed any bookseller with an enormous collection of travel books, militaria, maps, illuminated manuscripts, autographs, and Orientalia. Maggs's travel section alone would fill the average bookstore with first-edition, on-the-spot reminiscences by the likes of Stanley, Livingstone, Robert Falcon Scott, and Admiral Byrd. Whenever the stock gets dangerously low, it is replenished by 10 specialists who attend auctions around the world on a regular basis.

Maggs also boasts of a sizable autograph collection. Whether you're a bibliophile or not, you should visit Maggs to see just what a civilized delight book buying can be.

G. HEYWOOD HILL LTD.
10 Curzon Street, W1 (Tube: Green Park).

If **Maggs** is a showplace for books and autographs of the illustrious, nearby G. Heywood Hill on Curzon Street represents the cramped, Dickensian bookshop most visitors associate with literary London. For 50 years, Heywood has been a beacon to authors, librarians, and collectors around the world.

Although space is limited, the shop is packed to the rafters with books that meet the standards of its knowledgeable staff. You won't find the newest Judith Krantz novel here, but employees know the stock and can lay hands on thousands of volumes quickly. Moreover, while antiquarian books pay the light bills, Heywood stocks contemporary books on a variety of subjects merely to satisfy its clients' needs. (It is also probably the only bookseller that will refuse to sell its clients books that don't meet its Olympian standards.)

The shop specializes in books on design, architecture, gardening, and the allied decorative arts. There's also an extensive collection of biographies and a subspecialty in literary criticism; Heywood's bookishness has attracted many writers as steady customers, including Evelyn Waugh, Anthony Powell, Nancy Mitford (who worked there during World War II), and other Waughs, Mitfords, and Sitwells for several generations.

The shop's family feeling as well as its terrifically high standards often ensure them first crack at extensive private libraries when they become available. The location is right around the corner from the **Hilton Park Lane** and the **Connaught**, off Berkeley Square.

Piccadilly

BERNARD QUARITCH LTD.
5-8 Lower John Street, Golden Square, W1 (Tube: Piccadilly Circus).

In October 1847, Bernard Quaritch came to London, determined to become a bookseller. He succeeded, attracting such clients along the way as Prime Ministers William Gladstone and Benjamin Disraeli, publishing Edward FitzGerald's *The Rubáiyát of Omar Khayyám*, and being eulogized by *The Times* as "the greatest bookseller who ever lived."

By this time, Quaritch has attained an international reputation. Boasting perhaps the largest stock of antiquarian books in London and 32 experts in fields as diverse as Arabic, bibliography, and psychiatry, Quaritch has an atmosphere that is quiet, but not formal. The firm attends auctions on the Continent (sometimes bidding for the British Museum) and assembles collections that can run the gamut from Tibet and Henry James to rigging and shipbuilding.

Because of its size, Quaritch is able to air-freight its own crate of books to New York once a week; the contents are then sent separately to clients via UPS, bypassing the post office and possibly careless (and financially damaging) handling.

SOTHERAN'S OF SACKVILLE STREET
2-5 Sackville Street, Piccadilly, W1 (Tube: Piccadilly Circus).

Sotheran's has been selling books since 1761 in York and has been established in London since 1815. Charles Dickens was a regular customer, and when he died, Sotheran's sold his library. The firm also purchased a number of volumes from Winston Churchill's library and was the agent for the sale of Sir Isaac Newton's library to Cambridge. The firm specializes in ornithology and natural science.

Books line the extensive perimeter of the ground floor, and the atmosphere is neat, formal, and as silent as a library. A lower floor is given over exclusively to antiquarian prints and maps, drawings by book illustrators such as Kate Greenaway and Arthur Rackham, sporting prints, and military and naval subjects. There's also an attractive office in an adjoining building for private negotiations.

Sotheran's offers search service, handbinds serial publications such as the Bills and Acts of Parliament, restores books, and also maintains subscriptions to overseas periodicals for its customers.

PHILLIPS
101 New Bond Street, W1 (Tube: Bond Street).

Even though books are not on Phillips's weekly calendar (as are rugs, ceramics, furniture, and silver), the firm auctions books, maps, and autographs 13 times a year and provides auction catalogs in these categories by subscription. Look for English literature, militaria, modern first editions, and incunabula.

Charing Cross Road

Visitors searching for 84 Charing Cross Road will be disappointed to find a record store, not the bookshop that inspired Helene Hanff's bestseller; nevertheless, the long street is filled with other, equally engaging book emporiums, all of which are open Monday through Saturday from 9 A.M. to 6 P.M.

FOYLE
119 Charing Cross Road, WC2 (Tube: Leicester Square).

See description on page 133 of Chapter 8.

FRANCIS EDWARDS
48a Charing Cross Road, WC2 (Tube: Leicester Square).

Francis Edwards is the leading antiquarian bookseller on the street and carries natural history and militaria. Open Monday to Friday from 9 A.M. to 5 P.M.

EDWARD STANFORD
12-14 Long Acre, WC2 (Tube: Covent Garden).

Stanford is a mecca for maps, charts, atlases, and travel books, not the reminiscences that **Maggs** stocks, but rather the how-to variety. A particular specialty is guides for mountain climbers, skiers, and other outdoorsy types. Open Monday to Friday from 9 A.M. to 5:30 P.M., and from 10 A.M. to 4 P.M. Saturday.

Cecil Court and Covent Garden (WC2)

(Tube: Covent Garden or Leceister Square)

Cecil Court, a block-long street between Charing Cross Road and St. Martin's Lane, has some charming secondhand bookshops. Most are open from 9:30 A.M. to 6 P.M. Monday to Saturday. (Tube: Leicester Square)

Long Acre, the "Main Street" of Covent Garden, is also lined with bookstores on both sides of the road; it is a block from Cecil Court.

Harold Storey, No. 3: Naval and military prints and books

Bell, Book & Radmall, No. 4: English and American first editions

Pleasures of Past Times, No. 11: theater, music halls, juvenilia

Travis & Emery, No. 17: music, ballet, opera

Frognal, No. 18: law, economics, history, caricatures

Alan Brett, No. 24: *Vanity Fair* cartoons, topography, Acts of Parliament

H.M. Fletcher, No. 27: early English literature

COLLECTIBLES

> *St. George he was for England*
> *And before he killed the dragon*
> *He drank a pint of English ale,*
> *Out of an English flagon.*

On our first visit to London, and several times thereafter, we were offered that very flagon each time we ventured off to check out the collectibles market. But after the first few not-so-convincing pitches we began to catch on. Shopping for the real thing in London is a tricky business.

As time went on we learned that:

- England is indeed a nation of shopkeepers.
- Many of the shops they keep are crammed with collectibles.
- Some of these collectibles are as real as St. George's flagon or that grand old American collectible, the Brooklyn Bridge.

The collectibles shops Mike lists in this section, on the other hand, have stood the test of time—they are the real thing. Some are famous; others are our personal finds. When we checked them last, they were fresh out of flagons (thankfully). Instead, they offered books as sensuous to the touch as they are titillating to the mind, dolls so beautiful that they brought a tear even to our cynical eye, and toy soldiers as spiffy as anything you'll see strutting around West Point . . . but these little metal guys are just a tad older than the West Point version.

While furniture, fountain pens, and fine art also are available here, and while we know full well that people are capable of collecting *anything*, I wanted to give you at least a small taste of the tempting collectibles London has to offer to those who know that London is the first city of the world for collectors.

Collectors of antiquarian books, maps, and autographs, please see page 274.

Coins and Medals

SPINK & SON LTD.
5-7 King Street, St. James's, SW1 (Tube: Green Park).

If you've yearned for those glitzy costume-jewelry medals, you'll all-out faint and go stark raving mad with delight when you see the original medals that the current fad was based on. Why was a man always so dashing in his uniform? Because of his medals, of course. And chances are, they came from Spink. Spink has tremendous stock in Orientalia, paperweights, and Greek and Roman coins, as well as an ample supply of early English hammered coins in gold and silver and milled pieces dating back to the late 1600s; however, as **Hamley's** is to toys, so Spink is to medals. Along with sheer size, Spink offers an expertise born of creating decorations for Great Britain and 65 other countries.

In addition to fashioning the medals, Spink also has world-class experience in mounting and displaying them, and even publishes a guide to wearing them. (Medals on your evening gown? Wear on sash, please. Medals on your safari jacket? Hmmmm.) The company also issues the monthly *Spink Numismatic Circular*, which includes large sections on medals, orders, and decorations. Hours: Monday to Friday, 9:30 A.M. to 5:30 P.M.

B.A. SEABY LTD.
7 Davies Street, W1 (Tube: Bond Street).

Early coins bearing the likenesses of royalty from Corinth, Phoenicia, and Rome rub shoulders with tradesmen's tokens issued by coppers in Dover and fishmongers in Margate; each is presented with care, panache, and the necessary historical background.

The firm is deep in antiquarian coins, and that interest has led to sidelines such as collections of jewelry and copperplate from ancient Greece, Rome, and Jerusalem. Seaby publishes a magazine, the bimonthly *Coin & Medal Bulletin*, which is likely to contain scholarly pieces related to archaeological finds, as well as price lists of coins. Hours: Monday to Friday, 9:30 A.M. to 5 P.M.

Forman Piccadilly Ltd.
99 Mount Street, W1 (Tube: Bond Street).

Forman specializes in medals, but also sells carved ivories made by soldiers and sailors, and other specialized antiquities. But it's the gorgeous colored ribbons and enamel medals that drew us into the shop, to peer hungrily into the large wooden case. If you brush up on your Russian, you can read the inscriptions on medals awarded by the czars. We're fond of Napoleonic medals, complete with ribbons or sashes.

Armada Antiques
Grays Antiques Market, Stand 122, 58 Davies Street, W1 (Tube: Bond Street).

One of two important stalls in **Grays Antiques Market**, Armada Antiques is crammed with militaria of all kinds. Armada Antiques (Stand 122) carries mostly edged weapons such as stilettos and sabers, but also has some medals. For the total effect, shop also at **Seidler** (Stand 120)—together these two fabulous dealers give you a nice overview.

The Arches
Villiers Street, WC2 (Tube: Charing Cross).

Soaring rents have forced small-time dealers out of Cutler Street, long a Sunday-morning fixture at the

Petticoat Lane market; however, inexpensive coins still are available by the bagful at The Arches on Villiers Street, beneath the Charing Cross Road tube stop. This is where we got twenty coins from around the world for about $1.50. This is decidedly low-end, and major collectors will not be interested; however, the place is a lot of fun. In addition to coins, there are comic books, cigarette cards, military insignia, and used romance novels in this covey of little dealers nestled beside the tube station. Most proprietors are open Monday to Saturday from 9 A.M. to 6 P.M.

Collectors' note: In addition to the Spink and Seaby publications, there's also a periodical called *Coin Monthly*.

Scientific Instruments

TREVOR PHILIPS & SONS LTD.
75a Jermyn Street, SW1 (Tube: Piccadilly Circus).

A smaller version of **Arthur Middleton** (see page 284), Philips carries gyroscopes, English drafting instruments, sundials, stethoscopes, and a selection of books about scientific instruments. The shop also carries miniature instruments, such as pocket botanical microscopes, pocket globes, and exquisite orreries—small clockwork representations of the solar system. Hours: Monday to Friday, 10 A.M. to 6 P.M.

STEPHEN O'DONNELL
Grays Antiques Market, Stand 156, 58 Davies Street, W1 (Tube: Bond Street).

An interest in navigation led O'Donnell to begin collecting and restoring sextants, spyglasses, and telescopes. By this time, his collection is extensive, as is a fairly new sideline in antique postage scales. The scales run from $150 to $1,000, while telescopes start at $250, and sextants run anywhere from $700 to $3,000. Hours: Monday to Friday, 10 A.M. to 6 P.M.

Arthur Middleton
12 New Row, WC2 (Tube: Leicester Square).

Located between Leicester Square and Covent Garden, this shop is chockablock with antique clocks, telescopes, surgical instruments, and early dental equipment, all in splendid condition. Even if you're not a collector, you'll enjoy the spit and polish of these fascinating pieces. Hours: Monday to Friday, 10 A.M. to 6 P.M.; Saturday, 11 A.M. to 5:30 P.M.

Victor Burness
Specialty dealer at Bermondsey Market (Fridays only, 6 A.M.–1 P.M.); or by appointment; call 732-454-591.

Collectors' note: Collectors of scientific instruments should be aware of two specialty publications: *Rittenhouse Journal of the American Scientific Instrument Enterprise*, published by David and Yola Coffeen and Raymond V. Giordano, and *Bulletin of the Scientific Instrument Society*, published by the Scientific Instrument Society.

Stamps

The Strand (and offshoots such as King Street and Cecil Court) is a magnet for philatelists in London. All the shops are in the Strand area, although we label some as in Charing Cross Road/Covent Garden—this is the same neighborhood and is an easy walk. (Tube: Charing Cross)

Stanley Gibbons Ltd.
399 The Strand, WC2 (Tube: Charing Cross).

The shop has the largest collection of British Empire stamp material in the world as well as the most complete selection of stamp accessories—albums, tweezers, and perforation gauges—and its own well-researched catalogs.

Gibbons also sells extraordinary philatelic material. We were once shown an issued but unused full block of 12 of the Twopenny Blue with the original gum. Brilliantly colored and lettered "SG-TL" in the lower left- and right-hand corners (to prevent counterfeiting), this museum-quality piece was offered at a mere $20,000.

Such lofty material is viewed in private, secure surroundings on the second floor. On a more mundane level—the ground floor—Gibbons stocks a few topics such as birds and the Royal Family, and has specialists in first-day covers, plate blocks, precancels, overprints, color variations, etc. The firm gave up the coin and medal business several years ago but now carries a full selection of postcards and pertinent literature.

Gibbons is impossibly famous and therefore impossibly crowded—you may get less service, and they may not have what you are looking for. Don't be afraid to wander around the neighborhood and try the competition. Smaller and less-known dealers may be more fun.

DAVID BRANDON
77 The Strand, WC2 (Tube: Charing Cross).

The second in a row of three shops across from **Gibbons,** Brandon has a large stock of classic material and is particularly up on postal history items of Great Britain and the Continent.

STRAND STAMPS
79 The Strand, WC2 (Tube: Charing Cross).

Three dealers operate as Strand and deal in Commonwealth material. Even though **Gibbons** has a larger stock in this area, the Strand dealers often come up with particular items from India or Australia that the big kid on the block doesn't stock. Moreover, Strand isn't pricey and is particularly

ANTIQUES, USED BOOKS & COLLECTIBLES

patient with younger collectors. If you've gone to the trouble to seek the neighborhood, don't blow it now—you must stop in here.

Also try:

Harmer's
91 New Bond Street, W1 (Tube: Bond Street).

Phillips
101 New Bond Street, W1 (Tube: Bond Street).

Sotheby's
34-35 New Bond Street, W1 (Tube: Bond Street).

Spink & Son Ltd.
5-7 King Street, St. James's, SW1 (Tube: Piccadilly Circus).

Christie's
8 King Street, St. James's, SW1 (Tube: Piccadilly Circus).

Collectors' and shoppers' note: All these shops are open Monday to Friday from 10 A.M. to 5 P.M. (**Gibbons** opens at 9 A.M.) and the same hours Saturday, except for **Strand** and **Gibbons,** which close at 1 P.M. **David Brandon** is closed all day on Saturdays.

There are also several periodicals related to stamps, including *Stamp News*, and collectors also should keep in mind the large auction houses. **Phillips** has a postage stamp auction nearly every Thursday, and **Christie's** recently offered a collection that included proofs and essays from Bradbury, Wilkinson & Co., which has printed British stamps and bank notes for nearly 150 years.

Dolls and Toys

Parents and grandparents, please note: This section, in keeping with this chapter's theme, covers only collectible dolls and toys. For new toys for your darling ones, please turn to Chapter 8, "Toys & Kid Stuff."

Pollock's Toy Museum
1 Scala Street, W1 (Tube: Goodge Street).

Pollock's Toy Theatres
44 The Market, Covent Garden, WC2 (Tube: Covent Garden).

Nearly a hundred years ago, Robert Louis Stevenson wrote, "If you love art, folly, or the bright eyes of children, speed to Pollock's." Thousands still do and find a treasure island of toys housed in two adjoining buildings overflowing with dolls, teddy bears, tin toys, puppets, and folk toys from Europe, India, Africa, China, and Japan.

Exhibits of mechanical toys and construction sets fill the lower floor of Pollock's Toy Museum, and the second story has exhibits of the paper "toy theaters" and cut-out actors and actresses that have fired the imagination of British children for generations.

In addition to the museum, there's a second Pollock's, a toy shop, set up in Covent Garden when the original was destroyed in the Blitz. The shop sells the theaters, popguns, and dolls, and there's no admission charge. The shop is open Monday to Saturday from 10 A.M. to 8 P.M.

The museum is at the corner of Scala and Whitfield Streets, and is open Monday to Saturday from 10 A.M. to 5 P.M. Admission is 50p for adults and 20p for children and students. The museum also holds parties for up to thirty children.

London Toy And Model Museum
23 Craven Hill Road, W2 (Tube: Paddington).

In a case devoted to dolls based on the Royal Family, a German-made Princess Elizabeth doll, from 1932, sits next to a Princess Anne doll made in 1953.

This royal rite of passage from child to queen is nearly overshadowed by other dolls at the museum—poured-wax dolls; bisque (china) dolls;

a wax-headed Quaker lady in her original costume, from 1840; and a Topsy Turvy doll, which can be either white or black, depending on the owner's fancy.

In addition to dolls, the museum has 25,000 Matchbox and Corgi miniature cars, several working rocking horses, a collection of Paddington Bears, an entire room of toy trains, and a display of toy soldiers from Pierce Carlson (see page 289).

The latest addition is the Baywest exhibit, a computer-controlled model of 1,000 houses, 50,000 lights, a railway system, and a helicopter, and that requires a separate admission charge. There also are two smaller coin-operated versions by the same designer—a snow scene and a small town at twilight.

Hours: Tuesday to Saturday, 10 A.M. to 5:30 P.M.; Sunday, 11 A.M. to 5 P.M. Admission charge.

Collectors' note: *Doll & Toy World* covers these collectibles on a monthly basis, as does *Antique Toy World*.

Toy Soldiers

UNDER TWO FLAGS
4 St. Christopher's Place, W1 (Tube: Bond Street).

By the time toy soldiers became popular in America (during World War II), English children were celebrating the fiftieth anniversary of William Britain & Co. Britain went into the toy soldier business in 1893, creating a set of the Life Guards to honor Queen Victoria's forthcoming Diamond Jubilee in 1897.

Many Britain sets (including the first) are available at Under Two Flags on colorful St. Christopher's Place between Wigmore and Regent streets . . . just a stone's throw from Oxford Street and **Selfridges.**

The store also offers inexpensive lead soldiers for do-it-yourself painters; a selection of military books; magazines and prints; bronzes; porcelains; and curios, such as a chess set made of toy soldiers.

Hours: Monday to Saturday, 10 A.M. to 6 P.M.

Collectibles

PIERCE CARLSON
Portobello Road Market, Stall 27 (Tube: Notting Hill Gate).

There's a windowful of Britain soldiers at the **London Toy And Model Museum** on loan from Pierce Carlson. He runs a retail shop near the British Model Soldier Society and also maintains a stall on Portobello Road for those collectors of the famous Britain brand.

Miscellaneous note: While there are specialty publications for almost every collectible, two British periodicals cover collectibles in general: *Collectors Mart* and *Collectors Gazette*. These are filled with ads for cigarette cards (the British equivalent of baseball cards), "advertiques" (specialty advertising paraphernalia, such as ashtrays), porcelain bottles of spirits, and pre-1960 boxed sets of Lego—with the original instructions, of course.

Comic Books

Yes, we know you outgrew these years ago, but there are collectors out there who are buying up nostalgic reminders of the good old days with the speed of (Zap!) the Flash. Like our teenage son, Aaron.

Ten years ago, there were small comic-book departments in some of the better bookstores. Now, according to the comic cognoscenti, there are more than forty comic-book specialty stores in Great Britain, and a baker's dozen in London, each with a slightly different appeal.

FORBIDDEN PLANET
71 New Oxford Street, WC1 (Tube: Tottenham Court Road).

You are about to enter three strange worlds, one inhabited by aliens, a second in which fantasy princes and monsters reign supreme, and yet a third where comic-book characters rule, but that's not all. At

Forbidden Planet you'll also find videotapes of all 17 James Bond movies, trading cards from the original *Batman* movie, and the complete works of Al Capp (*Li'l Abner*). It's a comicoholic's dream. Where else would you find the unauthorized biography of *Superman* baddie Lex Luthor? The stock is vast, with some 10,000 different titles available. (Parents dragging kids should be aware that some are decidedly not for family consumption, such as *The Adventures of Johnny Condom*.)

While the emphasis is on new comic heroes, Dick Tracy, Superman, and Little Lulu are represented, as is, believe it or not, cowboy hero Tom Mix, who died forty years before current comic collectors were born. They also offer a limited stock of back issues. The shop also offers fantasy masks, an incredibly complete assortment of science fiction books and videos, and toys such as miniature versions of the original Starship *Enterprise*.

There are branches in Brighton, Glasgow, Cambridge, and New York. Forbidden Planet also sells most items by mail as well. The London shop is open 10 A.M. to 7 P.M. (8 P.M. on Thursday; 6 P.M. on Saturday).

COMICS SHOWCASE
76 Neal Street, WC2 (Tube: Covent Garden or Leicester Square).

Despite its fantastic selection, **Forbidden Planet** can be a noisy, hectic place to shop. If you prefer to browse for that hard-to-find early *Batman* comic book in peace and quiet, you should know about Comics Showcase. The place is organized in aisles like a record shop and has early work by *Pogo*'s creator Walt Kelly. They also have early issues of *Dr. Who* and *Batman*. The staff is knowledgeable and will excitedly show you *Newsboy Legion*, an early work by Jack Kirby, who later did the *Fantastic Four*. Comics Showcase also has branches in Oxford and Cambridge.

Collectibles

GOSH!
39 Great Russell Street, WC1 (Tube: Holborn).

Across from the British Museum on Great Russell Street is Gosh!, which dispensed with signs during the *Batman* craze and just hung an image of the Caped Crusader to attract passersby. Gosh! has a serene atmosphere very much in tune with museum goers. An employee confided, "We're dependent on the museum trade." As a result, you'll find, along with comics, complete histories of faded favorites such as *Captain Easy* and *Wash Tubbs* in eight volumes, and scholarly histories about cartoon strips and comic books. Gosh! is open daily, 10 A.M. to 6 P.M. Monday through Saturday and 1 P.M. to 6 P.M. on Sunday.

THE TINTIN SHOP
34 Floral Street, WC2 (Tube: Covent Garden).

If you know Thomson from Thompson and could pick the evil Rastopopoulos out of a police lineup, you'll be in heaven at this all-Tintin shop near Covent Garden. Tintin turned 60 recently, and his exploits have charmed children all over the world in over 50 languages—including Esperanto. The shop features all 22 Tintin adventures and other merchandise: drawing pads, unframed and framed posters. There's even an all-wool Tintin sweater if you're feeling expansive. If your kids have not yet discovered Tintin, now's the time.

Cigarette Cards

Just as baseball cards became wildly popular in the U.S. beginning in 1981, so cigarette cards have become highly collectible in England. Sets that used to sell for $5 or $7 in 1986 are now fetching $10 or $12.

You might expect that cigarette card dealers would be proliferating; just the reverse is true. With more cards being held by collectors (and investors),

ANTIQUES, USED BOOKS & COLLECTIBLES

> # Jean-Louis Ginibre's Secret List of Jazzy Record Dealers
>
> Jean-Louis Ginibre, the editorial director of Hachette Filipacchi Magazines in New York, has passed on his favorite sources for secondhand LPs and current CDs to me. What friends will do! They all deal exclusively in jazz, except for Honest Jon, who also sells rock and reggae. Direct from Jean-Louis...
>
> **JAMES ASMAN'S RECORD CENTRE**
> *23A New Row, St. Martin's Lane, WC2 (Tube: Leicester Square or Covent Garden).*
>
> **HONEST JON RECORDS**
> *278 Portobello Road, WC2 (Tube: Ladbroke).*
>
> **MOLE JAZZ**
> *311 Grays Inn Road, WC1 (Tube: King's Cross).*
>
> **RAY'S JAZZ SHOP**
> *180 Shaftesbury Avenue, W2 (Tube: Tottenham Court road).*
> See description below.

the number of sets that used to turn over at flea markets and in antiques stores specializing in ephemera has decreased. One of the best shops specializing in cards is:

MURRAY & CO.
20 Cecil Court, WC2 (Tube: Leicester Square).

51 Watford Way, Hendon Central, NW4 (Tube: Hendon Central).

Murray & Co. has become the mecca for cigarette card collectors around the world. Since 1967, the company has published the only annual price catalog in the field. Murray has also been active reprinting valuable old sets (clearly marked *reprint*) and publishing its own checklists and books; a recent one, *Half Time*, covers English football (soccer) cards.

Murray has two shops in London, one on Cecil Court just off Charing Cross Road, the other in Hendon, served by the Hendon Central stop on the Northern Line. The Hendon shop has far greater stock in all respects, while the Cecil Court shop is more convenient to central London (less than a hundred yards from Trafalgar Square) and offers a brief overview of what's available. If you've got any idea at all of becoming serious about cigarette cards, however, the trip to Hendon is an absolute must. To save time for all concerned, come equipped with a list of the sets you want and their manufacturers' names.

CDs & Records for Collectors

If the impersonality and sheer size of **HMV**, **Tower**, and **Virgin** have got you down, consider the following specialty sources for new and used CDs, LPs, and rare 78s. Otherwise, turn to Chapter 8 for the address of the nearest megastore near you.

Jazz & Classical Specialty Shops

RAY'S JAZZ SHOP
180 Shaftesbury Avenue, WC2 (Tube: Tottenham Court Road).

If what you're looking for relates to jazz, it's probably at Ray's Jazz Shop. New and used LPs and CDs, jazz books, magazines, and rare 78s. Some of the records are so rare that Ray's regularly auctions them off. Every month new records come up for auction, and bidders submit offers in person. The staff is more knowledgeable than employees in the jazz departments at the megastores, and very helpful. When a tourist asked to hear a used Billie Holiday CD, the manager sampled every cut on the compact disc to make sure it was all playable. You can wallow here in all things jazz from 10 A.M. to 6:30 P.M. Monday through Saturday.

TEMPLAR RECORDS
9 Irving Street, WC2 (Tube: Leicester Square).

While rock, pop, and jazz fans have been unabashedly pro–compact disk, classical music lovers have often been astonished at CD prices.

There are classical CD bargains out there, however. Templar Records, an unprepossessing classical CD specialist, features the work of name artists for as low as $8, while double-disc operas run upwards from $30. Open 10 A.M. to 6 P.M. Monday through Saturday.

Secondhand Records

If the record you're looking for can't be found by browsing the specialty stores, there are always secondhand shops; however, such stores are almost as used as the merchandise they sell. They're generally dirty, dusty, and jumbled up. (We like that in bookstores, but hate it in record stores.)

Gramophone Exchange may have that record of "My Tears Have Washed 'I Love You' from the Blackboard of My Heart" you've been looking for all these years.

GRAMOPHONE EXCHANGE
3 Betterton Street, WC2 (Tube: Covent Garden).

If you don't mind shopping for secondhand records in a place that's also devoted to Albanian trinkets, hit the Gramophone Exchange. It's covered with authentic dust, crammed full of records, and one of the house specialties is windup gramophones.

58 DEAN STREET RECORDS
58 Dean Street, W1 (Tube: Green Park).

When was the last time you saw a store display devoted to Doris Day's records? If you answered, "1958," you're halfway there. At 58 Dean Street, near Piccadilly Circus, you can check out Doris's greatest—"Que Sera Sera," and "A Guy Is a Guy"—recorded before she was a virgin.

VINYL EXPERIENCE
18 Hanway Street, W1 (Tube: Tottenham Court Road).

Maybe this is simply the vinyl solution: The shop caters to Beatles memorabilia and hard to find oldies. The records are downstairs; the ephemera is on the street level.

Chapter Eleven

LONDON SHOPPING TOURS

LET'S TOUR THE TOWN

London is a great walking city. You can get a fair view of the city, see some sights, and do some great shopping in about a dozen different locations. Pick a landmark and start marching.

If your idea of a landmark is **Liberty of London**, or Carnaby Street, or even **Harrods**, well, who am I to differ with you? Pick a store and then start marching. Or charging, perhaps.

Should your time be limited, you will have to pick and choose. Some of the suggestions in Chapter 1 should help you with this, or you may want to try these tours. They are devised to get you to a lot of places in a hurry. So grab your brolly, and maybe a tote bag for carrying your packages, and let's go shopping.

Do "look right." It's no fair if you get run over by a taxi because you don't know how to cross the streets in Britain.

PUBLIC TRANSPORTATION

In more complicated tours, you will want to jump between different neighborhoods either by taxi or public transportation. Before you begin your day, you may want to check routing for the number of

Mayfair Mayhem Day Tour 297

times you will be on and off the tube (or bus) to see if an all day TravelCard is a worthwhile investment. You need to use it at least three times just for it to pay for itself.

TOUR #1: MAYFAIR MAYHEM DAY TOUR

This is a complete tour of Mayfair with plenty of stops for real-people shopping, so don't be frightened away. Sure, lots of the stores on Bond Street and even Regent Street are out-of-bounds from a budget point of view, but I'm going to give you a little of everything, so hang on tight.

Feel free to pop into stores you pass that interest you, as this trip will take you right by just about every store in London.

1. Begin at **Marks & Spencer** on Oxford Street (No. 458), near Marble Arch. The British fondly refer to this store as "Marks & Sparks" or even "M&S." This is the only M&S branch that sells cashmere, so here's your first bargain tip of the day. Don't miss the basement, where you will want to buy ready-cooked foods in order to save money for clothes. I suggest the chicken *tikka*, followed by a tin of "Curiously Strong Mints." You may want to buy it now and keep it in your tote bag for a picnic lunch later. I do that all the time, honest.

    While at M& S, you may want to look at the men's department, where you can get an awfully nice silk tie for £6–£10. I also like the bath products, sold on the street level. The women's underwear, the St. Michael's brand, is a legend in its own time. Frankly, I buy from Victoria's Secret although in Britain there are statistics that say that something like seven out of every ten women in the U.K. are wearing St. Michael's knickers as you read this. Should you care to join the parade, now's your chance.

2. Next, cross Orchard Street and explore **Selfridges** (400 Oxford Street), a great British example of

one-stop shopping. Selfridges is a less glamorous version of **Harrods,** but they do have a good Filofax department which is handily near their branch of **Thornton's,** the mass candy marketeer that makes a toffee I am addicted to.

Don't miss **Miss Selfridge,** young and kicky—perfect for the teen-and-twenties set. It's on the ground floor. I buy stuff for myself here all the time. I'm a teenager at heart. So far, prices have been moderate.

3. Leaving Selfridges, go back onto Oxford Street. Proceed away from Marble Arch (turn left) on Oxford Street, and cross to the other side of Oxford Street. Be sure you look the right way. This street is crammed with buses and I don't want you crushed beneath a double decker. Look right!

   See that grocery store now? **Tesco Metro?** That's your next destination. You can take a miss on the street level if you aren't inclined to love grocery stores (I love them as long as they aren't in my home town), proceed downstairs and right into the health and beauty aids and the house-brand bath and aromatherapy products. Begin to shop in earnest. This is where I buy Bath By Chocolate, a bubble bath product.

4. Finished at Tesco, walk back across the street (look right) and right into **Body Shop.** Load up now.

5. From Oxford Street, turn right onto South Molton Street. By the time you get to South Molton, you will have passed many street vendors selling London souvenirs. Prices are best on the street, if you need this kind of stuff. Between Tesco and Body Shop, you should have all the gifts and souvenirs you are going to need.

   Once on South Molton Street, inspect all of the shops. The most famous is **Browns** for high fashion; there's a Browns discount outlet at No. 45. There are a number of shoe shops here and some fabulous costume jewelry stores, including **Butler & Wilson** (No. 20).

Tour #1: Mayfair Mayhem Day Tour

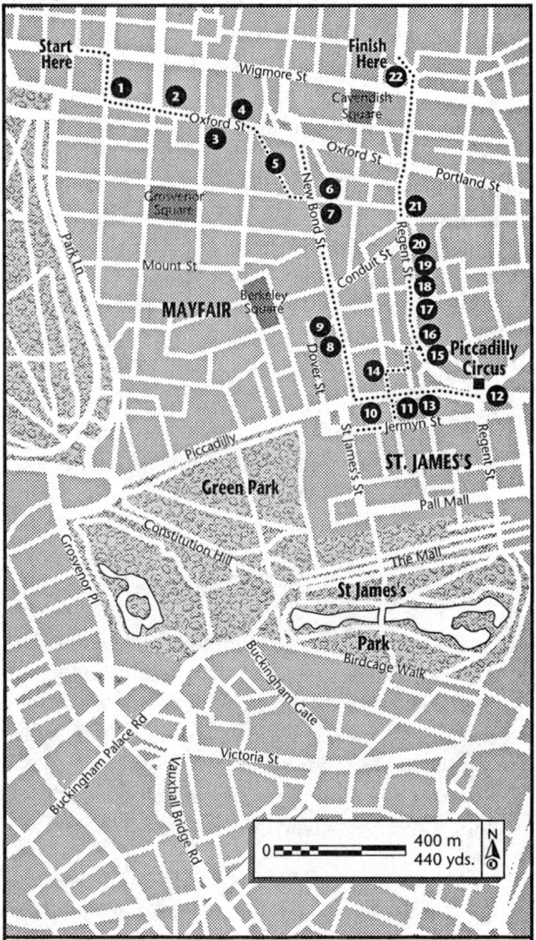

Alfred Dunhill 10
Aquascutum 15
Body Shop, The 4
Brown's Hotel 9
Burberry's 18
Burlington Arcade 14
Fenwick 7
Fortnum & Mason 11
Halcyon Days 6
Hatchards 13
Hamleys 19
Jaeger 20
Langham Hilton 22
Lawley's 17
Liberty 21
Lillywhites 12
Marks & Spencer 1
Reject China Shop 16
Royal Arcade 8
Selfridges 2
South Molton Lane 5
Tesco Metro 3

There's always **Grays Mews,** an antiques gallery, if you are more interested in your home than your closet. **The Hat Shop** has opened a branch on South Molton and no trip to London is complete without a half hour spent trying on hats. This is the perfect time to give your packages a rest; set them on the floor and get to working those mirrors. Hat, please (No. 9). If you've never been to **Twilight,** a spin-off from the multiple, **Monsoon,** this is also a good educational experience (No. 68); **Daniel James** is a very interesting kind of store—there are actually several of them around town and in convenient tourist places. Mr. James sells very upscale T-shirts; very chic, very artsy, not "Gram went to London and All I Got Was This Crummy T-shirt"–type T-shirts.

Finally, South Molton is your opportunity to visit **Whittard's** (No. 23), another multiple with branch shops in conventional tourist and shopping areas. They sell teas, coffees, and a few tea accessories like teapots, mugs, and the like. Tea, as you already know, is an easy to pack and moderately priced gift.

6. At the end of South Molton, take a left for a short block up Brook Street. Cross New Bond Street; visit **Halcyon Days** (14 Brook Street), where you will flip for traditional English enamel everything. While the presentation boxes are the most popular item, I've recently gone mad for the cuff links and am looking for some with frogs on them.

7. Retrace your steps back a few feet to New Bond Street and close your eyes and think of James Bond. No, no, no! Shop both sides of New Bond and then Old Bond streets. You will find most of the major designer boutiques on these two streets.

    I suggest you spend some time in **Fenwick** (No. 63), which is a small department store with moderately priced high fashion; it's the only store on Bond Street that I can afford.

8. If you need a break, take a stroll through the **Royal Arcade** (28 Old Bond Street), to . . .

Mayfair Mayhem Day Tour 301

9. **Brown's Hotel** at 34 Albemarle Street. Stop in for a wonderful and classic tea, which will include tea sandwiches and scones. Consider a quick trip to **Michaeljohn** for reviving aromatherapy (book ahead) or even a wash and blow-dry.

   Fortified and beautified, walk back through the Royal Arcade. Turn right and finish your shopping on Old Bond. Then take a left on Piccadilly, a right through the **Piccadilly Arcade,** and again a right onto Jermyn Street. Jermyn Street is one of London's best-designed retail streets for men's items. Go down one side of Jermyn toward St. James's and then come back on the other side toward Piccadilly. Buy the man in your life a shirt at **Turnbull & Asser** (No. 71), or at **Hilditch & Key.**

10. Walk to **Alfred Dunhill,** which is at the corner of Duke and Jermyn. At least look in the windows.

11. **Fortnum & Mason** is also here; don't miss the food hall toward the front of the store.

12. Go through the front of **Fortnum & Mason,** back out on Piccadilly, and walk to your right directly to Piccadilly Circus and the entrance of **Lillywhites,** the sporting goods department store. Come around and leave the store on Piccadilly, walking back toward the **Burlington Arcade.**

13. But before you go farther, now you need to weigh yourself down with some books. You can take in **Hatchards,** one of London's most famous bookstores, then cross over to the Burlington Arcade. Look right.

14. The **Burlington Arcade** is the prettiest covered shopping street in London. This arcade was built in 1819, and its atmosphere has remained delightfully British. The arcade is the only London area that maintains Regency rules of public conduct, prohibiting whistling, singing, or hurrying. Its 585-foot passage is watched over by two guards dressed in

302 LONDON SHOPPING TOURS

the ceremonial garb of officers of the 10th Hussars. Most of the 38 shops sell mainly British goods from cashmeres to linens to cashmere.

If you get the feeling that I've sent you in a circle, yes, I have. The last part of the route has been a bit of a loop-de-loop. You aren't dizzy, are you?

15–21. Exit the arcade at the opposite end of where you entered, take a right onto Burlington Gardens, a left onto Savile Row (home of the famous Savile Row tailors), a right onto New Burlington Street, and then a left onto Regent Street. You have now entered another major shopping thoroughfare. Walk toward Oxford Street, to complete your full circle tour—don't miss **Aquascutum** (No. 100), **Reject China Shop** (No. 134), **Lawley's** (No. 154), **Burberrys** (No. 165), **Hamley's** (No. 188), **Jaeger** (No. 204), and, finally, **Liberty** (Nos. 210–220).

22. Collapse at **The Langham Hilton** for tea, or maybe the week.

TOUR #2: KNIGHTSBRIDGE & CHELSEA

1. Begin at **Harrods** (Knightsbridge). Your visit here is optional—it's not un-American to bypass Harrods. If you've never seen it, tour the food halls and, if you are looking for china or souvenirs, or a wheel of Stilton, get them now.

   If you've done it and the store unnerves you, do not feel obligated to try it again. Frankly, this place can be a zoo.

2. Go out of Harrods via the front door—or begin the tour here without having gone into Harrods—and cross the street (look right), then walk to the corner, which is Montpelier Street. Cross this street, shop at **Genevieve Lethu** if you can't resist (hard to resist French table top), then turn right on Montpelier on the Lethu side of the street.

3. Go for a short block and turn left onto a tiny street called Cheval Place. I call it Pandora's Alley. Shop this entire block for gently worn designer bargains.

Tour #2: Knightsbridge & Chelsea

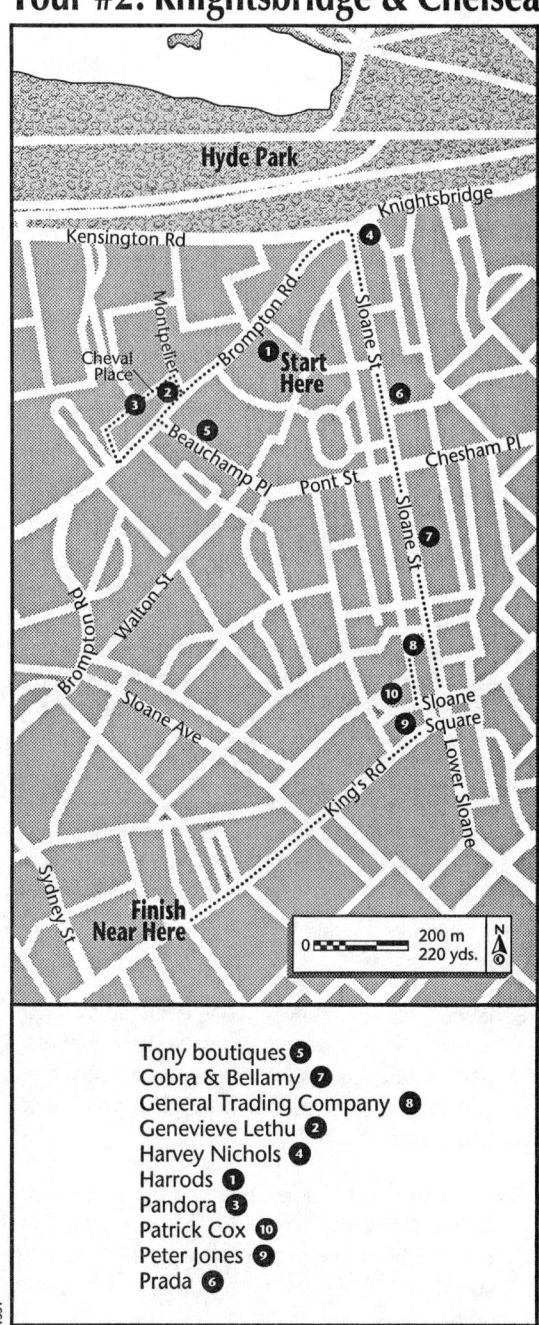

Tony boutiques ❺
Cobra & Bellamy ❼
General Trading Company ❽
Genevieve Lethu ❷
Harvey Nichols ❹
Harrods ❶
Pandora ❸
Patrick Cox ❿
Peter Jones ❾
Prada ❻

A bargain being a Chanel sweater for under £300. Every store has a selection; the most famous address is **Pandora,** No. 16.

4. Return to Harrods, but pass it as if headed to Mayfair along Brompton Road. Walk to **Harvey Nichols,** a smaller and more fashionable department store (corner of Knightsbridge and Sloane streets), known for its great selection of designer fashions.

   If you are hungry, stop at the fifth-floor coffee shop; you can browse the food halls after you've been fortified. Harvey Nichols is a lot easier to handle than Harrods; they have a very nice home furnishings floor.

5. Now you are ready to take the Sloane Street exit and walk toward Sloane Square. Sloane Street is a long, straight shopping avenue filled with fun, chic boutiques and all of Europe's big names from **Chanel** to **Valentino.**

   You now have to make a choice: to stay in Knightsbridge or segue on to a different type of nearby shopping. You can cut back toward **Harrods** from Sloane Square (or reverse the tour so you go to Harvey Nichols and then Harrods) and get on Brompton Road heading toward Beauchamp Place and the major museums on Cromwell Road. This is a short walk and then you turn left on Beauchamp, which is lined with tony boutiques selling high-end Sloane Ranger designer togs from **Kanga** to **Bruce Oldfield.**

6. If you want something funkier, continue on Sloane Street, where every big designer shop now has a branch. You are desperate to shop at **Prada,** aren't you? You do want to know what all the fuss is about, don't you?

7–8. Continue on Sloane Street, past the stores, past **Cobra & Bellamy,** the costume jewelry shop, and past **General Trading Company,** where you can spend the whole day, spend an hour, or keep on going.

Hot-to-Trot, Teenybop London Tour 305

9. Turn right to get to **Peter Jones,** a big department store.

10. Finished there, you want to go back out the front door, not the side door in the linen department, because you are going to Symons Street for a discreet stare in the windows at **Patrick Cox.** (No. 8) where pink patent leather loafers cost only about $200.

11. Now you are in the mood for King's Road, on the other side of **Peter Jones.** Turn right on King's Road, where you can walk for a mile or two and see everything trendy in fashion and furnishings. I walk King's Road up into the 500 block; most people will quit way before then. Hail a taxi to your next stop as there is no nearby tube stop. Your next stop will undoubtedly be your hotel and a hot bath or a stiff drink (consider both) because you have just had one helluva day.

TOUR #3: HOT-TO-TROT, TEENYBOP LONDON TOUR

This is really a half-day tour, best taken in the afternoon, since many of these shops don't open until 11 A.M.

1. Take the tube to High Street Kensington, which is a central shopping drag—you will emerge from the underground right in the middle of a lot of stores, many of which specialize in the New Wave.

2. Look on both sides of the street at the small boutiques, jeans shops, the market selling used clothes, army surplus, and the like, and the now famous **Hyper Hyper,** where up-and-coming designers try out their creations. The **Kensington Market** (Nos. 49–53) is an indoor den of dyed jeans and tie-dyed T-shirts and many leftovers from the 1960s, which are quite stylish now. (**American Retro** is on the basement level.) This is not for the Chanel customer.

306 LONDON SHOPPING TOURS

The market doesn't so much sell a look as it does pieces, so if you don't know what to do with those black studded things, this is not your kind of shop. There's also a branch of **Red or Dead** next to Hyper Hyper; there are some traditional stores mixed in here—don't be distracted by the likes of **Mothercare** and **Crabtree & Evelyn.** It's a nice adventure to get a little of everything.

Your main thrill will be at **Hyper Hyper** (Nos. 26–40), which is a two-level (go downstairs) supermarket of booths maintained by the up-and-coming designers who walk on the wild side. Even if you buy nothing here, you will be able to tell your friends about it for years.

3. Back in the tube, you're going to Covent Garden (you can taxi if you're feeling rich) so you are going to have to change lines at South Kensington.

4. Now that you're at Covent Garden, walk from the station toward the marketplace, but before you get all excited with it, hang a right on King Street. Cooool. It's the **Dr. Martens Department Store.**

5. Finished at Doc Martens, you are ready to collapse and eat at Covent Garden and then explore the shops.

6. Catch the tube at Covent Garden and go to Piccadilly Circus. Once at Piccadilly, pull out your *A to Z* or a map, as the Soho area is a rabbit warren of tiny streets that weave behind Regent Street.

7. Tour Soho, taking in **Workers For Freedom** (4 Lower John Street); **Academy** (yes, again—this one is fancier) (15 Newburgh Street); and **Dressed to Kill** (13 Newburgh Street).

8. Wind your way onto Carnaby Street. Mixed in with the tawdry sex shops and tourist attractions, you'll find some cheapie stores selling black leather, floppy hats, bandannas, and tie-dye.

Hot-to-Trot, Teenybop London Tour 307

9. Take Beak Street (this street is the length of your driveway at home) from Carnaby Street to Regent Street, where you'll be in the heart of traditional London. If you still want New Wave, don't look when you walk by **Burberrys.** Continue on Regent Street, passing all the hallmarks of British style, and end up at Oxford Circus but still on Regent Street. Pop into **H&M,** a department store devoted to cheap teenage fashion, and have a ball. Then move onto Oxford Street, passing **Shelly's,** the most famous shoe store landmark to teens everywhere, which is across the street from Hennes on the other corner of Oxford Circus. Done at Shelly's, you will turn right onto Oxford Street and walk one block to **Department X,** *the* word on mass-produced trendiness.

10. Not tired yet? Great. Walk toward Marble Arch on Oxford Street, passing several department stores and souvenir shops. I think **The Body Shop** is a souvenir shop, don't you? Be on the right-hand side of the street (if your back is to Oxford Circus) and take care to look for a tiny street called Gees Court off St. Christopher's Place.

11. Turn right (the only possible choice) and note that this is two-block street, which is a virtual secret to those not in the know. The first block is called Gees Court, which is filled with stores. Most of them are chic and expensive, but **Whistles** has some rock-and-roll clothes. Wander two blocks till the stores stop, then cut back to Oxford Street. In another block, you'll be at **Miss Selfridge,** which is maybe where you should have started. They have with-it clothes that aren't too weird or too expensive.

   Now then, assuming you would only do this with a teen or two in tow, I want you to walk two blocks over from Oxford Street and Marble Arch and drag your teens into The Dorchester (on Park Lane), where you can take high tea. Teach them how to aspire to the upper-middle class while you stare at their Doc Martens and laugh.

308 LONDON SHOPPING TOURS

TOUR #4: THE HOME DAY TOUR

Put on those walking shoes. I'm going to march you around town like the Black Watch Guards. Leave your bagpipes at home, but take along any swatches you might have brought with you, or a notepad to write down things of interest as you pass by. If you have business cards or credentials that admit you to the trade, bring 'em along.

1. Take the tube to Knightsbridge, enter **Harvey Nichols,** the department store, and take the escalator right upstairs to the home furnishings floor. Tour it slowly, taking mental notes. Then walk out of Harvey Nichols and onto Sloane Street. Ignore the fashion boutiques; this is a home furnishings tour.

2. Turn left on Harriet Street, right off Sloane Street, and walk right into the **Laura Ashley** shop. This is a giant home-furnishings store now, and will give you many ideas. Be sure to check the bins for sale items. As you leave the store, walk along Sloane Street toward Sloane Square (and away from Knightsbridge).

3–4. Things will be dull for a few seconds but will warm up quickly when you get to **Jane Churchill** at No. 135 and the **General Trading Company** at No. 144, where the tabletop is particularly interesting.

5. Dive into **Peter Jones,** the department store, to check out sheets, duvet covers, bed linens, and trimmings, then come out of the store on the King's Road side and head to the right. King's Road is very long, and the design sources are far-flung (the reason I told you to wear sensible shoes).

6. You'll pass several good antiques galleries on King's Road and should be quite warmed up for the chase by the time you hit **Designer's Guild,** one of the two Tricia Guild shops. You'll be panting when you leave (it's so exciting), but don't miss the second

Tour #4: The Home Day Tour

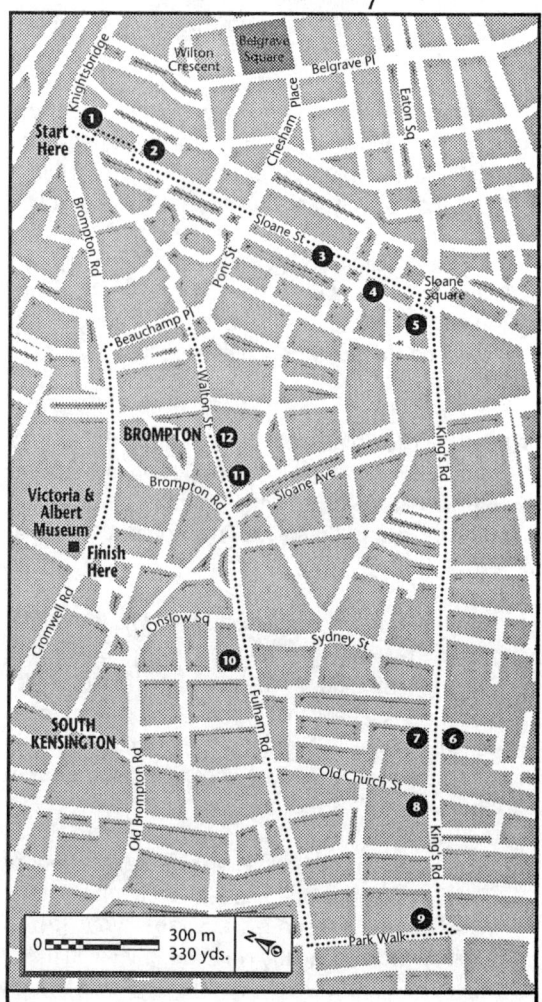

Colefax & Fowler ⑩
Conran Shop, The ⑪
Designer's Guild ⑥
General Trading Company ④
Harvey Nichols ①
Jane Churchill ③

Knobs & Knockers ⑧
Laura Ashley ②
Nina Campbell ⑫
Osborne & Little ⑦
Peter Jones ⑤
T. F. Buckle ⑨

shop a few doors farther down, where the fabrics are (No. 271 and No. 277).

7. **Osborne & Little** has a showroom across the street (No. 304), and there are many antiques shops here you'll want to browse. Keep on moving even if things get a little boring as the really chic stuff thins out.

8-9. **Knobs & Knockers** has a shop at No. 385 for brass fixtures; **T.F. Buckle** at No. 427 has the reproduction fireplaces that are all the rage. Of course, you'll dive into the antiques galleries as you walk past them.

10. Cut over to Fulham Road, which parallels King's Road, and find yourself more or less in the mid-200 block. Walk or bus to that number if you're too tired to search. **Colefax & Fowler** has a branch at No. 110.

11. Continue toward Knightsbridge now, on Fulham Road, taking in **The Sleeping Company, Divertimenti,** and maybe even **Smallbone,** where you'll see kitchens that will make you want to remodel right away. Finish up with a strong espresso at Michelin House, now known for **The Conran Shop.**

12. Restored from your coffee, go out the side door of **The Conran Shop** and head for Walton Street and more decorative shops (remember your trip to **Harvey Nichols?** All the **Nina Campbell** you didn't buy is still available at her shop at No. 9 Walton Street), then wander into the Victoria & Albert Museum, where you'll find decorative arts that will inspire you in your design decisions. Learn to copy the best and you'll never go wrong.

TOUR #5: SUNDAY IN GREENWICH

Since one has to plan ahead for the perfect Sunday in London, make sure to stop off at a newsstand or kiosk Saturday night if you want to read the

Sunday paper(s) the following morning. Otherwise, you'll waste precious time wandering from newsstand to newsstand on Sunday morning trying to find one that hasn't already sold out its stock of papers!

1. Order room service for breakfast (it *is* Sunday) or head for **The Ritz,** where their famous dining room serves a formal breakfast every morning. Usually only hotel guests are here in the A.M. hours, so you won't have to deal with the same crowds who come to The Ritz for tea. While the full English breakfast costs about £15, you can get coffee and pancakes a la carte for less while you enjoy one of the best sights London has to offer: the very dining room you are sitting in. Go ahead: Linger a bit over the paper you cleverly picked up the night before!

2. Plan to be at the Westminster Pier any half hour after 10:30 A.M. to catch the boat to Greenwich. The cab fare from the Ritz is about £3, but if there's two of you, that equals the tube fare—and this is an extravagant Sunday.

3. Catch the boat to Greenwich. It takes almost an hour to get to Greenwich; there is commentary on the sights all the way to the Tower. After the lecture, the captain will pass the hat; £1 is fine for two of you. Commentary quits at the Tower, where some people on the boat will disembark. Not you. Now watch the Docklands go by as you drift downstream to town. The Greenwich Pier is right at the edge of downtown and couldn't be more convenient. There are public bathrooms there.

4. You may want to let the husband (and the kids) explore the two boats and museums here, the three-masted *Cutty Sark* and the tiny *Gipsy Moth*. In fact, Greenwich has so many sights—and a fabulous park—that you will have to make choices in order to fit in everything you require for the perfect Sunday. If your time is limited, go right into the

Victorian marketplace where a crafts show is taking place.

5. Finished with the craft market—and all the adjacent stores which are conveniently open—leave the covered market and cross over to Greenwich Church Street and find the Greenwich Tourist Information Office, a small storefront that sells certificates (20p each) for standing on the Time Line (this is home to Greenwich Mean Time) or for walking under the Thames in the Greenwich Foot Tunnel. Excellent gifts for kids. Check out the brochures (free) and see if there is an additional antiques show that day at Town Hall.

6. Across the street is Bosun's Yard, where there is another crafts market. This one is more crass (featuring more imports) than the excellent official market, but still worth a peek. As you leave and head up Greenwich Church Street toward High Road, you'll pass **Goddard's Eel Pies,** a very authentic English-style diner where your entire lunch won't cost more than £2. Don't miss the fresh homemade berry pie (with custard on top) for dessert.

7. Keep walking up Greenwich Church Street to **Canopy Street Market,** a meandering market that sprawls along and sells mostly junk. We think it's great junk, although our friend Ian disdains this particular market. It's certainly not for the Sotheby's crowd.

8. Turn onto the high street and take in the outdoor **Greenwich Antiques Market:** Used clothes are toward the rear. This is a pretty good place for used paperbacks if you need reading material for your travels and are horrified by the price of paperbacks (and all books) in Britain.

9. You are now half a block from Town Hall (it's that unattractive modern building with the clock tower), where there may be another antiques show. These usually charge admission (the other markets don't),

Sunday in Greenwich 313

but add to the fun of the day if you are feeling flush. Since you are now half a block from the train station, and probably have a good number of packages in hand, you can zip on home via train and end up at Charing Cross. Follow The Strand for two blocks to the **Savoy,** where you can have high tea in one of London's fanciest hotels.

10. Refreshed? Good. Walk two blocks to Covent Garden, where the Sunday retail scene is happening.

11. Collapse!

Size Conversion Chart

Women's Clothing

American	8	10	12	14	16	18
Continental	38	40	42	44	46	48
British	10	12	14	16	18	20

Women's Shoes

American	5	6	7	8	9	10
Continental	36	37	38	39	40	41
British	4	5	6	7	8	9

Children's Clothing

American	3	4	5	6	6X
Continental	98	104	110	116	122
British	18	20	22	24	26

Children's Shoes

American	8	9	10	11	12	13	1	2	3
Continental	24	25	27	28	29	30	32	33	34
British	7	8	9	10	11	12	13	1	2

Men's Suits

American	34	36	38	40	42	44	46	48
Continental	44	46	48	50	52	54	56	58
British	34	36	38	40	42	44	46	48

Men's Shirts

American	14½	15	15½	16	16½	17	17½	18
Continental	37	38	39	41	42	43	44	45
British	14½	15	15½	16	16½	17	17½	18

Men's Shoes

American	7	8	9	10	11	12	13
Continental	39½	41	42	43	44½	46	47
British	6	7	8	9	10	11	12

INDEX

A

Academy, 216, 306
Accessorize, 103, 189
Accommodations, 30–40
  B & Bs, 37–38
  flats (apartments), 38–39
  hotels, 30–37, 39–40
Adolfo Dominguez, 128
Agnés B., 127
Airfares, 10, 12–14
Airports, 55, 58
Air travel, 12–14, 90
Alan Brett, 279
Alfie's Antiques Market, 266–67, 270
Alfred Dunhill, 92, 136–37, 158, 180, 181, 301
Alice's, 274
Ally Capellino, 91, 118–19
American Express, 10, 53, 54, 269
American Retro, 193–94, 305
Anna French, 248
Anne Higgins, 206
Antiquarian Book Fair, 258
Antiquarius, 267
Antiques, 26, 74, 93, 96, 99, 100, 102, 107, 143, 145, 230, 252–95, 308, 310
  fairs, 255–58
  markets, 106, 258–68, 312–13
  neighborhoods, 268–74
  shipping, 236–39
Apartment Company, The, 39
Apple Market, 163, 207, 259–60, 270
Aquascutum, 90, 114–15, 302
Arabesk, 170
Arches, The, 282–83
Armada Antiques, 282
Aromatherapy, 3, 6, 71, 109–10, 156, 298, 301
Art, 24, 134, 257, 259, 268, 280
Arthur Middleton, 283, 284
Arthur Sanderson & Sons Ltd., 251
Asprey, 157–58
Auctions, 232–36
Austin Reed, 187
Autographs, 274–79

B

B.A. Seaby Ltd., 281–82
Banks, 54, 55, 56
Barclay International Group, The, 39
Barkers of Kensington, 100
Beauchamp Place, 97–98
Bell, Book & Radmall, 279
Berkely Square Cafe, 48
Bermondsey Antique Market and Warehouse, 261
Bermondsey Market, 5, 227, 240, 260, 261–62
Bernard Quaritch Ltd., 276–77
Berties, 197
Betty Barclay, 116
Betty Jackson, 121–22
Beverley, 270
Bizarre, 270
Blairman and Sons, 269
Bleyle, 127
Body Shop, The, 2, 71, 88, 92, 111, 113, 187, 298, 307
Bond Street, 90
Bond Street Antiques Centre, 267–68
Bonham's, 234
Bonham's Knightsbridge, 234

316 INDEX

Books, 25, 100, 102, 131–34, 140, 143, 147, 167, 231, 246, 259, 301
  antiquarian, 133, 270, 274–79, 280, 312
  fairs, 258, 275
  travel and guide, 11–12, 132, 275, 279
Books for Cooks, 102
Boots the Chemist, 2, 3, 4, 20, 88, 92, 109, 111–12, 177, 178
Bosun's Yard, 264
Bourjois, 177–78
Bramah Tea and Coffee Museum, 24
British Antique Dealers' Association Fair, 258
British Home Stores, 76, 148–49
British Museum Shop, 22
British Tourist Authority (BTA), 12
Brompton Cross, 98
Browns Labels for Less, 116–17, 151, 298
Bruce Oldfield, 124, 304
Buckingham Palace Gift Shop, 6
Building Book Shop, 131–32
Bulldog Club, The, 27, 37
Burberry, 75, 90, 117, 302, 306
Burberry Factory Outlet Shop, 117–18, 151–52
Burlington Arcade, 91, 301
Buses, 15
Butler's Wharf, 106
Butler & Wilson, 169–70, 298
Button Queen, 134
Buttons, 73, 134

C

Camden Lock, 263
Camden Passage Market, 5, 261, 262
Camden Town, 105
Canopy Antiques Market, 264, 312
Carnaby Street, 91–92
Caroline Charles, 119
Car rental, 16
Cashmere, 78, 88, 146, 147, 202, 203–204, 206, 208, 209, 210, 262, 302
Cashmere by Design, 209
CDs. *See* Music
Cecil Court, 279
Céline, 9, 128
Ceramics, 4, 9, 225, 257, 258, 262, 267, 268, 273, 278. *See also* China
Cerutti 1881, 128
Chanel, 90, 96, 128, 304
Charbonnel et Walker, 72, 154–55
Charing Cross Road, 278–79
Charles Jourdan, 196
Chelsea, tour of, 302–5
Chelsea Antiques Fair, 257, 258
Chelsea Design Week, 232
Chelsea Galleries, 274
Chemists, 2, 3, 4, 20–21, 93
Chenil Galleries, 267
Cheval Place, 3, 99, 302
Children's shops, 6, 7, 22, 23, 24, 88, 89, 105, 130, 134–36, 212–17. *See also* Dolls, Toys
China, 4, 69, 75–76, 77–78, 92, 93, 104, 139, 140, 145, 150, 239–45, 302
Chinacraft, 104, 241–42
China Ware House, 92
Christian Lacroix, 9, 129
Christie's, 234, 286
Christophe Gollut, 272
Church's Shoes, 197
Church Street, 270
Cigarette cards, 283, 291–93
Cigars, 93, 136–37, 158
Clifford Wright, 272

Clothing, 22, 27, 91, 98, 103, 135, 147, 151, 172, 174, 182, 186, 187, 190, 191, 259
British, 66–68
children's, 115, 118, 134–36, 143, 145, 147, 148, 189
designer, 4, 69, 75, 114–31, 142, 143, 147, 148, 149, 150, 216, 300, 304
hip & hot, 118, 120, 121, 188, 212–17, 305–7
horse and rider, 167–69
knitwear, 4, 76, 78, 88, 100, 115, 124, 134, 135, 152, 160, 202–10, 262, 263
men's, 140, 142, 143, 145, 146, 148, 173, 179–86, 187, 189, 301
shirts, 183–86, 301
tartans/tweeds, 208, 209, 211–12
used, 99, 194–96, 300, 302–4, 312
vintage, 69, 108, 179, 263, 265, 270, 274
Cobra & Bellamy, 170, 304
Coffee, 155, 157, 246, 300
Coins, 234, 281–83
Colefax & Fowler, 248, 249, 250–51, 272, 310
Colingwood, 171
Collectibles, 74, 252, 265–68, 273, 280–95
Comic books, 221, 283, 289–91
Comics Showcase, 290
Conran Shop, The, 47, 98, 246, 272, 310
Cosmetics, 71, 111–14, 149 140, 142, 147, 148, 177–79
Covent Garden, 3, 4, 5, 18, 102–4, 270, 279
Crabtree & Evelyn, 112, 113, 306

Crafts, 104, 107, 108, 248, 264, 312
Crafts Market, 264, 312
Crate & Barrel, 9
Credit cards, 7, 52, 53
Crown Perfumery, 218
Crystal, 75–76, 239–45
Cuff links, 6
Culpeper the Herbalist, 3, 4, 6, 71, 103, 113–14, 187
Currency exchange, 53, 54–56
Customs and duties, 52, 62–63, 229
Czech & Speake, 92, 219

D

D.H. Evans, 148
D.R. Harris & Co., 93, 217–18
Dance and exercise line, 110
Daniele Ryan, 109–10
Daniel James, 300
David Brandon, 285, 286
David Fielden, 217
Davidoff, 93, 137
Davies Turner, 239
Debenhams, 147–48
Department stores, 2, 4, 18, 46, 138–50
Descamps, 128
Design Centre of London, 231
Designer clothing, 4, 69, 75, 114–31, 148, 149, 150, 216, 300, 304
used, 99, 194–96, 300, 302–4
Designer's Guild, 223, 247, 248, 271, 308
Designer Sale Studio, 152–53
Design Museum, 24, 106
Designs, 196
Dickins & Jones, 47, 149
Dillon's, 131, 231
Disney Store, The, 9, 130, 221
Divertimenti, 105, 310

DKNY. *See* Donna Karan
Docklands, 106
Dr. Martens Department Store, 3, 6, 77, 92, 103, 212–13, 306
Dolls and toys, 221, 280, 286–88. *See also* Toys
Donna Karan, 9, 45, 90, 130
Dorchester, 93–94
Dorothy Perkins, 190
Dress Box, The, 195
Dressed to Kill, 306
Duty free shopping, 25–26, 28–29
Dynasty, 196

E

Edina Ronay, 124
Edward Stanford, 278–79
Ehrman's, 100
Elizabeth Gage, 171
Embroidery, 98, 159, 217
Emma Somerset, 125
Emporio Armani, 45, 97, 128
Episode, 128
Erik Van Peterson, 170
Ermenegildo Zegna, 130
Escada, 128
Esprit, 130
Exchange rates, 52, 53

F

F. Pinet, 199
Fabrics, 98, 99, 140, 142, 143, 148, 227, 228, 229, 246–51, 310
Factory Outlets, 118, 150–53
Farah Lister, 170–71
Featherston Shipping, 238
Fendi, 128, 174
Fentons, 238
Fenwick, 46, 149–50, 300
Ferragamo, 128, 196
58 Dean Street Records, 295
Filofax, 6, 76–77, 173, 191–92, 298
Fior, 169
Fishing gear, 160, 200–202
Florists, 153–54
FoFo Club, The, 150
Fogal, 128, 176
Foodstuffs, 139, 144, 145, 154–57, 219, 246, 301, 302, 304, 306
Food guides, 42
Forbidden Planet, 289–90
Forman Piccadilly Ltd., 282
Fortnum & Mason, 47, 72, 91, 92, 144–45, 155, 301
Foyle, 133, 278
Francis Edwards, 278
Freed of London Ltd., 110
French Connection, 187
Frognal, 279
Fulham Road, 105, 271–72
Furniture, 108, 140, 147, 229, 246–49, 267, 268, 278, 280
Furniture Cave, 271

G

G. Heywood Hill Ltd., 133, 275–76
Gallery of Antique Costume & Textiles, 270
Gander & White, 239
Gap, The, 9, 89, 126–27, 130
Gap Kids, 130, 136
Garrad, 171
Gatwick Airport, 55
Gaultier Junior, 91
General Trading Company, 96, 158–59, 304, 308
Genevieve Lethu, 97, 99, 226
Genny, 129
Geoffrey Van, 274
Georgina Von Etzdorf, 125
Gianfranco Ferré, 128
Gianni Versace, 90, 130
Gidden, 169
Gifts, 157–60
Gina, 96, 198
Giorgio Armani, 9, 127

Glassware, 24, 140, 145, 224
Gosh, 291
Gramophone Exchange, 294–95
Grays Antiques Market, 266, 268, 269, 282
Grays Mews, 300
Greenwich, 107–108
  tour, 310–13
Greenwich Antiques Market, 260, 265, 312
Greenwich markets, 5, 263–65
Grosvenor House Antiques Fair, 257, 258
Gucci, 129, 174
Guidebooks, 11–12
Guns, 93, 60, 200–202

H

H.M. Fletcher, 279
H.R. Higgins, 155
Habitat, 226, 245–46
Hackett, 180–81
Hair products, 160–63
Hair salons, 18, 57, 141, 160–63, 301
Halcyon Days, 160, 300
Hamley's, 3, 6, 7, 89, 140, 221–22, 281, 302
Hampstead, 107
Handbags, 78, 149, 169, 172–75, 195
Hardy Brothers, 201–202
Harmer's, 234, 286
Harold Storey, 279
Harper & Tom, 102
Harrods, 3, 4, 20, 27, 46, 71, 72, 76, 94, 97, 98, 99, 139–41, 155, 169, 193, 222, 240, 242, 298, 304
Harvey Nichols, 46, 94, 116, 127, 140, 143–44, 155, 163, 193, 249, 304, 308, 310
Harvie & Hudson, 92, 186
Hatchards, 91, 132, 207, 231, 301

Hatmakers, The, 167
Hats, 69, 91, 93, 115, 144, 149, 163–67, 300, 306
Hat Shop, The, 165, 300
Heals, 245
Health and beauty, 111–14, 140, 146, 148, 187, 298. *See also* Toiletries
Heathrow Airport, 28, 55
Hennes & Mauriz (H&M), 215, 307
Henry Maxwell, 168
Herbert Johnson, 167
Hermès, 9, 129, 174–75
High & Mighty, 182
Hilditch & Key, 92, 183–84, 301
Hilton Park Lane, 35–36, 276
Historical reproductions, 97
HMV record shops, 88, 137, 138, 293
Hobbs, 198
Holidays, 18
Holland & Holland, 201
Home decor, 27, 76, 144, 173, 223–51, 308–10
Home furnishings, 116, 147, 149, 189 223–51, 304, 305, 308–10
Honest Jon Records, 292
Hope & Glory, 273
Horse and rider, 167–69
Hotels, 30–37, 39–40
  afternoon teas at, 50–51
  airport hotels, 39–40
  Athenaeum Hotel & Apartments, 33–34
  Brown's, 51, 301
  chains, 31
  changing money, 54
  Connaught, 93, 276
  Conrad, 81
  Dorchester, The, 32–33, 43–44, 80, 93, 201
  Dukes, 36–37
  Hilton Park Lane, 35–36, 276
  Hilton Mews, 32

320 INDEX

Hotels (*cont.*)
  Langham Hilton, 35
  Mayfair, The, 32, 36
  rates, 30–31
  Ritz, The, 34–35, 44, 50, 80, 90, 311
  Savoy, 104
  Stafford, 50
  tipping, 57–58
Housewares, 105, 140, 143. *See also* Home decor
Hunting, 93, 60, 200–202
Hyper Hyper, 6, 100, 214, 215–16, 305, 306

I

Imperial War Museum, 22
Insurance, shipping, 239
Interior design. *See* Home decor
International Ceramics Fair, 257–58
Irish Linen Company, The, 159
Islington, 106
Islington Market, 106
Issey Miyake, 129
Istante, 129
Italian Paper Shop, 193

J

J.A. Allen, 167
J. Dedge & Sons, 168
J. Floris Ltd., 218
J.J. Fox, 137
Jacadi, 129
Jaeger, 89, 122, 147, 302
James Asman's Record Centre, 292
James Bodenham & Co., 219
James Lock & Co., 93, 165, 168
James Purdey & Sons Ltd., 201
Jane Churchill, 97, 248, 308
Janet Reger, 176
Jasper Conran, 120
Jermyn Street, 92–93
Jerry's Home Store, 9, 223, 224
Jewelry, 22, 140, 157, 169–72, 259, 267, 268, 282
  costume, 169–71, 267, 298, 304
Jigsaw, 188
JJ Fox, 137
Joan and David, 9, 196
John Boyd, 97, 164–65
John Lewis, 2, 148
John Lobb, 93
John Sparks Limited, 269
John Stefanidis, 247, 272
Jo Malone, 98, 219–20
Jonathan Horne, 273
Joseph, 98, 123
Joseph Pour La Maison, 123
Jubilee Market, 207, 259, 260, 270

K

Kaffe Fassett, 223, 247
Kanga, 98, 304
Karen Millen, 188
Karl Lagerfeld, 90, 129
Katharine Hamnett, 121
Kenneth Turner, 154
Kensington, 99–102
Kensington Church Street, 100, 272–73
Kensington Church Street Antiques Centre, 273
Kensington High Street, 100
Kensington Market, 100, 214, 305
Kenzo, 129
Kiki McDonough, 171–72
King's Road, 96–97, 271
Kinloch Anderson, 211
Knickerbox, 25, 176
Knightsbridge, 3, 94–97
  tour, 302–305

Knits and Sweaters, 4, 76, 78, 88, 100, 115, 124, 134, 135, 152, 160, 202–10, 262, 263
Knobs & Knockers, 310
Krizia, 129

L

La Cigogna, 134–35
Lancer's Square Mall, 100, 272
Langham Hilton, 35
Language, 23
Laura Ashley, 76, 89, 115–16, 135, 186, 228, 248, 308
Lawley's, 4, 89, 240, 243, 302
Leather goods, 76, 91, 157, 158, 160, 172–76
Le Fax, 77
Leicester Square, 104
Les Olivades, 98, 226
Levi's, 9, 89, 130
Liberty of Londons, 2, 4, 76, 89, 142–43, 188, 302
Lillywhites, 147, 301
Lindka Cierach, 119
Linens, 105, 115, 143, 148, 302, 305, 308
Lingerie, 25, 176–77
Lipka Arcade, 274
Little Chelsea Antiques Fair, 257
Lockson Services Ltd., 238
Loewe, 172, 175
London
  accommodations, 30–40
  best shopping buys, 74–77
  neighborhoods, 83–108
  new phone numbers, 69
  public transportation, 14–16, 296–97
  restaurants, 41–51
  transportation to, 12–14
London Silver Vaults, The, 240, 244–45

London Toy and Model Museum, 287–88, 289
London Transport Museum, 22–24
Louis Féraud, 128
Louis Vuitton, 175
Lower Sloane, 272
Luggage, 157, 174, 246

M

Madame Tussaud's, 25
Maggs Brothers Ltd., 275, 276, 279
Manolo Blahnik, 197
Maps, 274–79
Margaret Howell, 121
Markets
  antiques, 258–65, 274
  collectibles, 265–68
  Greenwich, 263–65
  street, 258–65
Marks & Spencer, 3, 72, 76, 80, 84, 88, 146–47, 176, 180, 202, 206, 297
Marylebone, 270
Mary Quant, 124, 178
Max Mara, 129
Mayfair, 269
  tour, 297–302
Medals, 281–83
Merola, 171
Michael Foster, 272
Michaeljohn, 109, 161–62
Michelin House. *See* The Conran Store
Militaria, 275, 277, 278, 282, 283
Mirabilia Italiae, 193
Miss Selfridge, 142, 188–89, 298, 307
Mole Jazz, 292
Molton Brown, 163, 220
Money matters, 52–64
Monsoon, 69, 103, 189, 300
Morgan's, 193
Moss Brothers, 68
Mothercare, 89, 135, 306
Mount Streets, 269

322 INDEX

Moyses Stevens, 153–54
Mulberry, 123–24, 169, 173
Multiples, 4, 69, 88, 89, 94, 96, 100, 104, 107, 135–36, 186–91, 214, 215, 300
Murray & Co., 292–93
Museum of the Moving Image, 24
Museum stores, 5, 6, 22–24, 97
Music, 88, 137–38, 221, 270 292, 293–95

N

N. Peal, 206, 207–8
National Gallery Shop, 22
Neal Street, 3, 103–4
Needlecrafts, 76, 98, 100, 143
Neighborhoods, 83–108
  antiques, 268–74
  Camden Town, 105
  Chelsea, 302–305
  Church Street, 270
  Covent Garden, 3, 4, 102–4, 270
  Docklands, 106
  Dorchester, 93–94
  Fulham Road, 105, 271–72
  Greenwich, 107–8
  Hampstead, 107
  Islington, 106
  Kensington, 99–102
  Kensington Church Street, 272–73
  King's Road, 96–97, 271
  Knightsbridge, 3, 94–97
  Lower Sloane, 272
  Marylebone, 270
  Mayfair, 269
  Mount Streets, 269
  Portobello Road, 102, 273–74
  St. James's, 93
  Soho, 91–93
  Upper Knightsbridge, 97–99
  West End, 86–91, 275–76
New Century, 273
Newspapers, tabloid, 7, 73
Next, 89, 104, 136, 189–90, 216, 246
Nicholas Haslam, 248–49
Nicky Clarke, 162
Nicole Farhi, 45, 120–21, 191
Nicole Farhi Outlet Shop, 152
Nina Campbell, 144, 249, 310
No. 7, 177
Notting Hill Gate, 100–102

O

Objets d'art, 246–49
Objets Extraordinaire, 98, 159
Oggetti, 105
Oilily, 129
Oil & Spice Shop, 106
Old Cinema, 268
Old Cinema, The, 268
Oliver Sutton, 273
Olympia Decorative Arts and Antiques Fair, 256
Opera Market, 260–61, 270
Orvis, 131, 200
Osborne & Little, 249–50, 310
Oxfam, 69
Oxford Circus, 88–89
Oxford Place mall, 88
Oxford Street, 86–88

P

Pamela's, 98, 195–96
Pandora, 3, 4, 99, 194–95, 302–4
Paperchase, 192
Paper goods, 22, 191–94, 270
Past Times, 97
Patrick Cox, 197–98
Paul Costelloe, 120

Paul Smith, 181–82
Penhaligon's, 218–19
Perfume, 6, 28–29, 81–82, 140, 145, 189, 217, 218, 219
Personal checks, 54
Peter Jones, 96, 99, 150, 308
Peter Lipiteh, 271–72
Philip Treacy, 166
Phillips, 234, 278, 286
Piccadilly , 90–91, 276–78
Piccadilly Arcade, 301
Piccadilly Market, 263
Pied à Terre, 198–99
Pierce Carlson, 289
Pierre Cardin, 127
Pillows, 270
Pimlico Road, 99
Planet Hollywood, 90
Pleasures of Past Times, 279
Pollock's Toy Museum, 287
Pollock's Toy Theatres, 287
Polo/Ralph Lauren, 131
Portobello Antique Arcade, 274
Portobello China and Woollens, 4, 203, 210
Portobello Road, 102, 227, 273–74
Portobello Road market, 4, 5, 102, 261, 262
Postal codes, 83, 85, 274
Postcards, 5, 6, 22, 23, 24, 92
Pottery. *See* Ceramics, China
Prada, 172, 175
Prestat, 155
Principles, 190
Pringle, 208

R

R. Twining & Co., 157
Rachel Trevor-Morgan, 165–66
Racing Green, 190
Ray's Jazz Shop, 292, 293–94
Records. *See* Music

Red or Dead, 214, 215, 306
Regent Street, 89–90
Reject China Shop, 90, 98, 241, 243–44, 302, 304
Renate, 195
Resale shops, 173, 179, 194–96
Restaurants, 41–51
  afternoon tea, 49–51
  fixed price meals, 42–43, 68
  food guides, 42
  in-store meals, 45–48
  for lunch, 44–45
  luxury meals, 43–44
  snacking and shopping, 48
  tipping, 57
Riding supplies , 160, 167–69
Risky Business, 270
Ritva Westenius, 105, 216–17
Robert Lewis. *See* JJ Fox
Rochester Big & Tall, 9, 182
Rodier, 94, 130, 152
Royal Arcade, 300
Royal Crown Derby, 22
Royal Doulton, 21
Royal souvenirs, 26–27, 72, 73
Royal mail, 27–28
Royal warrants, 21–22, 157, 200, 208, 218, 219, 251
Russell & Bromely, 199
Russian Shop, The, 104

S

Sachets, monogrammed Victorian, 7
St. James's, 93
Sales, 68, 75, 117, 118, 145, 151, 179, 232
Sally's Own, 205, 207
Salou, 195
Santa Maria Novella, 178
Scams, 81–82
Scientific instruments, 283–84

Scotch House, 94, 205, 208–9, 211
Seidler, 282
Selfridges, 141–42, 155, 169, 189, 297
Selina Blow, 174
Shaker Shop, 223
Shelly's Shoes, 6, 92, 199–200, 307
Shepherd Market, 94
Shipping, 27–28, 229, 236–39
Shirin Cashmere, 209
Shirts, 183–86, 301
Shoes, 3, 6, 69, 77, 92, 93, 110, 135, 147, 168, 179, 182, 196–200, 212, 213, 220, 298, 305, 306, 307
Shooting and Fishing, 200–202
Shopping hours, 18–21
Shopping rules. *See* Shopping strategies
Shopping services, 27
Shopping strategies, 65–82
Shu Uemura, 178
Sign of the Times, 213
Silver, 145, 148, 239–45, 268, 278
Simon Spero, 273
Simon Tracy, 270
Simpson, 181
Simpson's In The Strand, 104
Size conversion chart, 314
Sleeping Company, The, 105, 310
Sloane Street, 96
Smallbone, 310
Smythson of Bond Street, 6, 192
Sock Shop, The, 176–77
Sogo department store, 90
Soho, 91–93
Sophie Henderson, 166
Sothebys, 234, 286
Sotheran's of Sackville Street, 275, 277–78
Souleiado, 226
Souvenirs, 25, 26–27
Spink & Son Ltd., 281, 286

Spode, 21
Sporting goods, 7, 104, 106, 140, 147, 301
Spy shops, 93
Stamps, 27, 104, 234, 284
Stanley Gibbons Ltd., 234, 284–85, 285
Steinberg & Tolkein, 271
Stephen O'Donnell, 283
Stirling Cooper, 214–15
Strand, The, 104
Strand Stamps, 285–86
Strelios, 195
Subway. *See* the Tube
Susan Woolf, 191
Sweaters and knits, 4, 76, 78, 88, 100, 115, 124, 134, 135, 152, 160, 202–10, 262, 263

T

T.F. Buckle, 310
Tapisserie, 98
Tartans, 208, 209, 211–12
Tax-Free Europe, 60, 61
Taxis, 15–16, 57, 68
  from airports, 55
Tea, 72, 144, 155, 157, 300
Tea, afternoon, 7, 49–51, 301, 313
Teapots, 24, 92, 210, 300
Telephones, 17–18, 69
Templar Records, 294
Tesco Metro, 2, 3, 7, 10, 114, 156, 298
Thomas Goode, 4, 47, 93, 242–43
Thomas Neals Mall, 4, 103
Thomas Pink, 6, 185–86
Thornton's, 156–57
Tiffany & Co., 171
Timberland, 131
Tintin Shop, 291
Tipping, 56–58
Today's Interiors, 272
Toiletries, 71, 111–14, 156, 187, 217–20
Tomasz Starzewski, 125
Tom Conran's Deli, 102

Tommy Hilfiger, 130
Tours, 296–13
   Greenwich, 310–13
   home decor, 308–10
   Knightsbridge and Chelsea, 302–5
   Mayfair, 297–302
   Sunday tours, 310–13
   teeny–bop, 305–7
Tower of London, 25, 84
Tower Records, 137, 138, 293
Toys, 7, 22, 24, 89, 139, 145, 220–22, 246, 286–89. *See also* Dolls
Toy soldiers, 221, 280, 288–89
Trains, 16–17
Train shopping, 25–26
Travel Bookshop, The, 102
Traveler's checks, 53
Travis & Emery, 279
Trevor Philips & Sons Ltd., 283
Tricker's, 168
Trotters, 135, 222
Trumper's, 92
Trussardi, 175
Tube, the, 14–15, 19
Tube shopping, 25–26
Turnbull & Asser, 21, 92, 184–85, 301
Tweeds, 160, 182, 211–12
Twilight, 103, 189

U

Under Two Flags, 288
Upper Knightsbridge, 97–99

V

Valentino, 96, 130, 214, 304
Valerie Wade, 249
VAT (value-added tax), 58–64
Victor Burness, 284
Victoria and Albert Museum Shop, 5, 6, 22, 97

Vidal Sassoon, 163
Vinyl Experience, 295
Virgin Megastore, 88, 137, 138, 293
Vivienne Westwood, 126, 153

W

Wallpaper, 115, 127, 228–29, 247, 248, 250, 251
Walton Street, 98
Warm and Wonderful, 205
Warner Brothers Studio Store, 131, 222
Warner & Sons Ltd., 251
Watches, 105
Watch Gallery, The, 105
Waterstone's Booksellers, 132–33
Wedgwood, 69, 72, 77, 134
Westaway & Westaway, 22, 203, 205, 209–10
West End, 86–91, 275–76
West London Antiques Fair, 257
Whistles, 190–91, 307
Whittard's, 300
William Evans Gun & Riflemaker, 93
Woodhouse, 91
Workers for Freedom, 91, 213–14, 306

X

X (Department X), 89, 190, 216, 307

Y

Yves Saint-Laurent/Rive Gauche, 130

Z

Zip codes, 83, 85, 274
Zwemmer, 133–34

ABOUT THE AUTHOR

Suzy Gershman is an author and journalist who has worked in the fiber and fashion industry since 1969 in both New York and Los Angeles, and has held editorial positions at *California Apparel News, Mademoiselle, Gentleman's Quarterly* and *People* magazine, where she was West Coast Style editor. She writes regularly for various magazines and her essays on retailing are text at Harvard Business School. She frequently appears on network and local television.

Mrs. Gershman lives in Connecticut with her husband, author Michael Gershman, and their son, Aaron. Michael Gershman also contributes to the *Born to Shop* pages.

Want to Go Shopping with Suzy Gershman?

What does Suzy Gershman do on vacation? She goes shopping, of course. But she takes people with her. If you've ever dreamed about shopping with the world's most famous shopper, this could be your chance.

Several times a year, Born to Shop Tours venture forth to Suzy's favorite destinations when she takes time to really show off her best finds. The pace is busy but relaxed compared to her regular schedule; several trips are booked through cruise lines to maximize the relaxation possibilities and to cut down on the stresses of transportation and dealing with luggage . . . but you do have to carry your own shopping bags.

Excursions often include lunch at just the right charming spot (perfect for resting tired feet), trips into back rooms and private warehouses not often seen by the public or opportunities to buy at special discounted rates reserved just for Suzy's guests.

While the schedule varies from year to year (last year, she hosted a shop-a-thon on the QE2 as she sailed from Istanbul to London), there's almost always a trip to Hong Kong, a trip to New York, and a Mediterranean cruise or two. Space is limited to ensure the intimacy of the group and experience. To find out about current plans or to inquire about arranging your own tour, call Acadiana Travel at 800/423-8661.

Frommer's Born to Shop guides are available from your favorite bookstore or directly from Macmillan Publishing USA.

To order by phone and pay by credit card, call 1-800-428-5331 (AMEX, MC and VISA cards are accepted). Otherwise, fill out the order form below.

Name _____

Address _____ Phone _____

City _____ State _____

Please send me the following **Frommer's Born to Shop** guides:

Quantity	Title	Price
_____	Born to Shop Hong Kong ISBN 0-02-860658-2	$14.95
_____	Born to Shop London ISBN 0-02-860659-0	$14.95

Available in Winter 1996

_____	Born to Shop Great Britain ISBN 0-02-860700-7	$14.95
_____	Born to Shop New York ISBN 0-02-860699-X	$14.95

Prices subject to change without notice.

Total for **Frommer's Born to Shop** Guides $ _____
Please include applicable sales tax

Add $3.00 for first book's S & H, $1.00 per additional book:
$ _____

Total payment: $ _____

Check or Money Order enclosed. Offer valid in the United States only. Please make payable to Macmillan Publishing USA.

Send orders to:
Macmillan Publishing USA
201 West 103rd Street
Attn: Order Department
Indianapolis, IN 46290